Counterfeit Community

Counterfeit Community

The Exploitation of Our Longings for Connectedness

JOHN F. FREIE

ROWMAN & LITTLEFIELD PUBLISHERS, INC.
Lanham • Boulder • New York • Oxford

ROWMAN & LITTLEFIELD PUBLISHERS, INC.

Published in the United States of America
by Rowman & Littlefield Publishers, Inc.
4720 Boston Way, Lanham, Maryland 20706

12 Hid's Copse Road
Cumnor Hill, Oxford OX2 9JJ, England

British Library Cataloguing in Publication Information Available

Library of Congress Cataloging-in-Publication Data
Freie, John F., 1947–
    Counterfeit community : the exploitation of our longings for
connectedness / John F. Freie.
        p.   cm.
    Includes bibliographic references and index.
    ISBN 0-8476-8871-2 (cloth : alk. paper). — ISBN 0-8476-8872-0
(pbk. : alk. paper)
    1. Community life—United States.   2. Community.   I. Title.
    HN59.2.F74   1998
    307.0973—dc21   98-17073
                                                                        CIP

ISBN 0-8476-8871-2 (cloth : alk. paper)
ISBN 0-8476-8872-0 (pbk. : alk. paper)

Internal design and typesetting by Letra Libre

Printed in the United States of America

∞™   The paper used in this publication meets the minimum requirements of American National Standard for Information Sciences—Permanence of Paper for Printed Library Materials, ANSI Z39.48-1984.

For Susan, Carrie, and Jamie

Contents

Preface

As I embarked upon the research trail to find out more about the topic of community, I was struck by the massive amount of literature that already exists and continues to be written on the subject. There are participation theorists, republican theorists, religious communitarians, global communitarians, existential theorists, critics of liberalism, feminist critics, radical democratic critics, and a host of other authors writing from almost every ideological perspective imaginable. While they disagreed about much (most fundamentally, the definition of "community" itself), almost all seemed to be in agreement that community in America was in decline or, as some put it, dead. It was the lack of community that first intrigued me.

When I began to look at society, however, to my surprise I saw claims of community in various guises almost everywhere. This finding seemed puzzling. On the one hand theorists and critics were bemoaning the demise of community, yet everywhere I looked new communities were being built: colleges were talking about their community atmospheres, businesses were experimenting with community in the workplace, communities were being created almost daily on the Internet, and even President Clinton announced that he was establishing a New Covenant with America that would extend and enhance community. Everywhere people seemed to be connecting with others; how could this be?

A closer look at the writings indicates that many authors were actually trying to develop solutions to what they saw as fundamental problems in American society. Traditionalists and some members of the communitarian movement, for example, seemed convinced that citizens had lost a sense of virtue or personal character, and this loss had led to dysfunctional social behaviors such as crime, teen pregnancy, drug abuse, divorce, and even poverty. Other communitarians and some republicans lamented the fact that politics was in a state of decline. Community organizers, approaching the subject from a more practical angle, thought that the problem was an unequal distribution of resources, and environmentalists felt that the world environment was in jeopardy.

What all these diverse perspectives had in common was that they all developed notions of community that would somehow solve the social problems they believed were leading to our demise. In social science terminology, these perspectives viewed community as an independent variable. Community was not an end in itself, rather it was a means to achieve other ends—to solve the problems they had identified. But, by looking at community in this fashion they had failed to see the claims of community that were being developed in all aspects of society.

This book started from a different premise. It began by asking the question: "What has happened to community in America?" By approaching the topic in this fashion it had the effect of shifting community from being the independent variable to becoming the dependent variable, thereby placing community at the center of the analysis. Consequently, the first order of business became an assessment of the status of community today.

This assessment eventually led to the formulation of the concept I call "counterfeit community," symbolic claims of community that are used to manipulate people. When we envision genuine community and then examine the claims of community as they are presented and as they actually function, we may begin to see what has happened to community in America, how it has become distorted and twisted into something barely recognizable.

This book does not challenge the assumption that community—or perhaps more accurately, the struggle for community—is a desired, even necessary, feature of human existence. It is a human goal worthy of pursuit. It is to the pursuit of community and how that desire has been distorted that we now turn.

Although it would be inaccurate to say that writing this book was a community effort, there are nonetheless many people who influenced my ideas, provided valuable criticism, supported me with time and resources, and, most of all, encouraged me when the project seemed hopeless. It would be impossible to identify all of them, but some deserve special mention.

The Faculty Research and Development Committee at LeMoyne College was an invaluable source of support. The faculty on that committee made it possible for me to obtain concentrated periods of time over the last several years and demonstrated confidence in the importance of the project by awarding me a sabbatical leave and a research grant. Neil Kraus and Joe Corso both read parts of my early drafts and encouraged me to continue. Dave Datelle's extensive comments on major sections of the book pushed me to clarify my own thinking, and his criticisms only served to improve the final product.

There is no doubt that without the confidence and helpful commentary of Jennifer Knerr at Rowman & Littlefield this book would not have taken the shape it did. Her ability to sense the direction the book was taking and her enthusiastic support made my job that much easier. Booth Fowler read the manuscript, in whole or in part, twice, and his support was critical for its completion.

There is no person who deserves acknowledgment more than does my wife, Susan Behuniak. She read every word I wrote and brutally and lovingly provided me with honest, careful, and thoughtful criticism. Our numerous discussions over the years helped clarify and focus the book, and her exceptional ability to make just the right comment at just the right time got me through the difficult times. Even more important, however, was her unwavering support for the project and her willingness to let me go into that "silly little room" and write. Without her assistance there would be no book.

1

Identifying the Counterfeit

> The great majority of mankind are satisfied with appearances, as though they were realities, and are often even more influenced by the things that seem than by those that are.
>
> —*Niccolo Machiavelli (1950, 182)*

On October 16, 1992, Bill Clinton, George Bush, and Ross Perot participated in something never before attempted—a nationally televised town meeting in which the three presidential contenders, sitting on stools, were surrounded by 209 randomly selected uncommitted voters who peppered them with questions for more than ninety minutes. Not far into the program the citizen questioners demanded that the candidates stop slinging mud at each other and stick to the issues. At least for that evening they did.

Even for the vast majority of Americans who have never participated in a town meeting, the symbolism of this event was powerful. Here was the format of the New England town meeting, the closest approximation of direct democracy in the United States, where the members of the community attend and participate in holding their elected officials responsible for their actions and, more significantly, actively participate in the discussion of issues themselves. At least once every year citizens are invited to attend the meeting at which reports about the status of the town are given, officials are questioned, and complaints are heard. The televised event, of course, differed significantly from real town meetings. Nonetheless, it was symbolically powerful by conjuring up nostalgic images of what most Americans believe has been lost—community.

The millions of viewers who watched were being symbolically linked to the candidates by the creation of the appearance of community. Each of the randomly selected citizens was voicing the concerns of citizens everywhere, and the candidates, while responding directly to the particular citi-

zen questioners, were really addressing the broader community of the entire citizenry. Each of the candidates knew that the real audience was not
the one in the studio, but the millions of television viewers across the country. Yet the candidate who dominated the format, Bill Clinton, was the one
who made it appear as if he was speaking directly to the person who asked
the question. America is a community, this town meeting was suggesting,
and our elected leaders must be held accountable to each and every member of that community. Even the president, one of the political figures perhaps most removed from the day-to-day concerns of the average citizen,
must be held accountable.

While political pundits spent most of their time trying to determine
which candidate benefited the most from his performance, what was perhaps more interesting was the town meeting format itself. Here was an effective use of the image of local democratic community to link citizens to
the electoral process and, by doing so, suggest that there is such a thing as
an American community. Regardless of age, ethnic background, race, gender, social status, or partisan affiliation (all randomly represented), we are
all a part of the American community. Although some commentators in
the media cynically scoffed at the format saying it was a "Clinton format,"
the responses of most viewers, regardless of their candidate preferences,
were overwhelmingly positive. The idea that we are all part of a community, even if only symbolically, was compelling, so compelling that the format was repeated in the 1996 campaign.

Still, there was a hollowness about it all. The town meeting format
seemed even more unusual in light of a growing body of social criticism
that describes America as a country characterized by rampant individualism, where greed predominates and citizens demand rights but refuse to
accept responsibilities. One critic has described America as a culture that
"leaves the individual alone and adrift in an often alien social and political
universe" (Merelman 1984, 6). Another has noted the dramatic decline in
civic engagement in recent years, a decrease in "social capital" (Putnam
1995). Others have described America as having evolved a "culture of separation" (Bellah et al. 1985) or having "swung too far toward the radical individualistic pole" (Etzioni 1993, 26), and social critic Christopher Lasch
has taken Americans to task for retreating into "purely personal preoccu-
pations" (1979, 29).

But, in many ways, the description of America as a country characterized by rampant individualism is related to the effectiveness of the symbolic appeals to community. Lacking genuine community, yet longing for
the meaning and sense of connectedness that it creates—the feeling of
community—people become vulnerable to even the merest suggestion of
community. For various reasons (many of which are unknown) people
have a need to be connected with other people: we have needs to be mem-

bers of a community. Sociologist Jessie Bernard, referring to community by using the preindustrial German term *Gemeinschaft,* described it this way: "*Gemeinschaft* is still the dream for millions of people, reflecting a deep longing. That *Gemeinschaft* in the longing sense is only a fantasy in no way detracts from its appeal. Untold thousands dream of living in a small, congenial, cooperative community of loving, understanding, noncompetitive relationships" (1973, 106–107). At least one social analyst has claimed that our longing for community is a part of our human nature: "Men in general have a natural allegiance to the community ideal, and would gladly see it carried out on a large as well as a small scale" (Cooley 1929, 52). Still, America has clearly moved in the opposite direction, toward individualism and a glorified sense of self as discovered in separateness, away from community and connectedness.

It is this disjunction between the longing for community and the reality of separation that makes us vulnerable to counterfeit claims of community such as the one illustrated by the presidential campaign town meeting. Sensing that we have moved too far in the direction of individualism and separation, we respond favorably to even the most superficial and obvious communal gestures. In doing so we not only open ourselves up to being exploited, but we provide support to social, economic, and political structures that, because of their very nature, cannot move us toward genuine community. Herein lies the focus of this book. Expecting and wanting to find community in places like our neighborhoods, our political arenas, and our churches, we are instead presented with counterfeit communities, structures that either distort genuine community or imitate communal structures that never existed. The desire for association and connectedness is so great, and our experience with genuine community is so limited, that we are easily deceived.

Counterfeit versions of community have been successful because of our failure to understand fully the conditions necessary for genuine community. Although there is considerable disagreement about what constitutes community, relationships are at the heart of all definitions. Above all, community is composed of webs of relationships. Members of communities have, in general, relationships of two sorts: first, relationships between the community members and the physical environment that defines the community, and second, relationships among the members of the community themselves. These two are intertwined, so that as people interact with their environment and with others in the environment, a feeling of community develops.

It is the sense of community, the feeling of connectedness, of solidarity with others, that is so often described as the essence of community. This emotional dimension is one of the unique characteristics of community. The feeling of sharing a common experience and working with others to achieve agreed-upon goals, so rare in our everyday lives, appeals to us at a deep emotional level. It is easy, however, to see the spirit of community and overlook the complex interactions that must first occur before it is realized. Too often we are presented with the relatively easy opportunity to "feel" a sense of community without undergoing the more challenging task of working through difficult and often uncomfortable relationships that are at the base of the communal experience. Counterfeit community severs our feelings of community from the web of relationships that link us to our environment and to others.

When we lose those relationships, we are left only with communal longings. Not realizing the critical importance of relationships to the existence of community, we are attracted to any appeals that suggest a feeling of connectedness. Counterfeit community attempts to satisfy those longings for community but without building the necessary relationships. In that sense, it is inherently exploitive. Perhaps because people initially feel a sense of connectedness, counterfeit community has gone unrecognized. Yet it has mutated like a cancer, extending into virtually all sectors of American life, subtly undermining the possibility of genuine community while masquerading as the very thing it prevents.

This book will first examine the state of the physical environment as it relates to community. Community is often associated with a sense of place: members often feel a special bond of attachment to the place. In the instances of residential housing patterns and the variety of arenas in which human interaction can occur (referred to as "public spaces"), it will be shown how recent developments have limited and restricted face-to-face interactions (primary experiences) and consequently made it all the more difficult for genuine community to develop. Turning to the social structure conducive to the maintenance of community, the book will next examine the workplace, politics, and religion and examine how each, in its own fashion, has undermined interactions and led to a separation between primary human experience and feelings of connectedness. Finally, the book will examine one of the latest arenas of counterfeit community—the Internet, which challenges assumptions about the importance of community being both grounded in a sense of place as well as based upon primary relationships among people.

As the book traverses the contours of American society, several patterns will emerge. The first is that counterfeit community does not "just happen": it is not a natural product of modern society. More commonly, it is explicitly created and promoted—it is an intentional social construct. Related to the prior observation is the book's second theme: counterfeit community is created and marketed in order to maximize profit or advantage for those in positions to do so. There is a not-so-hidden agenda to redirect American society away from forms of interaction that place highest priority on non-material values (community) and toward forms of interaction that encourage consumption. Third, the overall effect of the proliferation of counterfeit community throughout American society is to shape the fundamental identity of Americans by encouraging them to become increasingly privatized and one-dimensional. Counterfeit community will not create the kind of ethical, responsible citizens communitarian activists wish to create. Finally, it will be argued that movement in the direction of counterfeit community is not inevitable. Just as counterfeit community can be created, so too it can be prevented, and we can begin to build environments and encourage human interactions that build genuine community. This movement will not come easily, however. It will require a national commitment to build community that must begin locally.

Before examining the specific areas where counterfeit community becomes manifest, however, a clearer idea of what is counterfeit and what is genuine must be articulated. It is to that task that we now turn.

COUNTERFEIT COMMUNITY

Counterfeit community is composed of images, symbols, structures, and suggestions of association and connectedness that are false and ultimately exploitive. Unlike genuine community that demands that we actively participate, counterfeit community superficially and symbolically links us to others. It is more spectacle than substance. Counterfeit community projects images of community but keeps us at arm's length by never asking that we act responsibly to maintain the kinds of relationships necessary for genuine community.

Genuine community (which will be discussed in greater detail in chapter 2) develops as a result of the needs and wants of people who have at least some sense of consensus on basic values and beliefs. Counterfeit community, on the other hand, is imposed from outside the communal web of relationships and requires only that people sense a need or wish to fulfill a desire for connectedness. In counterfeit community, if you feel connected, you are—regardless of how you may actually relate to others or how you might behave. In many instances the structures that shape the patterns of human behavior in counterfeit communities actually exist prior to the physical presence of people. They are, quite literally, planned communities. Counterfeit community appeals to the real needs and concerns of people and their desires for association, but instead of creating environments and relationships that meaningfully satisfy those desires, it provides only the appearance of community and is, therefore, never fully satisfying. At best it is a "thin" version of community, but more commonly it is developed in order to exploit people for more sinister purposes, usually economic or political gain.

Counterfeit community thrives in a culture of individualism because it provides arenas in which individuals may express their feelings of community but does not require that community become so intrusive as to define their identity. For the modern individualist, society provides opportunities to express dimensions of his or her personality and social status. For example, a person may buy a house in a particular neighborhood or a particular brand of car, or may join a particular country club or the like, and by doing so, demonstrate to others what kind of person he or she is. In our highly individualistic society we have come to ascribe the accumulation of consumer goods with the expression of personality (Holsworth and Wray 1982, esp. chapter 2). In a like manner, counterfeit community performs the function of allowing a person to express the communal side of his or her personality in a safe way, without risking the type of intense communal involvement that might threaten the individualistic definition of self. Counterfeit community does not transform the individualistic self; rather it accepts individualism and, without tempering that individualism, elicits feelings of connectedness and community. It is more therapy than communal relationships. Community, in this sense, becomes a symbolic package of goods that are purchased to demonstrate our "communal side." The comments of a successful housing developer who used the concept extensively in his marketing campaign are appropriate. When asked what the word "community" meant to him, he candidly responded: "It doesn't mean—anything more than a marketing term" (Garreau 1991, 301).

Counterfeit community manifests itself in two ways: through distortion and through simulacra. One of the most common forms in which the counterfeits are presented is by distorting some aspect or aspects of genuine community to such an extent that a new form, quite dissimilar from the original, has been created. We can see how this has occurred in the example of the presidential candidates' town meeting. New England town meetings are important structures for communities. They are composed of people who know each other because they interact with each other throughout the year. Years ago, businesses in the town would close for the day of the meeting to encourage turnout and to allow everyone to participate. Issues would be seriously discussed and debated, and the elected leaders of the town would be held directly accountable to the members of the town who were present. Citizens were given the opportunity to set the agenda of the meetings and, at least politically, everyone was equal. Everyone had an equal opportunity to speak his or her mind and to try to influence others. The town meeting served important functions by obtaining citizen input, holding leaders accountable, building solidarity through interaction, obtaining support and legitimacy for decisions, and creating a sense of togetherness. It was not merely an electoral process; it was also a structure designed to encourage active citizenship and a sense of listening to and caring for others in the community.

As can be seen, the presidential candidates' counterfeit town meeting was only vaguely similar to the genuine form. Political advisors randomly selected the citizen participants, most of whom probably had never met each other before and had probably never met the candidates. There was a lack of connectedness among the people who played the roles of the town citizens and, consequently, the issues raised emerged not out of the common needs of the community (which would occur in a genuine town meeting) but from each individual's separate perspective and experience. While their participation in the event (and the vicarious participation of those who watched) may have helped them make up their minds about whom to vote for, it is unlikely that any citizens went away from the event with a richer and more complex sense of community.

In addition, the televised counterfeit community distorts the notion of democratic authority. Neither Clinton, Bush, nor Perot could be held responsible for promises they made or actions they took by the 209 randomly selected citizens because these citizens were not, in fact, the constituency. Unlike real town meetings where the people who attend are the entire constituency, neither the citizen questioners nor even the television audience could be called the entire constituency. Instead, the people in the immediate audience were merely symbols, used to create the appearance of a constituency. If the person eventually elected president were to renege on a promise made during the town meeting, it is unlikely that a member of the randomly selected group could contact the president and demand an explanation.

The second way counterfeit community becomes manifest is through the creation of simulacra. Simulacra are identical copies of things for which no originals ever existed (Jameson 1984). They are not just fantasies, but imitations of fantasies. Baudrillard (1994) refers to simulacra as being "hyperreal," as being models of reality without possessing any reference in reality. In effect, they are models of things that never existed. Because there is no reality upon which simulacra are based, there is no basis upon which to assess the validity of the simulacra: "It no longer needs to be rational, because it no longer measures itself against either an ideal or negative instance. It is no longer anything but functional" (Baudrillard 1994, 2). We must then ask: What are the functions performed by the simulacrum of community? While they most immediately are designed to elicit feelings of community, additional functions—less benign—may also underlie their use. An example will illustrate the use of simulacra and their effects.

In Terminal B in Boston's Logan International Airport, you will find a bar called Cheers. It is, of course, a blatant imitation of the Cheers bar from the popular television program of the same name. In this bar you find a vast array of props to remind you of the TV show, including Boston Red Sox pennants on the walls, logos taken from the television show's opening credits etched into the mirror behind the bar, and a menu of food and drink choices named after each of the TV characters (e.g., Woody's Polish Hot Dog, Sam's Screwdriver, Rebecca's Chili, Norm's Big Brewski). On each of the six television screens strategically placed throughout the restaurant, reruns of the TV program are constantly shown. But the major attractions in the bar are two large mechanical working-class dummies sitting at the bar who occasionally move their arms and heads and appear to ask for another beer (when traffic in the bar slows, the bartender will even place a glass of beer in front of the robots as if they were real).

The Cheers bar is a fascinating dimension of counterfeit community and represents pure simulacra. The TV program built its reputation on the friendships and connectedness of the characters (as well as humor, of course). It was presented as a place "where everybody knows your name." While the TV program could be said to be a distortion of the neighborhood bar where friends gather, the bar at Logan (and at other Cheers bars in other airports around the world) is one step beyond that—it is an imitation of a distortion.

Simulacra take on lives of their own because they so totally transcend our everyday experiences. There is no reference based on reality that can be used to set standards or make judgments. Baudrillard describes the dilemma with the following line of Huxleyan reasoning: "The simulacra is never that which conceals the truth—it is truth which conceals that there is none—the simulacrum is true" (1983, 1). The Logan Airport Cheers bar is, of course, itself a real bar. But the format is cleverly designed to make travelers feel comfortable and entertained. The friendly waitress furthers these feelings. Beneath these obvious ploys, however, one can easily see the functionality of the Cheers ambiance—to sell food and drink. While this should come as no surprise to most Americans, we must remember that genuine community is not traditionally an economic concept. Although communities must maintain a certain level of economic viability, the functions of communities have never been solely oriented toward encouraging consumerism. When we have lost touch with the real meaning of community, simulacra may be used for whatever purposes the creators desire. In the instance of the Cheers bar, it is to make a profit.

To some extent the reason for the success of community simulacra can be traced to our own limited experiences with community. Historically, there are few examples of community in the American experience. In the conclusion of his chapter "Rummaging through American History," Fowler (1991) finds few examples of community and instead concludes that the important thing is that there is at least the presence of an "idea" of community that still exists.

It is the hope that community is possible that provides fertile ground for the successful passing of community simulacra as the genuine articles. Having gone to extremes in the direction of individual freedom and self-absorption, society still holds an understandable longing for connected-ness. With little experience by which to judge communal forms of social organization, however, we lay ourselves open to the exploitation inherent in counterfeit community. For example, the Cheers bar with its numerous props designed to link us with the television program generates feelings of connectedness and friendship associated not with our own experiences of community, but with feelings of association that we attach to a television show. In doing so we become strangely nostalgic for something that never existed.

Still, there is more to the analysis of counterfeit community. The forms that it takes have, almost entirely, been conceptualized from a masculine perspective. Carol Gilligan (1982) and others have noted that women, more than men, are oriented toward relationships and the maintenance of relationships. Indeed, women tend to see their identity as defined within a context of relationships. Men, on the other hand, are more likely to describe their identity as associated with individual achievement, often accomplished through separation.

Even further, some have suggested that men fear relationships (Gray 1992). If this is the case, how is it that men, who are primarily in control of the resources to structure society, deal with concerns about community? Counterfeit community represents the masculine response to the desire for community in individualistic America. On the one hand, counterfeit community is a cooperative activity and even projects a concern about the well-being of others. On the other hand, the depth and intensity of relationships found in genuine communities are not required. Thus, the fear of intimacy is forestalled while the appearance of connectedness is asserted.

These gender differences are manifested in the call for the moral education of citizens among many who call themselves communitarians. Amitai Etzioni (1993), for example, wants to strengthen the family and the education system to support moral education, and Bruce Frohnen (1996) believes that the teaching of virtue must fundamentally be religious. Both assume that our difficulties are due to failings in our moral character. The re-establishment of community then becomes not an end in itself, but a means to an end—the development of character: "Communitarians argue that two requirements loom over all others, indeed are at the foundation of most other needs: to develop the basic personality traits that characterize effective individuals and to acquire core values" (Etzioni 1993, 90). Frohnen is even clearer on this issue: "Virtue rests on the notion that there are standards that tell us what is right. . . . It rests on a set of standards that

are 'imposed' on us by our pasts—by religion, tradition, and social and political institutions that existed before we were born" (1996, 5). Community,
so these arguments go, will provide us with moral guideposts and a sense of
discipline (and community coercion if all else fails) so that individuals will
behave morally and ethically. Given this vision of community, relationships
are valued not for themselves but only to the extent that they are effective
at controlling behavior (i.e., getting people to behave morally).

But, if Gilligan is correct, it is not possible to separate community and
relationships from morality because morality is integrated into the relationships themselves. What is right, at least for women, is the creation and
maintenance of healthy, ethical relationships. There are no abstract, core
ethical values to be applied to situations. To create community is, by definition, to relate to each other in an ethical fashion.

That counterfeit community is primarily a masculine agenda will become ever so clear when we look at claims of community on the Internet.
By some estimates 95 percent of the Internet users are men. The environments created are predominantly drawn from male assumptions about
what constitutes community. One arena in which Internet users claim
community is being constructed is in the thousands of MUDs that exist in
cyberspace. The term "MUD" originally referred to Multi-User Dungeons, a term adapted from the popular game Dungeons and Dragons.
(MUDs are also sometimes referred to as Multi-User Dimensions or Domains.) To a large extent the environments created in MUDs illustrate
male fantasies—in the early MUDs there were dragons, wizards, and evil
spirits. The use of power to control others is necessary in order to survive.
In MUDs virtually anything goes, with little social control exerted to temper behavior. The only control on behavior is one's own individual sense
of right and wrong. Relationships are not what is ultimately valued; the
predominate value on the Internet is a form of libertarianism—that you
may say whatever you wish to say and that no one has the right to limit
anyone else's speech. This principle flows not from female versions of interdependence or caring, but from the masculine ethic of separation and
independence.

At the very least we must examine the gender implications of claims of
community not just in terms of who benefits and who is disadvantaged or
who is included or who is excluded, but more fundamentally in terms of
the underlying premises regarding the conception of community itself and
its purposes.

PASSING THE COUNTERFEIT

Manifestations of counterfeit community—either blatant appeals using the
concept of community itself or the more subtle forms that appeal more to

our psychological urges for communal association—permeate American society. They appear in shopping malls, in restaurants and bars, in our politics, in our religion, in housing, and even in our high tech computer industry. Applebee's restaurant, a national chain, advertises itself as "a neighborhood grill and bar." Klahanie, a private residential development near Seattle, advertises itself in a promotional video in the following manner: "We're a real community, with sidewalks on safe streets, more than 300 acres of open space and, best of all, our commitment to the environment." The chain of Cheers bars from Boston to Las Vegas to Christchurch, New Zealand, all ask you to "Meet Me In Cheers." Willow Creek Community Church in South Barrington, Illinois, advertises itself as a "community with a cause." Howard Rheingold, in his "critical analysis" of the Internet (which reads like a promotional pamphlet), loftily claims that "the future of the Net is connected to the future of community, democracy, education, science, and intellectual life" (1993, 6).

In many downtown areas in our eastern and midwestern cities, attempts have been made to re-create historical districts and, in doing so, turn them into shopping districts. Baltimore has taken the lead in this respect with its Inner Harbor, but Boston's Quincy Market, New York's South Street Seaport, and Cleveland's Waterfront are all of the same ilk. Each instance represents an attempt to link us with the city's history by providing us with quaint images of our bygone past, appealing even more blatantly to our desire to be connected. Our malls have, in the words of Jim Wallis, "become the temples, shrines, and communal centers of modern America" (1995, 154). Consumerism, Wallis claims, has become the primary way of belonging in America and, if we can believe bumper stickers that read "I Shop, Therefore I Am," it has come to define our identity as well.

The presentation of counterfeit community comes to us through a new form of propaganda, called "palaver." Palaver is defined as "talk that charms and beguiles" (Combs and Nimmo 1993, 23). It is propaganda, but a special form of propaganda that provides us with profusions of lofty ideas, circular reasoning, circumlocutions, babbling, and sometimes even takes the form of riddles.

Hence, we see a large green neon sign on an Applebee's restaurant advertising it as a "neighborhood grill and bar," but the neighborhood it is a part of includes a Taco Bell, a Burger King, a large supermarket, and a newly paved asphalt parking lot—no people. Not long ago Washington, D.C., buses carried advertisements that read "I was saved at Potomac Mills" (a mall) and displayed a large picture of a dollar bill. An advertisement for a planned community near Dallas contains this bit of circular palaver: "Secluded from the world at large, yet close to all the finer things in life." Near Savannah, Georgia, promoters of The Landings, an exclusive planned community off the coast of Georgia, advertises itself as "truly a special place." In an attractive, colorful twenty-page brochure packed with glossy pictures of sprawling homes, green golf courses, clear blue skies, and sparkling water, the promoters claim, "We've made that dream a reality, giving naturally beautiful Skidaway Island the tasteful community it deserves."

Community has become a product to be marketed and sold, but the very manner in which goods are marketed through the use of palaver results in distortion and hyperbole. It makes little difference to the advertiser whether or not genuine community exists. The important thing is to make it appear *as if* it exists. The appearance of community, either through the form of distortion or simulacrum, has actually become easier to sell than genuine community. Genuine community involves qualification, avoidance of generalization, subtle analysis, and a sophisticated understanding of human behavior in order to be understood. It requires the stuff of community—face-to-face human relationships. This requirement does not bode well for a snappy marketing campaign. Counterfeit community, on the other hand, is easily marketed. It distorts and exaggerates genuine community and provides it with a unidimensional image well suited to palaver.

To some extent, the creation of counterfeit community has been consistent with changes in communication technology. While genuine community is dependent upon face-to-face communication in intimate groups, counterfeit community has become marketable because of the ability to communicate with large numbers of people while making it *appear* as if the communication is personal. An example from the world of cyberspace illustrates the point.

Many Internet users claim to be forming new communities by communicating with each other in cyberspace chat rooms. But because of the technology being used to communicate, one can never be exactly sure with whom one is talking. In fact, one clever computer programmer has devised a robot program named Julia that "lives" in the Carnegie Mellon computer in Pittsburgh. Once turned loose, Julia roams the Internet in search of people to talk with. She connects with humans (most of whom mistake her for a real person), talking about hockey and flirting. She is programmed to search for particular strings of characters in messages, and when she finds them, she responds accordingly. She uses statements and excerpts drawn from real news stories that she gleans from computer databases, and her responses are often filled with common typographical errors humans commonly make. She has been a viable member of numerous on-line communities. Modern technologies have made it possible to simulate human communication to the extent that, if we accept and extend the arguments of proponents of some forms of counterfeit communities, communities will be possible without even having humans in them.

REASONS FOR COUNTERFEIT COMMUNITY

While going through the case studies of counterfeit community that constitute the heart of this book, the reader may be struck by the obvious counterfeit nature of many of the examples. How is it, one might ask, that people do not easily see the false nature of the claims of community and reject them? How can people be so easily deceived into believing community exists when it does not? Certainly the counterfeit nature of some of the examples might be debatable. But other examples will fall far short of even the loosest definition of community, and yet few will object to their being called communities.

To some extent, at least part of the answer may be found in the simulacra nature of claims of community already commented upon. Lacking a reference point based in reality, we have no firm basis upon which to judge claims of community. Consequently, no assertion of community can be determined to be any more truthful or real than any other assertion. All become merely functional.

Nonetheless, additional reasons can be identified to explain the increasing prevalence of counterfeit community in our society. Some of these reasons may be traced to fundamental assumptions Americans accept about human behavior and reality; other reasons may be traced to the influence and power of the creators of counterfeit communities; still other reasons have to do with our ambivalent attitudes toward community itself. Each will be dealt with in order.

Individualism

Individualism provides the intellectual basis for an environment in which counterfeit community can flourish. The beliefs embedded in individualism lie at the core of American culture and provide us with assumptions about human behavior and reality. They also shape our beliefs about the purposes of politics that are supportive of counterfeit community, and they help make us cynical about the possibility of genuine community.

American individualism finds its roots in seventeenth- and eighteenth-century European political philosophy used in the struggle against aristocratic authority. The more recognizable proponents included political philosophers such as Thomas Hobbes, John Locke, Adam Smith, and the author of the U.S. Constitution, James Madison. The more fundamental elements have become "givens" in American culture, so much so that it becomes difficult to even envision alternative viewpoints. I will not provide a thorough discussion of individualism here, but will instead touch upon several basic beliefs associated with it that support the growth of counterfeit community. In essence, three components from the individualistic framework will be commented upon: certain assumptions about the self, an emphasis on individual rights, and the distinction between the public and the private.

Americans believe in the dignity of the individual. More accurately, the self is "the only or main form of . . . reality" (Coles 1980, 137). The strong, heroic individual standing apart from an often corrupt society and fighting for justice embodies American values. Thoreau had to withdraw from society to do what he believed was right, the Lone Ranger lived outside society and only intervened once a week in prime time on behalf of justice, and Gary Cooper in *High Noon* fought alone against the outlaws while the community deserted him. Closer to contemporary American life, Serpico, the New York City police officer, became something of a hero as he singularly fought police corruption, and *Washington Post* reporters Woodward and Bernstein fought to reveal the truth about Watergate at professional and personal risk to themselves. Examples of solitary heroes standing up for what is right against a corrupt system, thus confirming basic American values, are too numerous to list. What links these stories of heroism is an important truth: in America it is the individual who is sacred. What's more, the individual essentially must act in a solitary fashion to defend American values; the community will desert the just man.

Individual autonomy is thought to be so important that it permeates our entire child development and education systems. In the latest edition of his best-selling book on child rearing, Benjamin Spock (now with Rothenberg) says: "Youths have got to separate themselves emotionally from their parents in order to find out who they are and what they want to be. . . . They must pry themselves apart" (Spock and Rothenberg 1992, 566). A strong sense of individualism is created by placing children in dilemmas of their own and letting them struggle with making decisions by themselves. This, it is believed, builds strength of character and develops in children a strong sense of morality (Power 1989). Our belief in the self is so important that we have integrated it into our child-rearing and educational systems; consequently, it becomes an accepted part of how we see ourselves as human beings.

Beyond the formal educational structures, individualistic assumptions lay the foundation for how one should deal with problems that arise in life. Modern therapy focuses on the self and how to make people pursue the things in life that make them happy. "You must love yourself before you can love others" is a common refrain from pop-psychology, as if the self is devoid of a social environment.

The cultural view of human nature according to individualism is that it is dominated by self-interest. Individuals rationally pursue their own self-interest, usually thought of in material terms. The only rational motivation to join groups (appropriately called "interest groups") is to maximize one's ability to achieve some objective (most commonly the accumulation of material goods) considered vital to one's self-interest. These groups usually demand very little from their membership. It is not uncommon to be a member merely by paying membership dues. Group membership, because it is passive, does not so much shape one's personality as reflects it.

This view of the sacredness of the autonomy of the individual places severe restrictions on the ability to obtain legitimacy for any but the most superficial views of community. This is because, according to individualism, community is seen as smothering the ability of the individual to express him- or herself. Community is viewed as being in conflict with individual freedom. Counterfeit community plays directly upon the individualistic assumptions of self-interest by marketing itself as a safe environment, but more importantly, as a place where the choice to consume goods is expanded and consumption is facilitated. Counterfeit community provides environments where the linkage between a sense of self and the consumption of goods is made blatantly obvious.

Individualism places a high priority on the rights of citizens, especially liberty, so much so that any discussion of responsibility gets drowned out (Glendon 1991). The belief that individuals possess inherent rights and that these rights are almost absolute in nature has extended from civil rights to property, children, and even body parts (some even claim that potential people have rights). The assertion of rights eventually leads to the use of law for protection and a loss of civility and sociability, important elements for the viability of community.

Rather than challenging the manner in which rights have been formulated and attempting to determine how rights might be integrated into community, counterfeit community has either restricted rights to a single predominate one—the right to protect property, for example—or eliminated rights altogether by shrouding the idea of community in the blanket of privatization. Rights, as politically defined, usually apply to individuals as they act publicly. For example, individuals in court have the right to be treated equally regardless of social position, but housing developers may discriminate on the basis of social standing if they so desire. People have accepted such restrictions because they have reasoned that the protection of their property values or their safety is a more important value than the exercise of civil rights.

Restrictions of constitutional rights can legally occur because of the culturally accepted public/private distinction. The Bill of Rights protects citizens from government infringements and is seldom extended to private organizations. Most manifestations of counterfeit community develop structures and organizations that are legally private. This means that repressive, and at times oppressive, rules may develop to regulate behavior and that exclusion of people from participation is legally and culturally acceptable. Ironically, the rationale behind the limited scope of the public domain and the "hands-off" attitude taken toward private organizations can be traced to a firmly held distrust of the government. Yet today it is private organizations, often under the guise of community, that control, exclude, and repress members.

This public/private distinction is crucial for the existence of counterfeit community because counterfeit community, in order to develop the façade of community, must limit and restrict access and prevent public discussion and criticism. An important element in the success of the palaver of counterfeit community is the uncritical acceptance of images of community. To enhance the possibility that the message will be accepted, it is important to know the target audience so that the most effective advertising appeal may be developed. The effect of the privatization of community is to narrow the audience and, by doing so, frame the marketing message. If it is possible to control the social and economic demographics of the audience, it is also more likely that palaver will be less subject to critical analysis and scrutiny as long as it remains within the accepted parameters of the audience. Criticism emerges less from intelligence than it does from different life experiences and diversity.

The Creators of Counterfeit Community

It is probably true that most genuine communities start out unintentionally. People group together because they may share a common race, ethnicity, culture, religion, or they may simply enjoy each others' company. In some cases individuals may come to rely upon each other out of necessity. While some interactions may be planned, others might be spontaneous. Nonetheless, this does not deny that genuine community cannot be intentionally created or that at least the prerequisites for its development cannot be created.

On the other hand, all instances of counterfeit community are intentional. Because they are presented in a palaver-like fashion, their creation is often carefully thought out. Considerable planning goes into the formation of counterfeit community so that it may take on the appearance of genuine community. Research goes into developing marketing plans, surveys are often conducted to assess the interests of the target audience, resources must be secured, an organization must be created, and the plan must be implemented. This process requires considerable effort and skill on the part of the creators but, more significantly, it requires either power and money or access to those resources.

Although counterfeit community is becoming a more frequent occurrence throughout society, it is not emerging spontaneously. While it claims to satisfy our need for community and connectedness (which it does superficially), it is not primarily created for those purposes. Instead, it is used to extend the power and expand the wealth of those who are creating it. The primary function of genuine community, on the other hand, is to be found in the value and meaningfulness of the relationships that animate the community itself. People long for community out of a desire to find a meaning in their own lives that transcends their individual selves. But the primary function of counterfeit community is to be found external to those relationships, in the intent of the few who have created it.

This is not intended to suggest that the creators of counterfeit community are cynical manipulators (though that is surely the case for some). Rather, those possessing money and power enough to shape counterfeit community are not just believers, like the rest of us, in the dominant assumptions and beliefs, but they are avid supporters of those beliefs. It is by believing in the strength of the individual and the sanctity of private property that the creators of counterfeit community have become rich and powerful. Thus, even the most influential shapers of counterfeit community also approach the issue believing that they are creating genuine community. In many instances they believe their own palaver.

The Ambiguity of Community

There seems little doubt that the success of counterfeit community is a result of the desire for community as well as concerns about the disintegration of contemporary society. Just as the fundamental idea of individualism is ambivalently held (Bellah et al. 1985), so too does community present us with a case of ambiguity.

On the one hand, we believe that life has little meaning unless shared with others in community; but on the other hand, we have a strong desire for independence and self-reliance. We believe that it is important to be connected to something that is greater than ourselves, yet we also are suspicious of making commitments and skeptical of our ability to sustain them. We believe that people are essentially equal and should participate equally in community, but we also defend and justify vast inequalities in wealth and opportunity.

To some extent, the ambivalence of community may be traced to its history in America (which has not always been positive). Community has sometimes been used as a conservative attempt to reinstitute traditional forms of social control and exclusion. Certainly, the position of women in communities has not been liberating. In traditional communities they have been relegated to support roles, have been denied opportunities, and have been marginalized. Likewise, ethnic and racial minorities have found themselves excluded and oppressed in many communities.

The case of women in communities is illustrative of the ambiguity of community. One of the earliest and most repressive examples of the brutalization mainly of women occurred during the seventeenth-century New England witch trials. In the tight-knit communities of colonial New England, women who challenged the traditional roles assigned to them were often accused either of being "possessed" or of being witches. The effect of the witch trials was to eliminate women from the community either through excommunication or execution and to also send a message to other women that they must submit their own selves to male domination (Karlsen 1987).

The end of the witch trials did not, of course, end the repression of women. In one of the most ironic accounts of repression, Sara Evans (1979) describes the submissive role assigned to women in the civil rights movement of the 1960s. In the midst of organizations committed to engagement, liberation, and building a sense of community, males dominated and women, in the words of James Weinstein, "made peanut butter, waited on tables, cleaned up, got laid. That was their role" (Evans 1979, 160). The repression of women is not restricted to traditional communities and continues to flourish today, both within and outside of community.

Similarly, racial and ethnic minorities have not fared well outside of their own communities. Historians describe numerous examples of viable communities in America, but all too often these communities are marked by ethnic, racial, or religious homogeneity. While sameness may not inherently be a problem, communal views of differences seldom are benign. Minorities have experienced discrimination and repression and, for the most part, been oppressed by appeals to community. Indeed, many of those most vehemently opposed to the civil rights movement of the 1960s in the South justified their opposition in rhetoric that conjured up images of a unique, homogeneous southern community.

On the other hand, the power used by women and racial and ethnic minorities to fight against repression has often been based in community. One of the first steps women took to fight against repression in the feminist movement was to create consciousness-raising groups where women came together in friendship, shared their hopes, dreams, and frustrations, and developed a sense of connectedness and solidarity. These consciousness-raising groups performed many functions we might attribute to genuine communities. Similarly, the civil rights movement grew out of communally based organizations that already existed in the African American communities of the South or developed new organizations that pushed the civil rights agenda. Although in neither case were the movements totally successful at eliminating discrimination, the important point is that community was integral in creating a new sense of what it meant to be a woman or an African American and provided a base of psychological and political support necessary for action.

It is this ambiguity (illustrated in the woman's movement and the civil rights movement) that underlies our present debate about communitarianism. More significantly, it is this ambiguity that helps make it possible to pass off counterfeit community in place of genuine community. Counterfeit community exploits our urges for community that suggest liberation and solidarity as well as our fears of community that remind us of oppression.

The American cultural tradition contains within it a tension between a person's desire to act as a free and autonomous individual and the desire to be a part of a supportive network of people with a common purpose. Each of these dimensions contains words, symbols, and signs that represent a language—one of individualism and one of community. Although individualism has been the dominant discourse, it is not without its communitarian critics; likewise, the communitarian discourse has been taken to task by believers in individualism. Consequently, a healthy debate exists between how much individualism should be emphasized or how much communitarianism should be encouraged.

However, in recent years a new element must enter the debate—counterfeit community. Because the debate between individualism and communitarianism has often been so abstract, counterfeit community has been able to pass itself off as genuine community virtually without notice. What's more, because of its distortions, counterfeit community appears to fit nicely into both discourses with only modest objection from either. This book will examine the distorting nature of counterfeit community from the communitarian perspective. To do that we must first firmly establish what is meant by community. It is to that task that we turn in the following chapter.

2

Genuine Community

Community is not a place or a thing; it is a calling, a struggle, a journey.

—*Robert Booth Fowler (1991, 161)*

If we may believe the findings of archaeologists who deal with the origins of humanity, it would seem as if human beings have a need to live with other human beings. The human is "an animal with its own unique reason for living in communities" (Leakey and Lewin 1977, 157). While it is debatable whether such social behavior may be considered "natural," it seems clear that throughout human history the urge to cooperate is compelling. It is this compelling urge for sociality that makes community a reality but also makes its simulated version—counterfeit community—possible.

Community is organic, not contractual or artificial. In a sense it is a living organism that is continually changing and adapting to challenges in the environment. Just as it was impossible to impose democratic structures on Weimar Germany and expect it to become a democracy, it is not possible to impose communal structures upon people and expect them to become a community. The degree to which community develops is ultimately dependent upon the nature of the social, economic, and political fabric of a group of people. Community is not formed by people who get together and agree to sign their names to a document to form a community; rather, it is created over time as people form connections with each other, develop trust and respect for each other, and create a sense of common purpose.

As a community grows, it develops a history. Bellah et al. (1985) refer to this as a "community of memory," in which the story of its past is told and retold. One important way of telling the story of the community is through rituals. Rituals transmit knowledge about the community, confirm and maintain the existence of social groups and cultural forms, justify the power of the dominant groups as well as provide legitimacy to those groups that are weaker, moderate conflict, and affirm the legitimacy of the community (Nieburg 1973). The stories and rituals create a tradition and an ethos about what constitutes good character, what represents achievement, and what ties the present to the past.

This is not to suggest that community cannot be intentionally created—it can be. In fact, at some point there must be a consciousness about the nature of community if it is to survive and prosper. But community is not characterized only by the type of structures that exist. Communal structures are necessary, but not sufficient, for the creation of community. Equally important as the structures are the feelings of community, the character of the participants, and the quality of the human interactions.

The purpose of this chapter is to define the central concept of the book: community. This is not an easy task given the multitude of definitions that have been used. In 1955 one author identified ninety-four different definitions of community being used in social science studies (Hillery 1955). Twenty-two years later an examination of definitions of community by Willis (1977) found that the same degree of nonuniformity continued to exist. Unable to establish theoretical consensus, many social scientists merely discarded the concept altogether. But the reality of life in modern America has forced a reconsideration of community, and although definitional nonuniformity continues, discussions about the decline of community and calls to action to reconstruct it have become quite popular.

ON DEFINING

On their face, definitions seem innocent enough. They are simply words and phrases that describe the essential nature of something. They appear to be merely descriptive, helping us understand what something is like. In fact, however, definitions are far more powerful than that. They contain within them biases that identify what is important and what is not, what is essential and what is at the periphery. Definitions, as conceptual categories, identify what the definers think is worthy and necessary and what is irrelevant and should be pushed aside. This generalization is even more true of definitions of community because there is so little agreement about its true nature.

I will not be making any claim that the definition of community used in this book is the "true" definition and that, by implication, others are false. While the definition embraced here is based, to a large extent, on definitions others have used, it represents merely one (and certainly not the only) vision of community. It contains some elements that could be called conservative, other dimensions that come from liberal thought, and still other aspects probably best labeled radical. This definition was not developed with the intent of trying to touch all ideological bases in order to satisfy everyone. Instead, my attempt is to create a lofty vision of community, grounded in the reality of contemporary American thought and experience, which, although visionary, is still achievable. It so happens that such a conception incorporates ideas from a wide range of ideological positions.

The notion of community presented here represents more of a call for action than a blueprint for its achievement. My image of community is one that asks that we struggle to create a world that is more united, more connected, more sharing, and more meaningful for human action than the one we live in now. The vision of community sketched out in this book does not include a political action agenda that can be used to create community. While others have attempted to do so (Etzioni for example), it is my assessment that our experiences with community are far too diverse and varied to be able to fit into any comprehensive formula. Perhaps the best we can do is establish a vision, work toward that vision, assess and reassess our progress, and put in more work.

An idealized definition of community further makes it possible for self-criticism to occur. One criticism of communitarianism is that it is inherently conservative in that it embraces a romantic and unrealistic vision of the past and provides no criteria by which to change the status quo (Frazer and Lacey 1993). By starting with an ideal view of community we may continually subject communal experiments to examination. Self-criticism is possible because our vision is lofty, but it should also be built into the conception of community itself.

A final function that the definition of community must include is the provision of a vision that can be used to identify counterfeits. Identifying counterfeits is difficult. To be sure, the very purpose of counterfeits is to deceive, and the "better" the counterfeit is, the more difficult it becomes to identify. Definitions are helpful in this regard because they establish criteria that may be used to assess the counterfeit nature of forms that claim to be communitarian. To a large extent this represents the critical focal point of this book.

COMMUNITY DEFINED

Community is *an interlocking pattern of just human relationships in which people have at least a minimal sense of consensus within a definable territory. People within a community actively participate and cooperate with others to create their own self-worth, a sense of caring about others, and a feeling for the spirit of connectedness.*

People in community interact with others in complex and intricate ways. Just as people contain within them multiple sides to their characters, community provides safe arenas in which the different dimensions of an individual's personality may be expressed. While grounding us in the supportive environment of community, genuine community also allows people to take risks so that they may further discover aspects of their own identities. It is through serious confrontation of difference that a person truly discovers what he or she believes. Thus, genuine community devoted to human growth and discovery will encourage and support a diversity of interaction—diversity in terms of people as well as diversity in terms of the types of situations in which the interactions take place.

The demands of post-industrial society encourage fragmentation and specialization of our personalities. To be successful we must become experts in highly specialized areas. Community, on the other hand, buffers such tendencies and acts as an integrating force.

This process of integration is, in a sense, the building of character. By growing up in a communal environment, one learns about loyalty, commitment, and responsibility to a whole greater than oneself. In a community a person plays many different roles but, more significantly, identifies with a group that shares values and beliefs that can only be realized through cooperation and commitment. For the community to be successful, members must recognize their membership in it and develop an enlarged sense of self.

How does this process of character formation occur? Communities create a rich and varied number of public spaces and public rituals that function to involve members in common activities. At times, members may be involved in the governance of the community, at other times they may participate in entertainment rituals, and at even other times they may merely be involved in spontaneous interactions with other members. Healthy communities provide public spaces where both spontaneous and more structured gatherings may take place. Participants present themselves in different manners depending upon the audience and the environment. In doing so they reveal and express different dimensions of their personalities.

Alan Ehrenhalt (1995) describes three communities in the Chicago area in the 1950s. One of the communities he describes was the ethnically diverse St. Nick's parish on the southwest side of the city. Composed of Irish, Polish, German, Italian, and Lithuanian peoples, it was united by a web of formal and informal associations, each allowing individuals to participate in the life of the community in a different fashion. One of the most significant unifying institutions was the Catholic Church, which not only provided religious guidance but also ran the neighborhood parochial school for many children who lived in the neighborhood. But perhaps equally important for the expression of another side of one's personality was "High Mass at Hoffman's," the corner tavern where the men often drank, played cards, and entertained each other with clever stories.

While children received an education at the neighborhood school, the recreational center was the alley in the back of the house or, when adults were not around, the front stoop and front street. Thus, children played within the neighborhood, well within sight of adults who did not hesitate to help form character through the use of discipline even if the child involved was not one's own.

On summer evenings the front stoops became informal meeting places where neighbors carried on conversation well past dark. Even places of business were extensions of the web of relationships that existed in the community. Most shopping was done in the neighborhood, within walking distance of one's home. Shopping was not just an economic transaction; it was the establishment and maintenance of a relationship of trust and loyalty. Some business transactions even took on the flavor of community celebrations. Friday night at the Talman Federal Savings found hundreds of people socializing in the bank lobby as they had their quarterly dividends stamped in their books. The founder of the bank would often hire a piano player or the local church choir to entertain. The bank performed another function as well, for it held most people's mortgages. But people in the community got even more from the bank: they got a strong dose of conservative economic philosophy and psychological support. It was sometimes necessary for the bank to emphasize such values because loans were often given not on the basis of some abstract formula, but on the assessment of one's character.

Although the St. Nick's parish community was limited in some respects, it provided numerous opportunities throughout a person's life for individuals to develop aspects of their personalities. This was done within a communal context. To be sure, the community was not as racially or economically integrated as it could have been, nor was authority distributed or administered in anything approaching a democratic fashion, and, of course, the 1950s notion that a woman's place was in the kitchen prevailed here as well. But the fundamental structure for healthy psychological and moral development was present, if not fully realized.

Human interactions within communities are formal as well as informal, and both serve important functions. Formal interactions, sometimes taking the form of rituals, may take on highly structured appearances. They may be political elections, government meetings, religious holiday celebrations, school activities, sporting events, or parades. These things seem obvious. But they also include family structures, marriage, education, and patterns of work. Whatever the social arrangements, members of the community who take part link themselves to the community. Through their participation they demonstrate at least partially their role in the community. While differences in social status or rank may exist among the participants, participation in the ritual itself performs the function of cutting across such divisions and provides a source of cohesion. Furthermore, when the participants perform different roles in the rituals (in some cases high status roles, in other cases low status roles), the sense of connectedness is further enhanced.

Communities also encourage informal interactions. These may be accidental, incidental to the objectives of a formal organization, or arising from some personal desire or gregarious instinct. They may occur almost anywhere, although they are more likely to occur in "third places" (cafes, diners, bars, beauty parlors, etc.). It is in these informal interactions where friendships are formed, where attitudes and customs may form, where social skills are honed, and where one learns the habit of association. Third places provide safe arenas in which alternative ideas may be tried out, where frustrations may be vented, where authority may be harshly criticized without fear of reprisal, where cohesiveness to formal institutions may be developed, or where people may simply have fun. These informal interactions provide the community with both an additional mode to develop connectedness and a means by which change can be fostered.

Both formal and informal interactions develop as an outgrowth of the needs and interests of the members of the community; they are not imposed from outside. Organizations such as governance structures, businesses, civic organizations, entertainment events, sporting events, schools, and the like grow from and are sustained by the interests and needs of the members of the community. Because the organizations are community structures, the leaders of the organizations feel a sense of responsibility and obligation to the community that created them.

Communication within communities may include mass or secondary communication forms (e.g., newspapers, radio, perhaps even television) but, and perhaps more importantly, must include face-to-face communication (primary experiences). It is partially through direct, face-to-face communication that beliefs, values, and attitudes about the community are shared and formed as members discuss important issues or merely chat. It is through primary experiences that individuals develop skills of scrutiny and investigation and learn how to develop rapport with objects and other humans. "Perception in this sense is not merely mental; it is an act that best serves to unify mind and body; it is an achievement of the whole person who is looking, listening, scrutinizing, and discerning" (Reed 1996, 104). Secondary communication forms also help to define the community and articulate the agreed-upon beliefs within the community, although their more likely function is to inform the community about assets that are available· (Jeffres, Dobos, Sweeney 1987). Both forms of communication—primary and secondary—perform the important functions of building commitment and loyalty to the community. The complex web of formal and informal interactions creates a form of social capital that nourishes and enriches community (Putnam 1995).

The character of relationships in a community should be based upon notions of justice. This implies quite a bit. The governance of the community should be based upon principles of participatory democracy. The value of equality should be emphasized, and diversity and individual freedom should be tempered by the democratically agreed-upon consensus of the community. Justice in a community is not so much the imposition of principles of right or wrong on its members—of making "moral claims" on members as Etzioni (1993) suggests—as it involves trying to get people to live together in some sensible manner in which dignity, patience, trust, and mutual respect for each other occur. Morality, in this fashion, is more of an active way of relating to people than it is a set of disembodied principles.

The history of small groups in accepting and appreciating equality, freedom, and diversity has not been good. Indeed, some of the most oppressive treatments of women, African Americans, and various ethnic groups have occurred under the guise of community. If one of the objectives of community is to provide individuals with an environment in which they may pursue the development of the multiple dimensions of their personalities, there must exist a basic equality with respect to education, social status, and social power. Equality need not imply sameness; rather people must have appropriate access to resources needed in order for them to develop their potentials.

But in most communities resources are limited. Not everyone can, therefore, be provided with the resources he or she might wish to have. The principle of justice must be applied to the resources available to the community. Philosopher Michael Walzer (1983) argues that equality is easier to accept, psychologically, in some spheres than in others. Thus, it is easier to tolerate inequities in wealth that might allow individuals to buy luxury automobiles than it is to accept inequalities that control access to medical care, education, or the criminal justice system. Put another way, this means that the needs of all individuals must be addressed before the wants of individuals should be addressed. Wants are privileged; needs are not. Needs are more easily identified as being associated with the universal attributes of people. We all need food, but we do not all need to eat apple pie. It may be that some individual wants must be curtailed in order to satisfy the needs of all. This, however, actually benefits all in the community because all participate in the communal good. Once the needs of all (e.g., food, shelter, health, education) have been adequately satisfied, the wants may begin to be addressed.

The concept of justice also extends to the issue of diversity. Too often community and the belief that there must be a consensus associated with it are taken to imply sameness. Sameness often does produce agreement on fundamental beliefs and values, but it does so at the cost of creating an environment that makes it difficult for individuals to freely express themselves, and it places an additional obstacle in the ability to produce change. Sameness is more often associated with counterfeit community.

People possess different perspectives, skills, tendencies, temperaments, and values and respond to situations differently. But even more, they have within them a multiplicity of possibilities, talents, and skills. The nature of our society, however, is to limit and restrict those possibilities and channel people into socially acceptable forms of behavior. This, it might be argued, must be done to achieve harmony, but many social critics agree that the narrowing of human potentialities has occurred to too great an extent and has resulted in the creation of one-dimensional citizens who serve the status quo (Marcuse 1964). Many interests and abilities become repressed in the process. Community offers the hope that, because of the multiplicity and complexity of relationships that can be developed, a broader range of interests of community members may find expression. To expand the range, it is critical that diversity of thought and behavior not only be tolerated, but that it be encouraged and supported. Obviously, some limits would have to be placed on diversity (e.g., violence will not be accepted), but in fact the range of diversity that can be integrated into communities is far broader than we might, at first glance, realize. Whenever possible, decisions in communities should favor openness rather than closure.

Because Americans have been socialized in the language of individual rights, we have mistakenly come to believe that "freedom" and "equality," and even "equality" and "appreciation of diversity," are terms that are in conflict. This need not be the case and, in fact, all of these values may be incorporated into a participatory democratic community. The present rationale for individual freedom claims that, when individuals are allowed maximum choices, they may select the options (usually objects) that help them live the good life. The objective of community is no different, although the notion of the good life is modified. In community the good life is created through association. Through participation in the life of the community, the individual uses and develops his or her uniquely human capacities, talents, and attributes. It is through rich and varied communal participation that the individual comes to realize new abilities, and by individuals democratically relating to others, justice, as a process of human interaction, is achieved.

Communities are not characterized merely by the nature and extent of human interaction. For members of the community there is some sense of consensus both on values, beliefs, and mores of the community as well as on the boundaries, psychological as well as physical, of the community. There exists an awareness among members that they are part of the community. In many cases the community may have a particular name with which members identify. This sense of identification goes beyond identification with any of the particular memberships in any of the subgroups that exist within the larger community.

The conscious identification with the community provides members with a sense of rootedness and illustrates a sense of caring for others. Members of a community possess a sense of trust, common purpose, common respect, and a sense of connection. It is in community that the human potential for association and growth is realized and, in so doing, a spirit of caring and trust is developed. Members of the community care for the welfare of other members of the community, even though they may not personally know each and every one of them. In this way, identification with a community provides the basis for the development of an ethical perspective. Put bluntly, community helps build character. Before a person may answer the question, "What ought I to do?" one must first be able to answer the question, "Who am I?" Individual linkages that lack an ability to richly and firmly identify with a community will be thin and fragile and subject to destructive influences.

This should not be taken, however, to suggest that conflict is not present within communities. While at least a minimum of agreement on the fundamental values of the community must exist, other differences will be present. This is inevitable because of the diversity of human beings. Because people think differently (even though they may share common experiences), it will be difficult to achieve social consensus in any community. Conflict in a community is, however, handled in a fashion in which the individual dignity and worth of each participant are maintained while communal decisions are made. Politics does and should exist within communities. Indeed, politics should be encouraged because it is through a political life that individuals come to realize their full potential. Berry puts the case succinctly: "Individuals will become educated to *be* political; they will approach issues on a communal rather than a privatized individual basis. And the mode of education is through *doing* politics" (1989, 53).

The argument in favor of a vibrant form of politics does not stop with the individual growth argument. Provided with a vision of what it can become, members must have a means by which self-criticism can occur so that changes may be made to move the community further in the direction of the ideal. Consonant with this, individuals and groups must have access to mechanisms that will protect them from tyranny. The social history of community in America has too often been the history of authoritarian power and the oppression of the minority at the hands of the majority. One thing the individualistic focus of our society produced was an ethic of rights that provided a framework for the oppressed to obtain some degree of liberation. Communal forms and the behavior of members cannot be allowed to return to earlier forms of oppression. The protection of rights that have grown out of our individualistic preoccupation within a community is, as Berry (1989) has shown, possible as long as the community is a *democratic* community. Hence, democratic politics, participatory in nature, is a necessary element of our vision of community.

Although a democratic community should be inclusive, we must not be so naive as to think that all individuals can be or would want to be a part of it. Moon (1993) argues that in some instances moral values are in fundamental conflict and, consequently, only a very "thin" version of public life is possible. But such an argument places too great an emphasis on abstract principles (which, indeed, may logically be in conflict) and ignores the power of sociability. Oddly perhaps, one of the most effective ways to overcome fundamental differences that separate people is through apparently nonpurposive human interaction. It is through "mere association"—open-ended, playful, and nonpurposive—that vast moral contradictions may be bridged (though certainly not resolved).

"Community" is, by definition, a public term. But ironically, in order to create a rich and vibrant communal environment, an equally viable private arena must exist. To an extent greater than we would like to admit, human character is forged in the dynamic relationships between the private and the public, especially when the public is represented by genuine community. If community were to be all-consuming, it would be stifling as well as potentially authoritarian. Where community is non-existent, a pervasive nihilism runs rampant. Thus, to effectively create character we must maintain a healthy tension between the public (as represented by community and mass society) and the private (as best represented by the family).

Although dimensions of character (e.g., tolerance, morality, integrity, loyalty, responsibility) are arguably best developed in public arenas, the forging of identity occurs best within the private environment of the family. It is there where one's temperament and private virtues are initially developed and where a sense of self is initially created. In the environment of community, where individuals interact with others in the workplace, at school, and in the neighborhood, character is forged. In this sense, character is seen as an interpretation of the sense of self (which was created in the private environment of the family) in the light of the atmosphere and culture of the community.

In the family a person may develop a sense of caring, but it is in community where responsibility is acted out. In the family one learns the value of morality, but it is in community where moral agency is exercised. And in the private environment of the family one develops an active orientation toward life, but it is in the community where one develops a sense of commitment to a whole greater than oneself. In Robert Putnam's words, "Dense networks of interaction probably broaden the participants' sense of self, developing the 'I' into the 'we'" (1995, 67). It is in the dynamic interplay between the private and the public where an individual most fully develops character as well as the skills needed to function effectively in society.

Traditionally, communities have existed within definable geographical boundaries, not necessarily those consistent with political boundaries. Such a sense of place continues to be an important element of community: it provides a physical location and focus for human interaction. As will be shown in the analysis that follows, the undermining of place has had devastating effects not just on our ability to create community but on other behaviors as well.

Finally, a few comments about size are in order. Some have suggested that there exists, or more appropriately, should exist a global community. Those who advocate such a position claim that it is only by becoming globalists that we will realize our interconnectedness and that we will be able to cooperate to solve global problems. For some advocating global community, it is a matter of survival. Others suggest that a global community is possible because of advances in technology (e.g., the Internet) that have allowed people from different countries and different continents to communicate almost instantaneously. These technological improvements, so goes the argument, have drawn people closer together, making a global community a foreseeable reality.

My conception of community does not include the notion of global community. There are, I believe, size limitations on the concept of community (although what they are cannot be precisely specified). The critical element in community is face-to-face human interaction. Individuals in community must possess the ability to interact physically in multiple ways over extended periods of time. Formal and informal groups, structures, rituals, celebrations, and spontaneous meetings must exist to make it physically possible for any member of the community to meet any other member of the community. This is not to say that all members actively interact with all other members, but rather that the possibility exists that they could. This dimension limits the size of community, both in terms of the size of the population that could be included and in terms of the geographical area in which community can exist.

In a like fashion, to speak of a national community is to speak only metaphorically. The kind of intensity that community requires is not possible on such a broad scale. Nonetheless, as we will see when we examine politics, the theme of national community is often used by politicians attempting to mobilize support. When the notion of a national community is not linked with localized communities, it becomes a distortion—a form of counterfeit community.

What we are left with then is an ambitious and idealistic vision of community. Striving toward its realization is the necessary action that individuals consciously and unconsciously take in an attempt to fulfill themselves.

The driving force that attracts people toward community can be found in their natural desire to live in association with others and to find identity through participation in a greater whole. It is this desire to live in association with others that leads people not only toward communal life, but also, mistakenly, toward counterfeit community.

We are particularly susceptible to the lure of counterfeit community today because of the growing feelings that Americans have become too individualistic and that we are experiencing a moral crisis that can only be solved by reinventing community. Everything from crime to teenage pregnancies to personal bankruptcy has been blamed on Americans' obsession with individualism and their inability to act responsibly. In this atmosphere, virtually any claim of community will be taken seriously.

Perhaps more significantly, the concept of community has been found to be an effective marketing tool for a wide variety of purposes. It has been used to sell virtually every product imaginable, from houses to food to political candidates to religion. Claims of community have come to so permeate our society that they have become almost commonplace. Not surprisingly, upon careful examination many community claims turn out to be counterfeit.

THE DANGERS OF COUNTERFEIT COMMUNITY

What, one may ask, is the real danger of people living in counterfeit communities? After all, aren't people free to choose whether or not they want to live in community, and what is so bad about counterfeit community anyway?

As we shall see when we examine counterfeit community in a variety of settings, the particular dangers in each area vary somewhat. This is due to the fact that the specific nature of the counterfeit also varies. However, in one way or another, counterfeit community presents us with the following difficulties:

1. *Counterfeit community wastes resources.* Almost universally, counterfeit community is able to exist because it occurs in legally private rather than public realms. This is done to avoid regulation as well as to allow for the realization of private profits. In some cases members become, in effect, double taxed: once by the legal public government, and again by the private "government" in order to maintain the feature of the counterfeit. What's more, because the counterfeit must be marketed, considerable amounts of money must be spent on advertising, an inherently wasteful activity.

For example, developers build houses where none existed before. In order to get people to buy the houses, they must spend large amounts of money on advertising to convince people that it is the kind of community they would like to live in. But genuine communities do not exist prior to the existence of people, they develop slowly out of the character of the people and the nature of the human interactions. While there may be advertising by individual members if they decide to move and must sell their homes, the costs are born by the individuals, not by the community. In a similar fashion, businesses located in malls pay not just for their own advertising but also for the upkeep of the common areas in the malls and generic advertising to lure customers in. On the other hand, businesses that are integrated into genuine communities, although they certainly rely upon paid advertising, rely most heavily on word-of-mouth advertising by members of the community. Common services (parking, sewage, etc.) are paid for only once: to the local government, which is responsible for maintenance of common areas.

2. *Counterfeit community avoids social problems.* While at least part of the urge to embrace community comes from natural desires to be connected to others in some meaningful fashion, another aspect, often exploited by counterfeit community, is to avoid dealing with complex and uncomfortable social problems. Although vast resources have been committed to problems such as crime, racism, poverty, and environmental degradation, these problems continue unabated. Partially as a consequence of our inability to solve these problems, the American public has become highly cynical, believing that little can be done. Resigned to this, people with the opportunity and means to separate themselves from such problems withdraw into protected enclaves.

Thus, shopping malls provide pleasantly anesthetized shopping worlds away from the crime, poverty, and the uncomfortable mixture of lifestyles present in urban downtowns. And the new gated communities become seemingly secure havens where crime and poverty are only seen on TV or read about in newspapers. In this way, social problems become distanced from an important segment of society—those with the greatest resources to solve the problems. These issues are no longer a communal concern that requires active, responsible behavior on the part of members of the community and instead become relegated to government bureaucrats who develop programs to address the problems.

The avoidance of social problems by fleeing actually helps perpetuate those problems in three ways. First, when people leave areas where social problems occur, resources needed to address the problems are removed. By shopping in malls rather than urban downtowns, by living in lifestyle enclaves rather than in socially and racially integrated neighborhoods, by frequenting restaurant chains rather than neighborhood bars and restaurants, people redirect financial resources away from areas most likely to experience social difficulties. Second, leaving high-risk areas in favor of safe areas makes it even more difficult for people to work their way out of poverty and crime because those who could provide role models and help to organize important communal organizations have left (Wilson 1987). A potential criminal's role model in areas of poverty is not the person who chose the option of work and became successful in business (that person has left and is not seen); rather the only role model left is the drug dealer or the burglar.

Third, the social and racial segmentation of society removes social problems from their communal context. When the pattern of dealing with problems is avoidance and separation, the only remedy left is government intervention. However, this form of government intervention lacks a communal base and tends to produce programs developed by distant professionals who, lacking an understanding of the community, operate them often more for the benefit of themselves than the community (McKnight 1995).

3. *Counterfeit community doesn't address community concerns.* Counterfeit community is, by its very nature, elite-designed and elite-controlled. The physical space and social patterns present in counterfeit community are socially engineered in a top-down fashion. Problems that emerge are dealt with in a similar manner. Assessments are made by the elites, and solutions are developed and implemented by those same elites. The entire process is thus biased in favor of elite control. Elites determine what is considered a problem (if it adversely affects elites) and devise solutions that maintain their control.

Genuine communities, however, operate in a much different fashion. Problem definition emerges from the concerns of the active members of the community, and solutions are arrived at after community debate and discussion. An important criterion in communities is the extent to which solutions help maintain the viability of the community itself. In counterfeit community, on the other hand, the primary criterion tends to be the economic interests of the elites.

We will see when we examine the workplace, for example, that the attempt to create a sense of community has become a popular manipulation device used by management to improve the productivity of workers. Anything that interferes with increasing productivity is considered a problem, but concerns that workers might have about things such as corporate responsibility or the equal sharing of profits will not be considered relevant.

4. *Counterfeit community fails to produce psychological benefits for its membership.* The principle motivating force behind counterfeit community is economic, whereas one of the major benefits of genuine community is the psychological health of the people in the community. Relationships in community are based upon trust, respect, friendship, and mutual support—justice in practice. Counterfeit community is concerned with relationships only to the extent that they not become hostile to the point of

disrupting the status quo. To ensure that this will occur, counterfeit community places a reliance upon rules and regulations. When joining a planned community, for example, there is no requirement, or even expectation, that individuals treat others with respect or that they even have to know anyone else in the community. But, every individual, before being allowed in, will have to sign a several hundred page document that details all the rules and regulations that must be adhered to. The acid test for membership in genuine community has more to do with character as exemplified in human relationships, while the acid test for membership in counterfeit community has more to do with obeying rules and being able to pay.

5. *Counterfeit community separates us from reality.* Counterfeit community attempts to shift the traditional thick conception of community to a thin version of pseudo-community. It does this by redefining the meaning of community, passing off counterfeit forms through the use of palaver. The consequence of this shifting of the meaning of language—shifting the meaning of community—is to separate the concept of community from its reality. This is, of course, an effective political manipulation. If one is successful at getting people to adopt new meanings of community, at separating them from the reality of community, the effects are to produce an innocence toward the influences of class, wealth, race, and gender.

This is a more fundamental problem than avoidance, of fleeing from the awkwardness and difficulty of social problems. Counterfeit community represents an undermining of an important aspect of human association through the manipulation of images, sounds, and symbols. How else can we explain how residents of private gated community associations that impose hundreds of detailed regulations governing virtually every aspect of their lives can claim that they have little use for government? The notion of what government means has been separated from the activities government performs in our everyday lives. The effect then is to disconnect words from their worldly referents and produce citizens who claim to be a part of a community but feel no sense of social responsibility other than paying dues because the new meaning of community does not require anything more.

Mistaking counterfeit community for the "real" thing has significant implications, not only for social theory but for our own lives. If in seeking connectedness, we accept the counterfeit version of community, we will be using resources to distance ourselves from social concerns, from our psychological needs, and even from reality. Such a "communal" experience leaves us feeling alone, empty, and bewildered as to what has gone wrong.

The definition of idealized community that I have suggested helps not only to identify the counterfeit but to introduce an alternative that is responsive to human needs at both the public and the private levels. Community is a powerful concept, stimulating people to put aside narrow self-interest and act on behalf of justice. It is this activating force that is being undermined by counterfeit community.

SEARCHING FOR COUNTERFEITS

The discussion above provides us with some clues about where to look to assess the current state of community in America. In general, our examination of community will be broken into two areas—the physical setting and the social institutions. In reality, of course, these two elements are inseparable: place affects social interaction, just as social interaction leads to the construction of particular types of spaces. But for the sake of analysis we will first deal with the physical characteristics of claims of community and then turn our attention to social institutions thought to be relevant to the creation and maintenance of community.

Perhaps the single most significant physical aspect that helps to shape community is housing. The types of housing, the manner in which people relate to each other on the basis of their homes, and the governance of neighborhoods are all aspects of central importance to community. Chapter 3 examines recent trends in housing in America, focusing particularly on gated communities. These housing developments are becoming increasingly popular and are being presented as new forms of community. Taking our cues from descriptions of community, chapter 4 examines the public spaces necessary for community. To illustrate the importance of public space in communities and how it is distorted in counterfeit communities, three examples of public space are examined: shopping malls, third places (public places where people gather beyond the realms of home or work), and front porches. These particular spaces are not, by themselves, thought to be necessary conditions for community; rather, much like canaries in mines, they may be seen as warning signs about the erosion of genuine community and its replacement with counterfeit community. When public spaces disappear, community becomes problematic.

While physical settings are important, the essence of community is to be found in the character of the social interactions of the members of the community. Chapter 5 (the workplace), chapter 6 (politics), and chapter 7 (religion) all deal with social institutions important for the formation of community. Chapter 5 bridges the gap between the impact of the physical environment in shaping community and the effect of social interactions on community. In that chapter also, recent developments in management techniques are examined. The new participatory management approaches are examined and found to be examples of counterfeit community applied to the workplace. In chapter 6, the fundamental character of politics in contemporary America is examined as it leads us toward accepting versions of community that are inherently counterfeit in nature. We have come to accept a version of elite democracy that makes counterfeit claims of community in politics appear acceptable and natural. As will be seen in chapter 7, over the past several decades religion has embraced forms that have moved it away from playing a central role in communities to developing its own version of counterfeit community disconnected from people's everyday lives.

With both the physical and social dimensions necessary for community undermined and replaced with counterfeit versions, chapter 8 examines an arena that challenges our beliefs that community must be located in a physical space and that it must possess face-to-face social interaction. Making perhaps the boldest claims for creating community, the Internet will be shown to be fundamentally counterfeit.

What community is, how it may be created, and how it may be sustained are topics of interest for many who approach the subject from quite different vantage points. Chapter 9 briefly presents four popular approaches to the topic and finds that, while each makes valuable contributions to our understanding of community, each emphasizes (or fails to emphasize) key elements for the creation of genuine community, and none recognize even the existence of counterfeit community. The final chapter concludes by developing a program of recommendations to address the major barriers to the creation of community. To create genuine community in America will require a major national effort to reorient the way Americans live.

3
Housing

During the medieval era, banditry became widespread and was widely
accepted . . . as a populist revenge upon the defenders of the political
and social order. Unwalled cities and free citizens were replaced by
walled manor houses and serfs.

—*Lester Thurow (1995, 79)*

Twenty miles south of Atlanta, just beyond the beltway, among stands
of dogwoods lies Peachtree City. Without either a map or detailed
directions it would be easy to miss. All houses, industrial parks,
schools, and, to a lesser extent, shopping malls are set back from the highways, behind neatly manicured grassy berms and thick forests of pines. You
could easily drive down any of the two- or four-lane highways that slice
through the city and not even realize you had been through it.

Peachtree City has within it a planned community called Kendrick. It is
one of more than 150,000 private homeowner associations that exist in the
United States. Anywhere from 28 to 32 million Americans now live in housing, including condominiums and cooperatives, governed by private associations. Estimates are that the number of people who live in planned communities will continue to grow into the foreseeable future. Peachtree City
and the numerous planned neighborhoods within it represent the future
of housing in America.

East of Seattle, across Lake Washington, lies Bear Creek, a housing development of 500 residents where virtually everything is planned and private. The roads leading in to Bear Creek are protected twenty-four hours a
day by private security guards who limit access to residents and guests only.
There is no soliciting, whether it be vacuum cleaner salesmen, politicians
seeking votes, or Girl Scouts selling cookies. In Bear Creek the streets are
private, the sewers are private, the park is private, and even the government
is private. The homeowner association has imposed gun control, dog con-

trol (through the use of electronic monitoring devices), shrubbery height rules, house color limitations (either beige or gray) and even banned basketball hoops attached to garages.

Evan McKenzie refers to developments like Bear Creek and Peachtree City as Common Interest Developments (CIDs) and says they have the following characteristics:

> master planning of large-scale communities; isolation of the development from its surroundings and protection against change; capitalization on dislike of city life to attract residents; development of a government based on a corporate charter and attempts to replace politics with management; and creation of a government with greater powers than that of the city. (1994, 18)

CIDs are the most obvious examples of counterfeit community in America today, and the marketing of them as community is blatant.

The Urban Land Institute, founded by developers, was an early promoter of CIDs. In 1964 it came up with the following analysis of the urban situation:

> The explosive growth of our cities, their trend to gigantism, and the high mobility of their residents are rapidly destroying a sense of community among individuals in urban America. Constructive forces are needed to counteract these negative aspects and to utilize the opportunity that growth offers to build better communities. The best possible way to bring about—or to revive—a grassroots sense of community is for home owners to control nearby facilities of importance to them and through this to participate actively in the life of their communities. (McKenzie 1994, 24)

This analysis sets the stage for the creation of CIDs which exploited similar themes of community, grassroots participation, and fear of urban crime and poverty. It is in developments such as Peachtree City and Bear Creek that the future prospects for residential community are being presented.

But it should be made clear at the outset that the Urban Land Institute was not primarily concerned about reviving a sense of community. Composed of developers and those who would profit from development, it was interested in creating an environment favorable to a new form of development that would further maximize profit. The concern about the loss of community occurred only within that context. The CID represents a new form of residential organization that protects residents from the deterioration of urban American not by addressing the fundamental problems causing that deterioration, but by avoiding those difficulties and exploiting our longings for community.

COUNTERFEIT NEIGHBORHOODS

If there is any place at all where we might expect to find community, it is in our neighborhoods. It is here where the possibilities for interaction based upon social, economic, and political needs present themselves to the greatest degree. It has been in our neighborhoods where people have gathered on front porches to exchange gossip or argue politics, where boys played stickball in the streets or softball in the alleys, where girls played house in the attic, where women casually chatted at the neighborhood meat market, where men met in neighborhood bars for a few drinks and some light conversation after work, where people talked with each other as they leisurely strolled home from church on Sunday afternoon. Historically, neighborhoods have been the incubators of community.

But before we become overly sentimental about what used to be, we should note that even the most cohesive neighborhood communities lacked significant elements we would consider important for communal living today. Most allowed arbitrary authority to have its day, authority that was often corrupt and sometimes brutal; most excluded or oppressed those who were ethnically, socially, politically, or sexually different; and most communities severely limited the choices available to their members, particularly so with women who were responsible for home and children and not much else. Those were communities where equality was not achieved and was not even an issue, where justice was defined by authority and power.

What's more, the extent of neighborhood community was quite limited. Perhaps because of our longing for community today, we nostalgically look back to earlier times and find community where only fragments truly existed, and we tend to draw overgeneralizations about the pervasiveness of community based upon few real examples. Indeed, our limited historical visions may be even better than 20/20. Regardless of the time period selected, genuine community has always been the exception and never the norm.

It is into this nostalgic quagmire that a variety of forms of counterfeit housing communities have been introduced. Some are closed off and gated where only members or invited guests are allowed in; others take the form of high-rise condominiums. Virtually all of them have private governments and restrictive covenants attached to ownership. Because of their exclusivity, they lack diversity and spontaneity. Whereas in genuine communities public spaces provided a neutral meeting ground, public spaces in CIDs have been deadened, reduced to aesthetic complements for the neighborhoods rather than spaces for citizens to meet and converse. It is within these cocoon-like neighborhoods that counterfeit community, superficial in feeling and non-participatory in character, is being forged.

SELLING THE NEIGHBORHOOD

Counterfeit neighborhoods are marketed through the use of palaver that focuses on security, predictability, convenience, and scenic open space—images of bucolic communities of an earlier, imagined era. In the marketing process, an idealized vision of the American community is projected where streets are safe, life is predictable, houses are neat and tidy, and shopping, schools, and medical centers are only minutes away.

Virtually all CIDs are advertised as communities of one sort or another, whether they be retirement communities, singles communities, golfing communities, boating communities, ecological communities, or adult communities. By linking the concept of community with the targeted audience, developers market not just the houses but a preconceived concept of what certain kinds of people are like. One is encouraged to extrapolate from the social or economic characteristics of the individual to their individual beliefs. As one advertisement says, it "is more than a home, it's a lifestyle."

Critics of CIDs often take them to task for the lack of spontaneity. As Molly Ivins once said, "There is something inorganic . . . something utterly unspontaneous. I got the feeling there is nowhere you can get a bowl of banana pudding" (Garreau 1991, 231). The palaver of selling the CID, however, presents the potential buyer with the appearance of choice. One may choose from one of four or five floor plans, select any of three different colors of wall-to-wall carpeting, have a choice of lighting fixtures, and even opt for a partial or full membership in the private country club. By providing a modest variety of housing styles and accessories, the appearance of choice and voluntarism is projected. In reality, the range of choices is narrow and restricted to property accessories while regulations on behavior are strict, and the option of living or not living in some form of CID is becoming less and less a real choice. In Southern California, for example, a third of all new developments are CIDs, and by the year 2000 it is estimated that there will be 225,000 such developments nationwide (McKenzie 1994, 11).

But the primary marketing mechanism of CIDs is the concept of community. "We're a real community, with sidewalks on safe streets, more than 300 acres of open space and, best of all, our commitment to the environment," says one video ad. Another glossy brochure attempts to attract buyers by describing itself as "a special place to live [where] growth is controlled but not stifled." One CID in suburban Chicago advertises itself this way: "This perfect community is nearly complete . . . all it needs is you!" Another CID advertisement pictures a father and daughter hugging each other with the following caption: "Sundance Homes is building in the types of neighborhoods you remember as a child. Ones with trees, parks and wide open spaces. Where neighbors say hello, and have a real sense of community. Promises made, promises kept." Attempting to appeal to the ecologically sensitive, the Prairie Crossing CID markets itself this way: "A Conservation Community . . . where people reconnect with one another and the land." In an advertisement for one of the many CIDs that have been developed along the Atlantic Coast, the developers describe life there in the following terms: "A dream of a unique island community, marked by privacy, natural beauty and unmatched recreation. . . . Clearly set apart by an incomparable recreational package . . . also known for its special sense of community. And most importantly, [it] is distinguished by the striking resemblance of our reality to the original dream."

Community is thus effectively used as a marketing device to sell land and houses. This is done by convincing prospective buyers that, if they only purchase a house, they will become a part of a community: they will be connected to others who share similar beliefs and feelings. The special "sense of community" being sold comes not from interactions among members of the neighborhood; rather it comes because anyone who would purchase a house in the particular neighborhood already possesses values and beliefs similar to them.

DIVERSITY

From the early twentieth century until 1948, housing developments, aided and abetted by the Federal Housing Administration, used covenants to exclude African Americans, Jews, Asian Americans, and other minorities from owning houses in particular neighborhoods. Real estate agents actively cooperated with developers to ban minorities, justifying such exclusion in terms of protecting property values. The National Association of Real Estate Boards (NAREB), an alliance between real estate agents and builders, issued the following provision in their code of ethics: "Article 34. A Realtor should never be instrumental in introducing into a neighborhood a character of property or occupancy, members of any race or nationality, or any individuals whose presence will clearly be detrimental to property values in that neighborhood" (Abrams 1955, 154).

The Federal Housing Administration (FHA) not only failed to discourage racist practices, but actively promoted race and class separation. In their underwriting manual, the FHA set forth the following policy: "Satisfaction, contentment, and comfort result from association with persons of similar social attributes. Families enjoy social relationships with other families whose education, abilities, mode of living, and racial characteristics are similar to their own" (quoted in McKenzie 1994, 65).

One study conducted in 1947 found that 56 percent of all homes examined contained restrictive covenants (Dean 1947), and segregation continued as the law of the land until the Supreme Court in 1948 said the courts could no longer be used to enforce them. This, however, did not end housing segregation; it merely meant that new forms of exclusion would have to be found. One of the most effective exclusionary devices used today is the homeowner association. Through the use of numerous rules, regulations, and limitations of behavior, segregation has been, for the most part, maintained. Homeowner associations restrict how many families may live in houses, they ban excessive roomers, they may place age requirements on members, and they regulate the size of lots and establish maintenance standards: "In this manner, homeowner associations . . . shifted their emphasis to class discrimination, which is legal, from race discrimination, which is not" (McKenzie 1994, 78). The result is to exclude people who are perceived as being a threat to property values and thereby produce homogeneous neighborhoods. While there is not an explicit exclusion of people on the basis of race, the effect is to do so, as the economic disparities present between whites and nonwhites in America are allowed to be played out.

Some CIDs extend the idea of economic segregation beyond the entire development and institute it at the level of each block. Thus, one block might include only houses in the $200,000 to $250,000 range, while another block might include houses that range in price from $250,000 to $300,000. Further segregation is accomplished through marketing efforts that target particular types of people for particular neighborhoods. There are "working couples," "singles," "first-time buyers," "retirees," and the like who are identified by the builder to live in selected parts of the development.

In one of the more interesting strategies to create economic segregation, the Grand Harbor CID in Vero Beach, Florida, has segregated housing by island. On Victoria Island, the most inland of the twenty-some islands that make up the development, housing prices start at $194,000. But the choicest island is Harbor Pointe where housing starts at $400,000 and a "spectacular Indian River view" house starts at $697,500.

The effect of economic segregation is to further stratify people and encourage only interaction among people with similar incomes. Whatever sense of connectedness that develops becomes associated with economic status, so the "sense of who you are" emerges not from a richness of diverse human interactions, but rather from an objective assessment of one's income level (as imputed from the cost of the house you own).

This type of economic segregation is, of course, planned, and it is based upon grim beliefs about people's abilities to live together in harmony. Mark Pisano, executive director of the Southern California Association of Governments (the nation's largest regional planning association), sums up the viewpoint: "In a highly pluralistic society, it may be dangerous to bring disparate groups together too closely. A certain distance might be healthy" (quoted in Garreau 1991, 287). Nonetheless, this form of economic segregation is passed off as community.

Discrimination in CIDs occurs not only on the basis of economic distinctions. In the ironically named Phoenix suburb of Youngstown, an ordinance in the retirement community requires each household to have at least one resident fifty-five years of age or older, and people eighteen or younger can stay no longer than three months. In 1995 Jerry and LynnRae Naab took in their grandson, then sixteen, when he fled his home to escape physical and mental abuse from his stepfather. After they exceeded the three-month limit and several extensions, they were ordered by the CID board to move the boy out of the community or face stiff fines and possible jail sentences. This occurred even though it was agreed that the boy had not caused trouble, played with friends only outside of the community, and even worked part-time at a pizza parlor to help pay the bills. The common feeling in the retirement CID was that residents were tired of children, that they had already gone through that stage in their lives and simply did not want children around.

The problem with a lack of diversity in CIDs is not "merely" a problem of justice. The desire to associate only with people who are similar to oneself also represents the urges we possess as we go through the process of maturation, particularly associated with adolescence. As adolescents struggle to discover for themselves what skills they possess, what rules make sense for them, and what authority should be obeyed, they experience considerable anxiety. This anxiety represents, in effect, an identity crisis. While this may be seen as a natural part of the maturation process, it becomes pathological for the individual if it is embraced as a reason for avoiding that which is different, and it becomes destructive for genuine community when social structures and norms encourage interaction only with those who are similar to oneself.

The communal structuring of these patterns of avoidance of differences is referred to by Richard Sennett as "purified communities" (1970): "It is the social structure of modern urban communities of affluence that not only prolongs this adolescent pattern of avoidance, but also subsequently works to freeze adult lives in the same pattern, so that men are continually led to imagine meanings about all manner of experience they are afraid to have" (26). Purified communities are made possible because of affluence, and they stunt the maturation process. Rather than encouraging community members to discover their own identities by seriously encountering those who differ from themselves, they encourage a form of purified identity as a means of avoiding experiences that may be threatening or painful: "Communally painful experiences, unknown social situations full of possible surprise and challenge can be avoided by the common consent of the community to believe they already know the meaning of these experiences and have drawn the lessons from them together" (Sennett 1970, 38). Finding the differences in people and integrating those differences into our own lives are far more difficult than finding and sharing our similarities. This results in a superficial feeling of connectedness based upon sameness.

It is this sameness, structured into the residential patterns of CIDs, that forms the basis of feelings of community and makes them inherently counterfeit: "The sharing that occurs in deep relations of intimacy grows out of loving the distinctiveness, the uniqueness of the other person, not in the merging of selves into one homogenized being. But in the purification of a coherent image, fear rather than love of men's 'otherness' prevails. Out of this fear is bred the counterfeit of experience" (Sennett 1970, 39). Counterfeit communities produce counterfeit experiences.

Thus, counterfeit community replaces the heterogeneity that genuine community offers with homogeneity and instead of bringing people together, which genuine community would do, further separates people. The counterfeits "deprive people of societal resources and thus stultify their lives; promote isolation and conflict between residents of the community and the rest of society; stunt children's ability to relate to people unlike themselves; and leave residents frozen in their present way of life" (McKenzie 1994, 189).

MANAGEMENT RATHER THAN POLITICS

Americans, regardless of their age, social status, race, ethnicity, or political orientation, are alienated from politics. Everywhere people believe that government does not address the needs of everyday people and that it is run by the few, for the few. These beliefs (regardless of their objective accuracy) contribute to the attitudinal support for private homeowner associations (i.e., private governments) that tend to be far more restrictive and far more regulative than any government could even approach.

The distrust of government and politics can be traced back through history to the founding period and to James Madison, whose distrust permanently embedded itself in our constitutional structure. Madison explains his view of human nature in Federalist No. 51: "If men were angels no government would be necessary. If angels were to govern men, neither external nor internal controls on government would be necessary." Perhaps the development that has had the most significant impact on contemporary local politics occurred in the early decades of the twentieth century with the Progressive Movement. While there were many dimensions of the movement, the aspect of most interest here was the attempt to replace politics with management. Aiming their sights on urban political machines, which were primarily controlled by the urban working class, the Progressives pushed for efficiency and economy. Included in their reform package was the belief that the day-to-day administration of government should be separated from "politics," that trained experts should run city services, and that government should be run like a business, applying the principles of scientific management.

The Progressive reforms were not apolitical. They were aggressively supported by the middle and upper classes and opposed by the working class. Once instituted, the reforms hurt the urban political machines (although more fundamental demographic changes probably could be blamed for their downfall). More importantly for our purposes is the belief that emerged from the movement that the best way to run local government was through the use of management techniques rather than through politics.

Counterfeit communities, as represented in CIDs, emerge from the apolitical mythology advocated by the Progressive Movement that attempts to replace politics with management. In place of local governments are private homeowner associations. Although the specific focus that the associations take may vary somewhat, common elements are present: everyone who buys a residential unit automatically becomes a member (membership is mandatory); a set of covenants, conditions, and restrictions that are legally binding on the homeowner must be signed; a board of directors made up of neighbors is elected to enforce rules; and there is one vote per residential unit.

The range and scope of these private governments often go far beyond what would be acceptable for other local governments. The associations may impose standards of behavior on residents and guests and may enforce the regulations through the imposition of fines and, in extreme cases, the loss of one's home. Commonly, regulations include standards for repair and maintenance of one's house and restrictions on how long guests may stay, the number of occupants allowed, the age of occupants, and whether houses may be used for business. Most CID associations also have the right to enter individual homes as is deemed necessary in order to correct problems that might lead to an undermining of others' property values.

In addition to the enforcement of covenants and regulations, the associations are responsible for the common areas—parks, streets, pools, clubhouses, and the like. To support the building and maintenance of common areas, additional fees are imposed, thus leading to concerns by residents of double taxation—being taxed once by the local government and once by the association.

In genuine communities, rules and regulations emerge after extensive discussion and debate among members. They are codified and thus given formal legitimacy by local governments that give them the status of statutes and regulations. As is true in any organization, the rules have a tendency to become reified and resistant to change, but nonetheless, individuals may and often do alter them to best address changing circumstances. In sum, rules are created by the community to address the needs and concerns of the members who have identified problems as a result of their own communal experiences.

In counterfeit communities, however, the process of rule-making is reversed and is imposed upon the community from above: "First there is a plan; second, there is property; third, there are rules to protect the property; fourth, there is a physical 'city'; and last, there are people to live in the city and to follow the rules that protect the property. In short, a CID is a prefabricated framework for civil society in search of a population" (McKenzie 1994, 145).

What's more, the rules in CIDs are far more difficult to change than laws created by local governments. The very operation of homeowner associations tends to violate traditionally accepted democratic principles. Although members of the homeowners governing board are elected by a majority vote, it does not follow the "one man, one vote" principle. Instead, each property unit (not person) is given one vote. Furthermore, associations commonly require a super-majority vote, often as much as 80 percent of all eligible voters, to change restrictions. Finally, these private governments have been provided legal protection in most states that allows them to be immune from many complaints (and lawsuits) of disgruntled members. Legally, the restrictions are called "equitable servitudes," devices that allow someone to sell land but still control how the land is used.

The loss of politics that occurs in counterfeit communities produces consequences few Americans, if they were fully aware of them, would willingly accept. One beneficial consequence of an active democratic form of politics is that it may become a catalyst for change, both systemic and personal change. Politics inherently involves conflict, as support is mobilized behind issues affecting the community by competing individuals and groups. But more fundamentally, politics represents a form of self-determination whereby individuals empower themselves and others (in democratic forms of politics) to take control and responsibility for forces that might otherwise control them (Moon 1993). In a world in which individuals feel as if they have no control over decisions made by distant bureaucrats or behind closed doors by business and political elites, democratic politics provides a form of collective freedom. This is possible only if there exist practices and institutions that encourage citizens to present their views, discuss, debate, and deliberate with other citizens who hold opposing viewpoints, modify their views, and arrive at some vision of the common good. Needless to say, the forms of counterfeit neighborhoods discussed in this chapter discourage democratic politics.

On an individual level the elimination of politics undermines personal change. In one strain of democratic political theory, it is argued that participation in democratic politics performs an important educative function, developing in each citizen an ability to link the public with the private, to increase the value of freedom, and to create in each individual a feeling that he or she belongs in the community (Pateman 1970). Politics should perform the important function of building democratic character. But in counterfeit community, potential political issues are suppressed and dealt with within the managerial context.

Because of the virtual elimination of politics from CIDs, residents are given few options to redress their grievances should management decide against them. One of the few strategies open to residents has been court action. But the courts have, for the most part, not been sympathetic to the pleas of residents and have instead given homeowner associations almost complete freedom to operate as they wish, reasoning that CIDs are private, voluntary organizations, not governments and therefore not subject to the rules that would limit governments. Thus, by accepting a nonpolitical model of governance, CID residents have closed an important avenue by which change and protection of rights could be accomplished—politics.

DEAD PUBLIC SPACE

Lively public spaces have long been considered vital for the existence of community. It was in public arenas—parks, streets, markets, squares, "third" places—where a wide diversity of people could be encountered, where the habits of association could be developed, and where the roots of democracy could be cultivated (Oldenburg 1989). From a more esoteric perspective, the public realm allows those dimensions of the human personality associated with will and artifice to be expressed while the private dealt more with the accidents of individual character (Sennett 1976).

Regardless of the specific reasons for the importance of public space for communal development, there has been a consistent elimination of such environments and a deadening of the few that remain. A multitude of causes for this trend have been identified: the rise of capitalism, the fear of crime, the advent of new technologies such as the automobile, the TV, the Internet, the growth of suburbia and edge cities, the development of shopping malls, or merely our own psychological fear of meeting people who are different.

The planners of counterfeit neighborhoods have at least symbolically included public spaces into their designs. Yet, while spaces exist where residents may meet, the vital community-building functions traditionally associated with them have been replaced with the symbolism of public space. Public space in CIDs is designed to enhance social control and maintain property values. This is accomplished through the careful placing of public arenas, the banning of some "undesirable" third places, and the establishment of strict rules governing their use.

Third places, as discussed by Oldenburg (1989), are simply the informal gathering places for people beyond the family and work. They include cafes, pubs, corner stores, pool halls, coffee shops, barbershops, parks, and other hangouts. They are oriented primarily for conversation and free play. They have been typically modest, inexpensive, and small, where people met spontaneously to entertain each other without hidden agendas or clearly defined purposes.

Suburban growth represented one of the first attacks on third places, as zoning boards carefully controlled the location and number of such places that could be established. CID developers took the attack one step further, banning private third places from residential neighborhoods and isolating those allowed to exist to clearly defined commercial areas, accessible only by car. To frequent such places requires more than merely a spontaneous urge to walk down the block; it requires a specific reason to drive several miles—it requires a purpose, the very motivation that runs counter to their existence.

In place of third places that encourage spontaneity, CIDs have pools, parks, and clubhouses "for members only" where particular social activities are allowed and events are planned and scheduled. Loitering, lounging, or hanging-out are activities not just frowned upon but in many cases banned by the homeowner association. In some common areas such as green spaces, forests, and aesthetically pleasing man-made lakes, any human activities at all are prohibited. All activities considered acceptable must only take place in appropriately designated areas. To discourage the use of the front stoops as gathering places, the CID house has eliminated them altogether. Instead, gatherings have been moved to family rooms or to decks attached to the rear of the house where little interaction with neighbors will occur (this change is discussed in greater detail in chapter 4).

These changes reflect changes in the way people treat each other throughout society and illustrate further the decline of community: "The modern urban environment accommodates people as players of unifunctional roles. It reduces people to clients, customers, workers, and commuters, allowing them little opportunity to be human beings. It constricts and constrains" (Oldenburg 1989, 207). This is very different from the manner in which people are treated where community exists. For example, Ehrenhalt (1995) describes community in St. Nick's parish in Chicago as including the integrating functions performed by the neighborhood grocery stores, vital third places. Early each weekday afternoon the women would wheel their shopping carts a few blocks to buy groceries. The mom-and-pop grocery stores would record each family's debt without charging interest (the debts inevitably would be paid off on paydays). On Monday and Thursday evenings the small business areas would be crowded with residents, some shopping, some just talking: "The very act of shopping was embedded in the web of long-term relationships between customer and merchant, relationships that were more important than the price of a particular item at a particular time" (Ehrenhalt 1995, 99).

Counterfeit communities as they are manifest in CIDs further the segmentation that exists in society by establishing common spaces that either prevent any activities whatsoever or that allow only narrowly defined, planned activities. Most third places of the type Oldenburg refers to are banned altogether from the CID boundaries. In doing this the CID distorts the meaning and significance of third places and, in reality, turns them against community.

CITIZENSHIP

Americans have never developed a clear consensus about the meaning of democracy or what it means to be a "good citizen." Throughout U.S. history there have been periods of intense grassroots political movements (e.g., the Revolution, the Populist Movement), but at other times politics was considered unimportant (e.g., the 1950s). In recent years, however, there is reason to believe that a more passive form of citizenship has taken hold. Individuals today tend to view their roles as citizens primarily in terms of rights rather than responsibilities. At best, they feel an obligation to vote at election time, a rather passive form of political activity.

Orientations toward citizenship, whether they be active or passive, are not inborn. People are not, at birth, imprinted with active or passive political genes. Instead, citizenship is culturally conditioned. People learn by growing up in society, by watching and listening to others, by modeling behavior, and by making conscious choices about what it means to be a citizen. It is here, of course, where community plays such a critical role. In genuine community, members are actively engaged in civic life and, by being engaged, they further learn the democratic skills needed to be effective and adopt the values associated with democracy.

Most residents of CIDs play a passive role in governance and the structures of the homeowner associations tend to be dominated by an oligarchy. Citizenship roles, like so many other aspects of CID life, are defined by the overarching goal of maintaining property values. Citizenship "consists of making house payments, paying association dues and assessments, and conforming to a set of lifestyle restrictions that have the sole stated purpose of preserving the value of the commonly owned property" (McKenzie

1994, 149). Membership in CIDs violates most commonly accepted norms of genuine community life: membership is mandatory not voluntary; obedience to rules is forced rather than based upon a commitment to the community; participation is motivated by the narrow self-interest goal of protection of property values rather than a recognition of communal interdependence.

The limited and limiting role of citizenship is also reflected in the structure of the homeowner associations—the private governments. The character of the structures themselves emerges from the corporate business world. Indeed, they are usually drawn up by the developer and imposed on the development as the developer completes the house-building phase and seeks to move on. Most commonly, the developer sets up the homeowner association following guidelines found in the *Homes Association Handbook*. The governance rules and procedures make it extremely unlikely that they will be modified because super-majority votes and a several-year waiting period usually are required before changes can be effected.

Serving on the board of directors of a homeowner association is often a thankless task. Members meet frequently, receive no pay, and are concerned primarily with the rather bland world of finances, assessment of fines, and rule enforcement. Unpleasant and acrimonious feelings often result as the board members must enforce decisions against their neighbors that sometimes involve substantial financial penalties and, in rare cases, loss of homes. It is not surprising then to find that members of governing boards possess strong authoritarian tendencies (McKenzie 1994). More significantly, the boards of homeowner associations, as is true of most private governments, are inclined toward oligarchy (Berle 1954). Thus, rather than being open and inclusive, they tend to be controlled by what is perceived of as a small group of powerful neighbors (Barton and Silverman 1987).

The entire culture of citizenship in the CID leans in the direction of the acceptance of a passive membership role to an even greater extent than exists in most of public life. Yet this limited view of citizenship is occurring within the context of supposed community. While passive involvement in the civic life of one's neighborhood may be beneficial for the business elites who have built common interest developments, it undermines attempts to create more viable forms of community which must rely upon the active involvement of the membership. Above and beyond issues of property values lie more significant issues of equality and justice, issues that require inclusiveness and participation for their realization.

JUSTICE

Based upon the prior analysis it should come as no surprise that CIDs are woefully inadequate in being able to achieve, or even begin to address, issues of justice. In many respects they are designed to avoid dealing with un-comfortable issues such as inequality, fairness, and discrimination. By sepa-rating residents from the results of fundamental inequalities manifest in deteriorating urban neighborhoods, declining city schools, homelessness, and deserted downtowns, counterfeit communities never allow issues that relate to the unequal distribution of resources to even be placed on the po-litical agenda. (Of course, the replacement of politics with management further helps eliminate issues of justice from the discourse.)

Planned communities market themselves as safe havens away from the deteriorating social and political environment. This image is further en-hanced through the use of mandatory security measures such as security guards at entrances, electronic security systems built into each housing unit, the elimination of names from mailboxes, and the construction of walls and gates to limit access. Rather than remaining within urban areas that experience difficulty, Americans who possess the economic means have fled, first to the suburbs and now to CIDs. With the flight they have taken with them valuable resources that could otherwise be used to help solve the very problems that led to flight in the first place. The exodus from the city has added to the undermining of the tax base, has eliminated from participation many middle-class citizens who would otherwise partici-pate in local urban organizations (the PTA, religious organizations, etc.), and has removed important role models for children growing up in disad-vantaged neighborhoods.

Attempts already exist by residents of CIDs to exempt themselves from a variety of local taxes that go to support services duplicated by home-owner associations (e.g., police protection, road maintenance). Increas-ingly, residents are seen as formidable voting blocs that threaten to oppose the use of government funds to support programs for the urban disadvan-taged. Robert Reich refers to this as "the secession of the successful": "In many cities and towns, the wealthy have in effect withdrawn their dollars from the support of public spaces and institutions shared by all and dedi-cated the savings to their own private services" (1991, 42).

What's more, one must be concerned about the education of children who grow up in gated communities, associating only with people who are similar to themselves. While American society continues to become more and more ethnically diverse and where inequalities in wealth are becom-ing more and more pronounced, the life experiences of people—espe-cially people who can afford it—are becoming more and more homoge-neous. Community should provide an environment in which people of diverse backgrounds and diverse ideas interact in a nonconfrontational manner. Instead, the form of counterfeit community that is emerging in the form of CIDs is leading to an even greater and more visible separation of people.

CONCLUSION

Our environments affect us; they help shape our thoughts, our feelings, and our actions (Altman and Low 1992). Environments can increase the pace at which we move or slow us down, they can make us feel helpless or in control, they can depress us or stimulate us, they can isolate us or bring us together. But our relationship with our environment is not a one-way street. Just as our environment affects us, so too we can shape and influence our environment. We may pollute and poison our environments or we may live in harmony with them; we may build environments that are ugly and lack character or we may create environments that are beautiful and unique. To build genuine community in America we must pay attention to our physical surroundings—first and foremost to our neighborhoods. We need places that support and integrate our lives rather than fragment us, places that help us balance our lives rather than reinforce the feelings of alienation we experience elsewhere.

Perhaps one of the saddest things about CIDs is that they lack character: they fail to provide any sense of uniqueness to place. A CID in Georgia could just as easily be mistaken for a CID in New York or Oregon. Following the oft-heard adage of the real estate professionals that if you want to sell your house it should not have anything permanently attached that might offend prospective buyers, CIDs have created sterile and bland neighborhoods. Everything must be kept neat and tidy, houses must be painted inoffensive grays or beiges, all houses must be made to conform to others in the neighborhood. Rather than allowing houses to become statements of individuality and an extension of one's tastes and personality, residents of CIDs are forced to adhere to one overarching principle—the protection of property values. CID houses seldom become homes to the extent that the house represents a celebration of the achievements of the owner and a representation of family life. Instead, they are good financial investments.

The view that one's house is first and foremost a financial investment has resulted in a homogenization of neighborhoods and undermined the possibility of creating a place with uniqueness, character, and community. The neighborhood environment created in the CID isolates and alienates residents by disconnecting them from social problems and discouraging human interaction. By deadening public space and treating residents as investors rather than citizens, the CID discourages the emergence of feelings of community based upon face-to-face meetings with neighbors. Community feelings and loyalties consequently are created (if they are created at all) through the use of abstract symbolic appeals. Sameness masquerades as community.

CIDs also disrupt the important linkage between the family and the community. Families have traditionally been viewed as important building blocks for community. Some have even contended that "a stable family unit and village system is the foundation of civilization" (Wachter and Tinsley 1996, 4). In order for them to function in this capacity there must be environments conducive to the promotion of the interaction of families and family members within the community. But the private nature of the CID environment severely limits and restricts interaction. The emphasis in CIDs is for planned interactions for specific, defined purposes. The definition of what constitutes a family is often defined by covenants, and the public spaces where interaction may actually occur are limited and controlled. Family units are treated as private, separate, and disconnected.

The resulting environment in the typical CID is a clustering of houses, often aesthetically pleasing, with no uniquely definable sense of place. Notions of community are asserted (and often felt by residents), but they are shallow because they are disconnected from genuine forms of human contact. They are, then, not new experiments in community, but counterfeit communities.

4
Public Spaces

I Shop, Therefore I Belong.

—*Jim Wallis (1995, 154)*

People come from around the world to experience the West Edmonton Mall in Edmonton, Alberta, Canada. It is the world's first mega-mall, containing more than 800 shops, 11 department stores, 110 restaurants, a full-size ice-skating rink, a 360-room hotel with theme rooms, a lake, a nondenominational chapel, 20 movie theaters, and 13 nightclubs. In the artificial lake, real submarines wind their way through a simulated underwater world of imported coral, plastic seaweed, fake waves, and electronically controlled rubber sharks. Interspersed among the plastic and rubber simulations are live penguins, real Siberian tigers, and dolphins that perform in front of Kinney's Shoes. The 5.2 million square foot mall is open twenty-four hours a day, employs over 15,000 workers, and generates an income of $300 per square foot, almost twice what a normal mall will bring in.

Although the West Edmonton Mall is located in Canada, it represents the prototype shopping mall that American mall developers envy. Large malls under a single roof have come to dominate the retail market. In the process they have helped change the character of American community life, perhaps permanently, and challenged traditional beliefs about the meaning and significance of our public spaces.

Throughout history, shopping areas have been important public spaces where community socializing has occurred. The agora of ancient Athens, the forum of the Roman Empire, the oriental bazaar, the medieval town square, Main Street, U.S.A., the street corner in urban America, all were important gathering places for local communities—focal points where friends and neighbors met and talked as they casually walked and shopped. Main Street, U.S.A., was where the retired would sit on benches along the storefronts and chat with passers-by, where store owners would catch up on the lives of patrons, and where even those who disliked each other were obliged to provide at least curt greetings. It catered to the rich and poor alike and provided shopping, eating, and drinking establishments for all. Main Street provided an integrating focus for local community life allowing the unique character of the community to be expressed while encouraging sociability.

In urban America the street corner or the front porch (also in rural America) served as public spaces where community residents would gather to pass the time on a warm summer evening. Porch sitting developed into a graceful art of entertaining neighbors and acquaintances as people would stroll up and down the block, stopping to visit with neighbors relaxing on their porches. Neighborhoods throughout America were dotted with dingy corner taverns where men from the area might stop for a beer after work before going home or where they might gather in the evening merely to participate in the lively art of conversation. The neighborhood cafe similarly provided an environment where friends could gossip or joke about the trivial or the serious over an endless cup of coffee. These environments represent only a few of the many types of public spaces that have existed in American communities and that today are disappearing. Their demise will significantly hamper the ability to recreate communal life in America.

PUBLIC SPACES AND COMMUNITY

Public spaces are crucial for the maintenance of genuine community. In public spaces (marketplaces, parks, street corners, cafes, taverns, front porches, etc.), members of the community meet, usually informally and often spontaneously, to socialize. It is in this area of neutral ground that people feel free to gather, to come and go as they please, to argue, or to playfully discuss topics with no particular purpose in mind. Because these areas are neutral, people feel welcome and protected from the expectations of private environments.

Effectively functioning public spaces need not be physically attractive (in fact, they seldom are). More significantly they must be unpretentious and comfortable and must engender habits of association. Where association is encouraged, the basis for democratic community becomes possible, even as it exercises a measure of informal control over its members. In reference to third places (the first place being the home, and the second place being the workplace), Oldenburg comments: "The third place is a force for good. It affords its habitués the opportunity for more decent human relations than prevail outside, and it is their habit to take advantage of that opportunity" (1989, 78). It is not so much that individuals talk about politics in such environments (though they may); rather it is that public spaces provide opportunities for people to develop habits of sociability and mutuality which are so important for democratic political dialogue. Only by participating in face-to-face dialogue with others does one learn the importance of public dialogue.

Public spaces emphasize the value of equality as all members of the community are allowed access to them, and the status distinctions originating from other areas of life (e.g., the workplace) have little significance in them. Genuine public spaces act as leveling devices and serve to expand the possibilities of interaction among participants, whereas formal associations tend toward limitation, restriction, and exclusion. People are accepted not because of who they are but merely because they are members of the community. Because of this, individuals will be more likely to share and express the fullness of their personalities and come to know others more thoroughly than in other more restricted social settings. It is here where the mousy office clerk can become the vivacious life of the party or where the computer nerd is able to impress friends by reciting Shakespeare.

Public spaces tend to have upbeat, lively atmospheres. Because the primary activity that occurs in such places tends to be conversation, clever conversation is valued and encouraged. People enjoy each other's company, relax, and joke with each other. Even in serious conversations the feeling tends to be light-hearted and cheerful. In many ways these spaces act as a form of therapeutic relaxation when people can forget about problems and discuss anything that comes to mind. As Tony Hiss puts it: "Once we know that there are environments where people from all cultural backgrounds can come together and feel comfortable and relaxed, we are in a better position to address stress in modern life" (1990, 37).

In effect, public spaces help provide the glue for genuine community. Not only do they provide a form of refuge for community members and link them together in informal, relaxed settings, but the public spaces, if carefully situated, physically and symbolically link people together. When public spaces function effectively, they overlap and reinforce the patterns of interaction that occur in the broader community and help define community boundaries. Front porches allow friends to interact and further solidify community dialogue, shopping areas become spaces where we might expect to bump into friends and neighbors, coffee shops and taverns attract the usual morning or evening crowds. Those who interact tend to come from areas within walking distance and are attached to these spaces because of the ease of access.

Just as our ownership of private property helps us define and express who we are as individuals, so too our participation in public spaces helps us define and express who we are communally. Genuine community cannot exist without viable public spaces. But instead of cherishing such environments, we have let them fall into disrepair or eliminated them altogether. Neighborhood marketplaces have been put out of business by suburban shopping malls, front porches have been moved to the rear of houses and become patios, and third places have been forced to close because they cannot compete economically with chain restaurants and bars. Rather than protecting public space we have seen its erosion and we have produced, in the cynical words of James Howard Kunstler (1993), a geography of nowhere.

In this chapter I will examine attempts to replace public spaces with counterfeit versions through a brief examination of three areas: marketplaces and shopping areas, front porches of houses, and third places. The selection of these areas is not meant to encompass all of what is meant by public space; rather it is intended to illustrate common patterns that are undermining community and replacing it with counterfeits. In the case of shopping areas the most dramatic change in recent years has been the spectacular growth of malls. Perhaps no single factor has been so effective at destroying neighborhood shopping areas as has been the shopping mall. The reasons for this are assumed to be economic, but in reality they are social. In addition to the hype that one may find the best prices at the mall (seldom true), malls have systematically exploited our desire for connectedness by offering a subtle, yet powerful version of counterfeit community.

Over the years the front porch has been moved to the side of the house and finally to the rear as a deck or patio. Its physical change has symbolized the social transformation of the American family, from a family connected to the neighborhood to an increasingly privatized household. The patio remains an environment for social activity, but the activity that now occurs there has become far more exclusive than what took place on the front porch.

Likewise, genuine third places such as local restaurants and local bars have declined only to be replaced by fast-food and chain restaurants. Realizing that people patronize eating and drinking establishments for more than just the food or drink, chains have also attempted to appeal to consumers through the use of subtle appeals of community. Simulated friendliness has replaced genuine friendship, and plastic symbols of community have come to decorate the walls.

THE MALL

Malls have not so much replaced Main Street, U.S.A., as they have smothered and crushed it. In place of Main Street we now have another dimension of counterfeit community that creates a false sense of connectedness, further exploits our fear of difference, constructs barriers to human inter-action, and contributes to the deadening of public space. In the process meaningful linkages between property—both public and private—and community have been severed, resulting in a communal disconnectedness that has made us vulnerable to the attraction of community simulacra in other environments.

Selling the Mall

Shopping malls have become so embedded in the everyday existence of middle-class America that little publicity needs to be generated to lure shoppers to them. Malls "have become the temples, shrines, and commu-nal centers of modern America" (Wallis 1995, 154). Since the construction of the first shopping center in 1923 (the Country Club Plaza in Kansas City), and after a slow beginning (only eight such centers in 1946), malls have come to dominate retail trade today, accounting for upwards of two-thirds of the total retail purchases in the United States. By 1975 there were more than 16,000 malls, almost 23,000 by 1981, and more than 28,000 today. When we think about "going shopping," our first thoughts turn to the mall.

Still, direct advertising for malls themselves is miniscule. Unlike com-mon-interest housing developments which rely upon blatant appeals to our desire for community, the communal appeal of malls is far more sub-tle, ironic, and manipulative. Mall management will seldom even men-tion the word "community," yet the promotional strategies they pursue are designed to exploit our desire to belong. This is accomplished by en-couraging the disorientation of the consumer and, at the same time, pre-senting him or her with a non-commercial focus. The shopper is pro-vided freedom to wander in what appear to be public spaces, yet these public spaces are legally private spaces limited to safe, non-controversial activities. And while there appears to be an incredible amount of sponta-neous human contact and interaction occurring in the mall, in reality human interactions are minimal and highly structured. Contrary to some who have touted malls as the modern and improved versions of Main Street performing many of the same community-building functions (Francaviglia 1977; Keyes 1973; van Cleef 1970), malls are simulacra—they present us with counterfeit images of non-existent community. George Lewis makes the point succinctly: "The important thing, from a marketing perspective, is to create the warm *illusion* of community while at the same time quietly stacking the deck against its actual development" (1990, 123).

To a large extent, the success of malls has been the result of the ability of mall managers to understand the concerns of consumers and to provide features that appear to satisfy them. This has produced a "science of

malling" in which virtually every behavior of the consumer is carefully examined—from determining how far a shopper will walk from his or her car
to the mall entrance (600 feet), to the precise moment at which a "destination shopper" with a specific purchase in mind, slows his or her pace and
becomes transformed into an impulse shopper (referred to in the trade as
the Gruen Transfer). I will not sketch out all the dimensions of this science; Kowinski (1985) has already humorously done so. Rather, I am interested only in those aspects that bear on the theme of the chapter—malls as
examples of counterfeit community.

False Belonging

The primary and fundamental objective of shopping malls is to sell as
many products as possible. All other activities that occur in the malls are
subordinate to, and consistent with, that objective. Events, behaviors, or activities that are in opposition to, or inconsistent with, that objective will either be excluded from the mall or refashioned in such a manner as to
bring them into conformity with the profit motive. This is what has happened to our urge to belong.

Genuine communities satisfy our need to belong by linking us to other
people in a variety of complex ways, through formal as well as informal
human interaction. With the existence of some minimal level of agreement in the community the members obtain a sense of rootedness, some
sense of a firm center. This connectedness is reinforced symbolically
through special community rituals and on a day-to-day basis through the
myriad of informal interactions that occur among the members. While
some interactions may be primarily economic, or social, or political, all are
tempered by a non-instrumental communitarian requisite. Indeed, in
some instances the communal dimension even takes precedence over any
of the other motivations.

For example, in the book *The Lost City* Alan Ehrenhalt (1995) found
that residents of the St. Nick's parish in Chicago patronized local stores
even though they paid more for the same goods found at national chain
stores only a few blocks further away. This kind of communal loyalty existed not just for small products but for big-ticket purchases as well: cars,
appliances, and furniture. Going to the neighborhood commercial area in
the evening was not just a shopping experience; it was a social experience.
"On Monday and Thursday nights," he reports, "Sixty-third Street was
crowded with knots of local residents who came out to window shop and
make conversation, whether they intended to buy anything or not. Late
shopping nights were a neighborhood social occasion, an important element of the word-of-mouth network" (Ehrenhalt 1995, 99). This practice
occurred because the neighborhood was an integral part of the web of re-

lationships that existed in the community and, as such, offered something chains could not—trust, honesty, and social interaction.

While there has been an erosion of community in America over the last several decades, our urge to belong has not waned. It is this need to belong that is being exploited by the presentation of counterfeit community in the mall. How does this occur?

We have long since moved from a time when commodities were produced and sold because they satisfied particular needs (referred to as "use value"). Today, through the magic of advertising, commodities are presented as "objects of desire" (Forty 1986). In a time of overproduction the use value of items is no longer a compelling reason to buy, and the marketing approach consequently has shifted to focus on the social and psychological desires of the individual. Lacking a stable community with which to identify and find a sense of status and belonging, Americans have increasingly turned to the acquisition of products in order to make symbolic statements of belonging: "Consumerism offers us its own sense of community" (Wallis 1995, 154).

Perhaps more than ever before, commodities define our lifestyle and status. The brand of clothes we wear, the type of car we drive, the neighborhood we live in, all send powerful signals to others about who we think we are. As central institutions in this ideology of consumption, shopping malls continually structure and restructure our sense of self as new products are introduced and old products become "new and improved." In just this way our sense of belonging, which could most thoroughly be satisfied in community, is instead exploited in order to sell products.

The ideology of consumption being suggested here has subtle psychological roots. As commodities become more numerous, manufacturers attempt to distinguish theirs from similar products by continually creating minor variations in features. Advertising attempts to link each of these features to the psychological desires of the consumer, but this is also accomplished by the act of shopping itself. As shoppers go about the process of "just looking," they familiarize themselves not just with the product they will eventually purchase, but also with other products they may desire but cannot then afford. While they attempt to belong by buying, they have also established within themselves a sense of dissatisfaction by imagining yet another product—another lifestyle to be purchased.

This psychological process is not unknown to the gurus of the science of malling. The mall is physically designed to exploit and encourage this disorientation. Within the mall exists a status hierarchy of shops, each projecting a different version of what the consumer can belong to by purchasing a product there. With limited entrances, escalators only at the ends of

the mall, and a minimum of benches inside, a slow, meandering traffic flow
is created, encouraging shoppers to spend time looking at all the products
on display.* The effects produced by the repetitive white corridors and the
"white noise" of Muzak numb the shopper into a semiconscious state ideally suited for impulse buying.

Malls further exploit our urge to belong by including activities that
symbolically conjure up visions of community. The number and variety of
special activities and services are endless: ice-skating rinks, fashion shows,
petting zoos, symphony concerts, trading card shows, high school proms,
raffles, visits from Santa, gift wrapping services, Fourth of July fireworks displays, military recruiting, post office services, craft shows, art shows, car
shows, magic shows, and even lion-taming performances. Many malls have
"community rooms" that are rented out to local groups for meetings. The
activities and services that appear—all safe and non-controversial—simulate a pleasant vision of community life that never existed. Hidden from
the enclosed mall is the uncomfortable side of community life. Nowhere in
the malls are you likely to find bag people, beggars, controversial political
activities, protesters, soliciting, or just people hanging out (other than
teenage "mall rats" who are usually carefully isolated by placing stores that
tend to attract them to dead corners of the mall).

Even the communal activities that are allowed in malls are carefully analyzed by mall scientists. They have discovered that the deadening numb-
ness that the malls create can be temporarily alleviated through the inclu-
sion of such activities. This performs the function of keeping consumers in
the mall longer and, by doing so, making it even more possible to sell more
products. In the business it is referred to as "indirect commodification," a
process whereby non-commercial activities are placed into commercial environments thus allowing noncommodified values to enhance commodities.

Thus, malls present us with two primary ways in which a counterfeit
sense of belonging is achieved: first, by creating a disorienting physical environment that encourages belonging by purchasing products, and second, by including counterfeit communal activities that subtley associate
the non-commercial values of community with commodification.

Barriers to Interaction

In an attempt to draw more shoppers to Shoppingtown Mall in suburban
Syracuse, New York, a program was developed whereby the bus fare for
every person who wanted to go to the mall on a spring Saturday was paid

---

* Mall experts have been successful. The average mall visit has increased from
twenty minutes in 1960 to nearly three hours today.

for by the mall management. By the afternoon the mall had attracted hundreds of inner-city African American teenagers whose loudness and very presence created what was considered by mall management as a "near riot" situation. After several brief altercations with mall security, the adolescents were placed back on the buses with the aid of the local suburban police and returned to their neighborhoods. Free bus rides to the mall were never again offered.

The marketplaces in genuine communities are open to all, regardless of social status, race, ethnic background, or lifestyle choice. It is on the street level where people meet and talk, where they catch up on news, where some merely pass the time of day, but where the variety that exists within the community is on display. These are public places, and every member of the community has equal access to them.

Malls, by their very design, but also through the use of management policies, have constructed barriers to human interaction and created a structured environment that disconnects people. This is exactly what is intended. From the very conception, placement, and design of the mall to the management policies, malls attempt to exclude undesirable social elements and reduce human interaction in the mall to a minimum.

The location of a mall follows some basic rules of thumb by the developer: first, the mall should have at least 250,000 people within a fifteen-minute commute. Second, malls should rely primarily upon automobile traffic. For all practical purposes this means that malls will be located along interstates, often at the intersection of two of them. Third, malls should be built in relatively open spaces. This is primarily an economic consideration. Undeveloped land will be less expensive, and it also allows the developer to purchase more land than is needed adjacent to the mall, which can be resold later to the myriad fast-food chains and strip mall developments that inevitably surround the enclosed mall. These principles of mall location have the effect of excluding the poorest in the city, who rely disproportionately upon public transportation, from "going to the mall."

Although placement seems, at face value, to be a rather benign dimension of the mall dictated more by economics than class or race, incidents from time to time challenge that belief. The death of a black teenager in January 1996 in Buffalo illustrates the point. Cynthia Wiggins, a seventeen-year-old mother, took a bus from her home in the predominantly black section of Buffalo to her job at a fast-food restaurant in the Galleria Mall in suburban Cheektowaga. While the mall was being built in 1988, the Pyramid Company, one of the largest mall developers in the Northeast, lobbied successfully with the local transit authority to prevent buses that went through the heart of Buffalo's black community from stopping at the mall. Instead, the bus made several stops on the busy seven-lane highway that passed by Galleria. Cynthia Wiggins was crushed by a dump truck as she tried to negotiate her way across the street.

Malls also attempt to control the type of interaction that occurs by declaring them private, rather than public spaces. Although recent Supreme Court decisions seem to be moving in the direction of considering malls public spaces, mall managers are united in their opposition to this trend. Many malls post signs like the following: "Areas in this mall used by the public are not public ways, but are for the use of the tenants and the public transacting business with them. Permission to use said areas may be revoked at any time." By considering mall space private rather than public, a host of "disruptive" citizenship activities (picketing, petitioning, leafleting, etc.) may be legally excluded, and "undesirable elements" (bag people, African American teenagers, etc.) may be banned. Thus, what interaction does occur in the mall occurs only among the population the mall managers have targeted as their clientele; in most malls that is the middle-class white suburbanite.

The final barrier to human interaction occurs within the mall itself in its original design. Malls are designed to discourage loitering. You will not find people in malls playing checkers or chess, pitching horseshoes on the green areas, or even just sitting and talking for very long. While all malls contain benches, these sitting areas are too few and far between to accommodate the volume of traffic in the mall, and they are usually so uncomfortable that they provide little comfort to the weary shopper. Many malls contain food courts with fast-food chains, but the emphasis is on "fast." The sterility of the food court encourages people to move on, and in most malls the seating capacity is too small to handle the crowds during peak hours.

The result is an enclosed environment that discourages the interaction of different kinds of people, pre-selecting who will come to the mall by choice of location, and controlling the extent and type of interactions through management policies and structural design. The vast majority of interactions that occur in the mall are business transactions among strangers.

Regardless of this, the mall presents images of community to the suburbanite. One of the paradoxical consequences of suburban life has been the intensification of the urge for human contact. With their singular emphasis on low-density residential development, suburbs have failed to provide residents with public spaces. The enclosed mall, with its geographical centrality, its appearance of public space, and its human density, contains elements that are commonly associated with community. At least symbolically, the mall provides a focus for the suburbs. But, as the preceding analysis has shown, the focus is consumer-based. In the process of going to the mall, the suburbanite is presented with the image of citizen as consumer and is offered products to purchase as a way of belonging. Malls "are not a 'core of community involvement' but they are a gauge of it, and one that renders rather pitiful readings" (Oldenburg 1989, 120). The undermining of real public marketplaces and the attempt to satisfy our longing for connectedness through the purchase of goods have pushed us further in the direction of redefining community to embrace the counterfeit. Although feelings of community, of connectedness, emerge as a result of the social interactions that occur in genuine community, community is not singularly viewed as feelings alone. Genuine community is composed of *both* primary interactions and experiences with others as well as feelings of connectedness. Malls, however, have severed the primary experiences from our desire for connectedness and redirected those feelings for community to turn us into consumers.

THE FRONT PORCH

Prior to the popularization of the automobile, the character of the residential street was far different from what it has become today. Streets were truly public spaces where people stopped to talk with each other, where friends met, where children played, where neighbors would feel comfortable picnicking. Even with the occasional disruption of the passing of a horse and rider or a wagon, the street performed an important social function for the community. Sociability dominated the residential street.

Complementing the social character of the street were houses with front porches that linked the privacy of the family inside the house with the publicness of the community in the street. In the summer months in the North and year-round in the South, the porch was an appealing blend of indoors and outdoors, of family and community. Family events such as birthday parties were often hosted there, young ladies could receive gentleman callers in the porch swing, or neighbors could gather in the evening to exchange news, argue, and gossip. Porches functioned best as informal gathering places for family and friends. Neighbors would stroll by and strike up a conversation with porch sitters who might invite them up to "sit a while." Visiting on the porch was a way to be sociable without the formalities associated with a visit inside. The front porch represented a physical area where one could be sociable to a wide range of guests without embracing them as close friends.

Importantly, the porch emphasized the human scale of community. Porches differed in size and shape, and individual homeowners would decorate and furnish them to reflect their own tastes. There were front stoops in urban neighborhoods, colossal porticos that rose the full height of the house on grand Southern houses, verandas that wrapped around the side of the house, and the uniquely American dog-trot porch, which physically divided the house in half. Rich people had porches, middle-class people had porches, poor people had porches. Porches were often furnished with swings, comfortable rocking chairs, tables, and potted plants to add warmth and color. Often birdcages or fishbowls would be moved to the porch in the summer, and dogs and cats would use the porch to lazily watch the traffic in the street.

But the popularization of the automobile brought with it a transformation of how streets would be used and, in turn, how front porches would be used. They brought with them noise and pollution and demands from car owners that streets be paved to facilitate the movement of traffic. Streets lost their sociability function and became seen as primarily designed for the flow of automobile traffic. Cars became more important than people, and sitting on the front porch no longer was an attractive feature of living: "The unwillingness to think about the public realm of the street in any other terms beside traffic, shows how little value Americans confer on the public realm in general. . . . No thought has gone into the relationships between things—the buildings to each other, the buildings to the street, the pedestrian to the buildings" (Kunstler 1993, 138).

At about the same time, the television was developed and became popular. The television further accelerated the decline of the front porch as it first drew the family into the living room in the evenings and then, as families could afford multiple sets, separated family members themselves as the children deserted the family viewing time for watching television in their own rooms.

Front porches satisfied an important need: in a real sense they linked not only the indoors with the outdoors, but they linked families with the neighborhood community. In an informal, semi-public atmosphere spontaneous relationships could flourish. Builders attempted to satisfy what they believed to be the essential components of the front porch—the desire to be outdoors and the desire for a social environment—and began to build houses with patios and decks on the rear of the house, often hidden by fences and shrubbery from passers-by. Today, this model prevails. Houses are closed off from the front facing the street and open out to spacious decks and patios in the rear. Automobiles have also been catered to as architects have incorporated garages into the house design itself, often having the garage facing the street in the front of the house. With the development of the automatic garage door opener, the resident is able to drive directly into the garage and enter the house through a door linking the garage to the house, never having to get out of the car to open the garage door and never having to even enter the front door. This has further resulted in a deadening of the street as an arena for social interaction.

Along with these architectural changes have come changes in social patterns. When front porches were in use, spontaneous conversations could be developed between the porch sitters and passers-by (it was, of course, also difficult to ignore a prying neighbor). But with the development of the patio, spontaneous interactions have been replaced by planned invitations. The planning of social occasions such as backyard barbecues tends to result in a restricting of interactions to only those people one knows already. In place of the diversity of the street, residents now tend to interact primarily with others who possess characteristics and beliefs similar to themselves. This has resulted in a weakening of neighborhood and community ties and a homogenization and narrowing of perspectives.

Like the impact of the mall on the undermining of public space, the elimination of the front porch and its subsequent relocation to the rear of the house have thinned and reduced communal interaction. Living in a particular neighborhood no longer means being connected to others as part of a complex web of social interactions. With the decline of sociability we now tend to view living in a particular neighborhood as an abstract feeling. Sunning oneself on the patio, isolated from the sociability of the street, we are allowed to view community as a "feeling of connectedness" without ever encountering those we consider part of our community. The acquiring of a sense of community is no longer obtained through social interaction; rather it becomes a psychological act of projection. When this occurs, we open ourselves to the possibility of being manipulated through the use of images and symbols that conjure up feelings of community without providing genuine interaction with others.

Such manipulation is perhaps most visible in the real estate industry. One of the most pithy yet revealing adages among real estate agents is that the three most important words to keep in mind when purchasing a house are "location, location, location." Neighborhood is used as a marketing device for the selling of homes. But what exactly is meant by "location"? Real estate agents seldom mention anything about the nature or quality of social relationships in a neighborhood to a prospective buyer. Instead, location is meant to refer to the price of other houses in the area. Those prices have nothing to do with the quality of relationships and everything to do with square footage, how well the house has been maintained, if the house has a deck or patio (rather than a porch), how modern the kitchen and bathrooms are, and, of course, the market value of the houses in the area. The shrewd buyer will attempt to use the idea of location to advantage and purchase the least expensive house in the neighborhood, knowing that the value of the house will likely increase rather than decrease.

Thus, the idea of a neighborhood is used as a marketing ploy but, more than that, in the process of doing so the concept of a neighborhood has been altered. It is no longer used to describe a complex of social interactions and instead is used as a strategy to maximize profit, both for the real estate agent and for the buyer. Once the buyer takes possession, identification with the neighborhood community then occurs through a psychological process of projection rather than a social process of interaction. One may live in a neighborhood for years, and even develop a sense of identification with it, but never even know the names of one's neighbors.

THE DECLINE OF THIRD PLACES

Critical to the growth and maintenance of community are distinctive informal gathering places—third places. If the home provides a domestic environment where one's true personality may be expressed and the workplace is where gainful and productive economic activity takes place, third places are characterized by playful sociability. Conversation is the main activity in third places, and often the most popular people are those who are successful at spinning a colorful yarn or demonstrating skill with a clever line. Functionally, third places are integral for providing people with a sense of belonging and participating in communal life. Oldenburg quotes one woman who used to frequent a local diner to show her children that there were alternatives to the hamburger chains. About it she said, "The atmosphere is relaxed and friendly, everyone is spoken to and many people see friends there. Their style is entirely reliant on the personality of the people. It's old and a bit rundown but it's an excellent place to go when one wants to feel better, have a sense of belonging, or relax" (1989, 206).

Unfortunately, third places are rarely found in newly built environments in America and, more and more, they are disappearing from older neighborhoods. In their place we find "nonplaces," where "character is irrelevant and one is only the customer or shopper, client or patient, a body to be seated, an address to be billed, or car to be parked" (Oldenburg 1989, 205). It is in these new nonplaces, often attracting people because of their familiar logos and predictable ambiance, where the counterfeit sense of belonging is promoted.

The counterfeit replacements use a variety of techniques to exploit our desires for belonging, but each version has two features in common. First, counterfeit third places attempt to satisfy our feelings for connectedness through the use of symbolism rather than developing primary interactions with others; and second, the environments are designed in such a way as to maximize profit rather than encourage human interaction. Although profit is not irrelevant for the owners of genuine third places, often of greater importance are the interests of the guests—the creation of an ambiance conducive to conversation.

Genuine third places are becoming increasingly rare, so rare, in fact, that few people today even recognize the profusion of reproductions in modern America. In every city plastic reproductions of historical third places are being constructed with the goal in mind to conjure up emotionally satisfying images of bygone times, when community meant something. Though, in fact, the form of community reconstructed may have actually been quite oppressive, reality is not the issue. The images are designed to elicit feelings, not historical analysis.

One way counterfeit third places are promoted is through the creation of an overly friendly atmosphere. This is not merely being polite or courteous to patrons; it is designed to suggest a degree of personal familiarity usually reserved for friends. On its face it appears to be the same atmosphere one would encounter in a third place filled with friends, but the friendliness comes entirely from strangers. One manifestation of this phenomenon we have all observed is the birthday dinner. Birthdays are traditionally events for friends and relatives, when a gathering of those closest to the honoree occurs. The birthday event at counterfeit third places is predictable: waiters and waitresses parade through the restaurant following the one holding a cake aglow with candles; as the cake arrives at the table, the restaurant employees launch into an upbeat version of "Happy Birthday" while friends of the birthday person are relegated to the status of an audience. In keeping with their passive role, they enthusiastically applaud after the performance. Thus, an important family and friendship ritual is being replaced by the scripted corporate version of the birthday party.

Still, underneath this friendliness is a serious attempt to keep the customer flow moving to maximize profit. In genuine third places, conversation receives the highest priority. Customers in neighborhood taverns, for example, may, over the course of several hours, consume less than one full draft of beer or an endless cup of coffee. The furnishings and atmosphere, though usually dingy, are nonetheless comfortable. But in counterfeit third places the bartender or waitress, under the guise of friendliness, will be highly attentive and, by doing so, encourage consumption. In fast-food places, the air conditioning is often turned down to make it so cool that it becomes uncomfortable to linger.

A second approach to the replacement of genuine third places is built into the architecture of the buildings themselves. Although it is occurring throughout America, it can be seen most visibly in places such as Boston's Quincy Market, Harbor Place in Baltimore, Fisherman's Wharf in San Francisco, the Riverwalk in New Orleans, or the South Street Seaport in New York. Under the guise of urban revitalization, substantial amounts of money have been spent to rediscover (and in many instances reconstruct) the look and feel of the city as it used to be. In New York one may cross the street lined with towering corporate skyscrapers and enter an architectural promenade composed of upscale boutiques, restaurants, and tourist shops located inside of rediscovered merchants' countinghouses and cast-iron warehouses built in the early nineteenth century.

Interspersed throughout the South Street Seaport district in New York are art galleries, bookstores, clothing stores, and the South Street Seaport Museum complete with a reception center. Thus, in the midst of a bustling city of millions of strangers, one is reminded, through the use of simulacra images of the past, that New York is composed of quaint communities within the larger city.

The theme is extended to the inside of buildings as well. These buildings and the products they sell must conform to the overall theme. There, long-since abandoned buildings have been refurbished and turned into upscale marketplaces. The aim is to create a new vision of the city and yet maintain connections to the past. This is done by constructing images that remind one of the past, or at least the past we would like to believe. Nineteenth-century façades are recreated, once functional tools typically used in the area are used as ornaments, and street performers dressed in period costumes roam throughout the area. In effect, parts of the cities are being turned into simulated art forms.

Once the theme is set for a third place, all of the decorations and furniture are made to conform. Where once the old general store served as a meeting place in rural America, we now have a chain of Cracker Barrel restaurants replete with decorations including pitchforks, old license plates, and a variety of tools, all hung on rough wood walls reminiscent of an old building. Menu items continue the theme and offer hearty breakfasts and filling dinners for hard-working folks. Waitresses, dressed in period costumes, are prompt and courteous, and if they don't encourage maximum customer flow, the frigid temperatures will certainly discourage lingering. In the entrance area where you will be asked to wait until your table is ready (even though many tables are empty) are displayed thousands of souvenir items to remind you of your visit. You may purchase taffy and fudge, models of old cars, traditional Christmas ornaments, replicas of Coca-Cola bottle openers, and the like.

These reconstructed forms of a bygone era are designed to provide us with satisfying memories of American communities. They are, of course, partial and incomplete images—but they attract us because they appeal to the need for connectedness that we lack in our daily lives. Wanting to become a part of that reconstructed (and counterfeit) community, we participate in it through the purchase of the goods being marketed.

The reconstructed historical items are used for decoration and are not presented for their utility but instead become a part of a system of commodification: "The further away the commodity seems from the functional, the useful, and the necessary, the more appealing it appears. When the commodity is placed within a system of signs symbolizing entire lifestyles and supporting environments, the system itself seeks to increase consumption by suggesting that a particular lifestyle requires the acquisi- tion of not one but an entire series of goods" (Boyer 1992, 200). By creat- ing nostalgic environments we encourage consumption by patrons who, once they have opened themselves to the simulated environment, wish to become a part of it by purchasing goods.

PROPERTY, COMMUNITY, AND HUMAN INTERACTION

Our possessions have symbolic meaning. They exist within a status hierar- chy, and ownership of particular types of property helps orient people within that hierarchy system. What's more, possessions satisfy psychological needs, giving us a sense of individual worth and self-esteem. The feelings of self-esteem connected to the ownership of property are also embedded within the status hierarchy system. Thought of in terms of the broader community, property and the type of work undertaken to accumulate that property are statements of what our community stands for and how we re- late to others. Thus, communities become known as working-class commu- nities or middle-class communities, fishing communities, mining commu- nities, or farming communities.

In our examination of malls we saw consumerism gone wild. Many so- cial critics have taken Americans to task for being too concerned about commodities and not concerned enough about nonmaterial values. It is not my intent to condemn consumerism; rather I want to use it as a way of understanding the relationship of property to community and why com- munity has been allowed to deteriorate in America. Why have so many well-intentioned people embraced the consumer lifestyle? Why do Ameri- cans go to such extremes to consume? Why are we unable to see the envi- ronmental degradation and economic exploitation that occur as a result of our desire to consume? Why have we allowed community to wither and die? Why do we have so little respect for public space?

Answers to these questions lie in understanding the importance of two crucial relationships: one links property to community, and the second links human interaction to feelings of community. Because both linkages have been severed, Americans have become vulnerable to the seductive ap- peals of counterfeit versions of community.

As has already been discussed, property ownership (whether it refers to land, money, or personal belongings) is fundamental to a sense of self-esteem. We feel a sense of personal violation when people break in to our homes. We are protective of our property, and we feel we are in the best position to determine what to do with it—property is an exten- sion of who we see ourselves as being. At a political level, property conveys a sense of power (if we can believe public opinion polls, most Americans think that those with the most money control American politics). More fundamentally, property ownership allows us to be rooted, to have a home, and to connect with other property owners to create a community. To be homeless is to be uprooted and to lose a sense of being a part of a community.

But property ownership should do more than simply satisfy our status, ego, and power needs. If we think about where commodities come from, what energy systems exist in order to make them possible, what economic relationships have been created in order to produce them, what political decisions have been made to enable entrepreneurs to build factories to manufacture them, we may begin to see how our relationship to property entails responsibilities. Every commodity embodies environmental costs to create it, to market it, and eventually to dispose of it: "Just as property serves to reinforce autonomy, it continually reiterates interdependence" (Thomashow 1995, 83). In this way, property *should* provide a critical link between the individual and the community.

In genuine communities, a sense of connectedness to a place develops, and property ownership helps to forge a common bond. Regardless of one's social status, racial or ethnic heritage, or ideological identification, a sense of place unites the community as people dependent upon the same physical environment value that place. The fact that people occupy a common space with which they identify brings them together to protect it, and it is the process of active participation among people who value that space that creates community. When this linkage occurs, property ownership becomes tempered as one realizes the implications for the community of excessive commodification. Where property is linked with community, people have not just rights to own property but they also have responsibilities to assure that the property they own is well maintained and imposes minimal damage on the environment and the community.

This critical linkage between property ownership and community has been severed in America. Lacking a concrete community with which to identify, we no longer possess the ability to assess the social, economic, or political implications of the purchase of any particular commodity. We are left alienated and vulnerable to suggestions that property will, by itself, provide the sense of belonging we are seeking. The private feelings of status and power that we enjoy with the purchase of a product are no longer tempered by the community. Social conventions that come into play in communities and function to provide social meaning for the property we possess are absent without community, and so the palaver of counterfeit community steps in to fill the void. Malls have helped sever this connection by contributing to the decline of the communal marketplace, and the decline of third places has further weakened social conventions that come from interaction.

It is not my intent to criticize the linkage between property ownership and a sense of self-esteem; others have done so. Indeed, I believe that this is an important and positive relationship when it occurs within the context of genuine community. However, where property ownership is severed from community, the result is excessive commodification with little purpose. Property loses its social value—and retains only its monetary value—because the communal referents have been undermined by the disappearance of community. The only ways left to determine value are the forces of the marketplace. Further, when people become disconnected from a common place and the social interactions there, they lose a sense of responsibility that should be attached to property.

The second linkage that has been severed is the linkage between human interaction and feelings of community. This split has occurred partially because of the decline of public spaces, where human interaction should flourish. In order to create genuine community there must be public environments where the members of that community come to know each other through both playful and serious interaction. While formal governmental mechanisms are designed to deal with the more formal dimensions of communal interaction (discussed in a later chapter), the more playful social dimensions must also be allowed to express themselves. These environments, referred to in this chapter as public spaces, have declined in number and been deadened in character.

It is through human interaction that individuals seek and create meaning. When individuals, amid the context of a web of relationships, create meanings for their lives that transcend themselves and include others with whom they interact, a sense of community is created. This feeling of community, of connectedness with others, is something that most people experience at some time during their lives, whether it is a temporary feeling in times of crisis or a more sustained feeling for those who live in genuine communities. Whenever it occurs, and whatever the circumstances, it is a compelling experience that we want to recreate and sustain.

CONCLUSION

When public spaces disappear, the desire to experience feelings of connection become torn from their social and physical contexts. As public spaces vanish, we turn inward and become all that more private. Just as the front porch, an inherently social space that linked the family to the community, moved to the rear and represented a further undermining of our social selves, so too the deterioration of all of our public spaces has privatized our lives and made us vulnerable to manipulation through the use of simulacra of community.

Public spaces provide arenas in which individuals may practice and learn sociability. To a considerable extent, interaction in public spaces may be seen to tame the personal impulses that exist in our private lives. The civility of public interaction tends to limit and temper one's own feelings and beliefs: "The public world put a limitation on the principle of happiness as a full definition of reality. Although the realm of conventions could not alter or change nature, *in esse* nature transcended any social situation, public culture served a purpose in taming the effects of nature" (Sennett 1976, 98). With the decline of public spaces, we may subsequently anticipate a decline in civility and tolerance of others.

5

The Workplace

You will be assimilated.
Resistance is futile.

—The Borg

ederal Express (FedEx) is touted as one of the most progressive corporations in the world. Begun in the spring of 1973 with a handful of Falcon aircraft, FedEx has expanded to include more than 575 aircraft, 38,000 vehicles, and 127,000 employees worldwide. It serves 211 countries and moves approximately 2.5 million packages a day—a far cry from the 183 packages it handled in April 1973. FedEx operates out of 1,400 service centers and almost 32,000 drop boxes, and each night it shuttles packages throughout the world through 325 airports. While all of this is occurring, FedEx guarantees that each and every customer at any time day or night can find out where his or her parcel is located among the company's maze of aircraft, vans, and baggage handlers.

But the real claim to fame for FedEx is not the impressiveness of its organization to transport packages quickly and efficiently, or even its spectacular growth or its impressive profit margins—rather, it is its corporate philosophy of people first. As founder and Chief Executive Officer Fred Smith puts it: "We discovered a long time ago that customer satisfaction really begins with employee satisfaction. That belief is incorporated in our corporate philosophy statement. People—Service—Profit" (quoted in Waterman 1994, 91).

Federal Express is only one of thousands of businesses that, since the 1970s, have embraced the theme of worker participation. As seen by advocates, it represents a paradigm shift in how business should operate. Rejecting traditional business beliefs in hierarchical organization, scientific management, and expertise, it embraces decentralization of decision-making, informality, and the importance of vision, while emphasizing the val-

77

ues of cooperation and empowerment of all employees. The new paradigm claims to create a learning environment in the workplace where communication is enhanced to produce quality products and service. Ultimately, it claims to encourage workers to connect with other workers and to the organization, and to create a feeling of community.

The internal operation of Federal Express illustrates how this is accomplished. One of the keys for FedEx is to match the people in the organization with the appropriate jobs. Consequently, it conducts a rigorous screening process for those who will fill leadership positions. Management positions are advertised and usually filled from within the organization. Those wishing to become managers first attend a one-day class entitled "Is Management for Me?" The reality of management is honestly explained, and many applicants decide at that point not to pursue the position. Those who continue on then undergo an exhaustive review of their past work history and are examined with respect to how well they compare to a list of personality attributes FedEx believes are correlated with good management (charisma, courage, integrity, etc.). Following the review, they are interviewed by a panel of senior managers. If the management candidates successfully pass these hurdles, they then proceed to a one-week course at the FedEx Leadership Institute, where they learn the values, philosophy, expectations, and guidelines of a FedEx manager. Over the next several years these young managers will take a series of classes such as "coaching," "beyond unions," "diversity," "ethics," and "interpersonal dynamics." As they work in the field, they are guided by a 400-page manual that details the philosophy and practice of managing at FedEx.

Much of the assessment of how effective the organization is functioning is conducted through small problem-solving groups called "Quality Action Teams" (Qwats). Each Qwat reviews particular problems as well as the day-to-day operations for the members of the group. An annual review is conducted in the spring of each year when employees complete an attitude survey that assesses the atmosphere of the work group and, based upon that survey, the manager receives a leadership index score. Each year a goal is set for the leadership index, and if the company fails to achieve the goal, the top 300 managers in the company don't get a bonus (which, if they receive it, is about 40 percent of their pay). Managers who receive poor scores fall into a category called the "critical concern" group, and their work group must take the survey again after another six months.

In an attempt to put people first, FedEx has a no layoff policy, and it further attempts to protect its employees by guaranteeing that their voices will be heard through a Guaranteed Fair Treatment policy (GFT). The GFT is a program designed so that anyone who has a grievance can go all the way to top management if necessary and have his or her problem re-solved within twenty-one days. If an employee's manager fails to solve a problem, the employee may appeal to the manager's manager who must respond within seven days. If the employee is still not satisfied, he or she may appeal to division vice presidents and senior vice presidents. All hear the case and conduct deliberations.

Federal Express is not merely in business to please its employees, of course. In order to please its customers and to increase efficiency in the de-livery of packages, it has developed the SuperTracker system, a new tech-nology designed to monitor package movement. Every time a parcel changes hands, employees pass a small hand-held scanner over the pack-age's bar code. The scanner sends its information to a unit (often in the courier's van), which in turn sends the information to a transmitting sta-tion, which then sends the information via satellite to the home computing complex in Memphis. With all this information FedEx can not only tell the customer where his or her package is at any particular time, but the data may also be collected and analyzed to assess the efficiency of the entire op-eration or any parts of it.

Federal Express is an example of the popular new paradigm shift oc-curring in business today that attempts to achieve financial success by cre-ating a sense of community and connectedness among employees. These participatory approaches include getting employees to feel as if they are in control, to believe in the value of their work, to be challenged, to cooper-ate with others, to take individual responsibility for their actions, to engage in lifelong learning, and to be recognized for their achievements (Water-man 1994). Although the specific approaches needed to accomplish these objectives go by a host of different names, they are all focused on creating environments in the workplace associated with community. At least one or-ganization that conducts seminars for businesses to introduce such tech-niques, the Foundation for Community Encouragement (FCE), clearly ar-ticulates its goal as introducing community into the workplace: "As organizations struggle to find appropriate structures for a new paradigm in business, they need to incorporate the principles of community. If they wish to become learning organizations, they need to realize that the learn-ing organization is by definition a community" (Gozdz 1993, 107). Most of the characteristics the FCE uses to describe community are, in fact, quite similar to the multitude of programs that may collectively be referred to as participatory approaches to management.

What's more, this new paradigm extends beyond the internal opera-tions of the corporation and recognizes that business has a sense of re-sponsibility in the broader environment as well. One such corporation, Procter & Gamble (P&G), explains its community linkage this way on its web site: "To our communities, we provide a source of stable employment at competitive wages, and, through our business success, a foundation which will encourage support industries to develop and prosper. Our profits generate significant tax revenues that support numerous functions in the community. In addition, corporate contributions and volunteer efforts of our employees support schools, charities, and other community activities. Further, our facilities are managed with the utmost concern for the environment." As evidence of this commitment, P&G contributes millions of dollars each year to community organizations (almost $45 million in 1995–96).

However, before endorsing these new people-first approaches to management, we must examine the underlying dynamics of the techniques. Although participatory approaches in general tend to improve worker morale and create worker loyalty, they are, in reality, closer to counterfeit community than to genuine community. This is true because the specific participatory techniques employed occur within a set of institutionalized parameters that prevent genuine community from developing. For example, three fundamental assumptions are present in almost all corporate participatory models: (1) the commitment to maximizing profit for the corporation; (2) the belief that managers ultimately make the most important decisions for the business; and (3) the structure that prevents real employee ownership of the business itself. Because of these assumptions, employee participation will be allowed to occur only on the day-to-day operations of the business where activities do not directly threaten the character of the organization.

Once again, Federal Express illustrates the limitations of the participatory model of management. Although FedEx has a stated "no layoff policy," when it began to experience modest losses in the early 1990s after years of soaring profits, it wasted no time in laying off 6,000 European employees, arguing that the no layoff policy did not apply "under extreme emergency conditions." Similarly, although FedEx is touted as an organization that provides its employees with unusual amounts of freedom to do their jobs and guarantees them a process to redress their grievances, a spate of recent firings of FedEx veterans who had excellent job performance ratings but were engaged in unionization activities calls the participatory model into question. Participation, it appears, is to be encouraged so long as it does not challenge the underlying philosophy of the organization as defined by top management and ownership.

Seen within this context, as operating within a system of limiting assumptions, the communal environment created by the people-first philosophy at Federal Express more closely resembles the community of The Borg in the Star Trek movie *First Contact* (and earlier in the television series) than it does genuine community.* The Borg has no obvious central control as it goes about assimilating new members into the collective. Once totally assimilated, each member takes on the thoughts and ideas of all the others in the collective. As The Borg says, "Assimilation is inevitable, Resistance is futile." As operated through Quality Action Teams, the FedEx ideology is imposed not from above, but horizontally through peer pressure. It is through decentralized networks that FedEx employees are socialized into the corporation's ideology. When socialization is complete, central coordination is not necessary: everyone within the organization is placed in an "appropriate position" on the basis of personality screening and performance reviews. All workers know exactly what is expected of them.

Pushing the analogy even further, The Borg are an interesting combination of human life forms and mechanical attachments which allow them to plug into the collective. The mechanical parts of The Borg allow for greater coordination and more efficient operation. As if imitating The Borg, the FedEx SuperTracker system not only can trace every package being shipped to see where it is at any particular time, but it is also used to track its couriers. Based upon the SuperTracker data, management can assess the efficiency of the entire organization as well as particular parts of the organization and even particular couriers. At all times the courier in the field is plugged in to the FedEx collective and his or her behavior is monitored.

CORPORATE BUSINESS

Business plays an important role in genuine community by providing an economic base, and the interactions business managers and owners have in the community, in turn, temper their urge to make decisions solely in terms of economic criteria. The relationship is complex and reciprocal. In this chapter we will first examine the relationship of business to local communities in America. It will be argued that, for the most part, corporate business has been a force that has weakened and undermined genuine community.

Second, we will examine recent participatory management trends within the workplace. These techniques, seen within the context of the relationship between business and community, represent counterfeit at-

---

* This analogy is not originally mine. It is cleverly suggested by a disgruntled Federal Express employee, Kevin Osiowy, who has created a web page, "Fed Up," to share his frustration with others and build support for the unionization of FedEx employees.

tempts at creating community. They are based on an exploitation of workers' longings to be part of meaningful work that contributes to genuine community. The dominant forms of business today—corporate forms—inherently undermine genuine community. Still, workers long for a sense of connectedness and want to believe that work is meaningful and socially worthwhile. Sensing this, corporate leaders have developed new models to manipulate workers through the use of techniques that simulate community and connectedness in the workplace. These techniques work (in the sense that they are successful at redirecting worker loyalties) at least in part because of the failure of community elsewhere. Yet, these new participatory workplace techniques fail to fundamentally alter relationships that must be changed in order to produce genuine community. No matter how well the techniques work to improve efficiency, morale, and profits, these approaches will, at best, create feelings of community that are not sustainable because they lack the kinds of social interaction and power relationships necessary to create community. Genuine community requires real control over one's work, not the illusion of control. Consequently, the new paradigm shift that has occurred in the workplace is merely another version of counterfeit community.

Corporate Business and Community

Traditionally, work has been instrumental in defining the character of local community. The type of work that has dominated particular areas has carried with it values, beliefs, and habitual patterns of association that have shaped local communities. There are fishing communities, farming communities, steel industry communities, coal mining communities, and the like. Workers in each type of business bring the beliefs and values they adopt and internalize from their work environments into their communities, and those beliefs, in turn, help shape the character of the community.

For example, the automobile industry had a tremendous impact on Detroit and the towns surrounding Detroit when the industry experienced both booms and down periods. Not only did the auto industry influence Detroit financially by providing jobs (or unemployment during layoff periods) and through the payment (or non-payment) of taxes, but the nature of the workplace itself emphasized particular values, beliefs, and skills which similarly carried over into the civic aspect of the workers' lives. Early on, the U.S. auto industry realized the importance of a skilled and stable workforce in order to produce quality products and meet demand. Likewise, the fact that automobiles were produced in large factories requiring thousands of workers made it much more likely that unionization was likely to occur. Although, as in many early unionization attempts, there were wildcat strikes and violence, the advent of unions in the auto industry and management's acceptance of them led to liberalization of the industry as well as the local politics of the area. The United Auto Workers has a history of liberal politics, General Motors and Ford have led the way in attempting to adopt participatory management techniques, and the city of Detroit has a history of being the training ground for liberal and even radical politicians.

Similarly, the paternalistic company towns in the coal mining areas of Appalachia have hurt local communities by helping to create feelings of frustration and hopelessness in the workforce. The isolation of towns in the hollows of Appalachia, the need in the industry for muscle but not an educated workforce, and the almost totalitarian control of coal mining corporations have made it difficult for any organization of citizens to occur. Although coal miners have been one of the most oppressed labor forces, attempts to unionize them have been extremely difficult. In the Great Plains, wheat farmers realized early on that they were at the mercy of the weather as well as the railroad industry that they used to ship their grain to market. Consequently, they recognized the importance of using government action to protect themselves by obtaining crop insurance as well as regulating railroad shipping rates. It is not surprising therefore to find that the most avid supporters of the Populist Movement were farmers in these areas.

For genuine community to exist, it must be able to sustain itself economically. This does not mean that local economies must be socialized; rather it means that in order to control and shape one's culture the members of communities must control, in some fashion, the sources of power within those communities. One of the most fundamental and powerful spheres of power is the economy. Consequently, the first part of our inquiry will examine the relationship of business to local communities.

In his emotional analysis of the decline of community in America, Wendell Berry (1993) attributes the decline, at least in part, to local economies becoming subject to larger economic forces external to the communities themselves. As the economy has shifted from small businesses, locally owned and locally controlled, to large corporations with absentee ownership, giant corporations have become less concerned with the impact of their operations on the local communities and more concerned with maximizing profit for others. Able to undersell local business, corporations have put them out of business and forced owners to become wage earners rather than owners.

In rural areas perhaps the most visible impact of corporate decision-making that ignores the needs of local communities has been the destruction of local environments as corporations have moved in, hired local people to work for them, and brutally extracted the resources with little concern about the lasting effects on the land. Although this pattern has occurred throughout America, one of the most visible impacts has occurred in the coal mining areas of Appalachia.

Driving through towns in Appalachia, it is difficult to believe that it is one of the richest areas in America. Huge deposits of coal have generated massive profits for coal mining companies, most of which are owned by absentee corporations. But this wealth is distributed so unequally that the vast majority of people in Appalachia live at poverty or bare subsistence levels while absentee owners reap the profits. Huge earth moving machines have gutted the once lush mountains, resulting in ecological devastation. Streams and rivers throughout the region are highly acidic, and enormous gullies are cut into the slopes with each rain: "The rubble that gathers on the valley floor creeps upward as the mountain is sliced away, until the entire range is obliterated. In its place is a wasteland of displaced soil, slabs of rock and slate, and shattered residues of coal and sulfur. All that is left of what was once a tree-covered, living ridge is a vast mesa where nothing moves except the clouds of dust on dry, windy days, or the sluicing autumn rains that carve new creekbeds across its dead surface" (Caudill 1973, 106). Corporations have not only severed the linkage between business and community by extracting wealth from the area with little or no thought given to the economic status of the people in the area, but they have also aggressively and consciously attempted to undermine local attempts to build community.

An example drawn from John Gaventa's book *Power and Powerlessness* (1980) shows how corporations see attempts to build community as threatening and so attempt to destroy them. In the 1970s, in the wake of the War on Poverty, community development corporations (CDCs) sprang up in poor rural and urban neighborhoods across America. CDCs were nonprofit grassroots organizations that attempted to build community self-sufficiency and self-determination by developing and supporting locally controlled political and economic institutions. Although receiving no federal assistance, a CDC emerged in Clear Fork Valley, Tennessee, in an attempt to address the community needs of the area:

> With the help of a community organizer, a twenty-five-member board was formed composed of miners, other workers, unemployed and retired poor people, a shop-keeper, and an office worker. With the assistance of church or foundation funds, a community-owned, -operated and -managed pallet factory was opened, providing badly-needed jobs. In an area of immense health needs, there developed four community-owned clinics, each governed by a local board of directors. (Gaventa 1980, 210)

While non-controversial projects such as improvements in garbage collection and health care ran into little opposition from the dominant coal company in the valley, when CDC participants began to develop viable alternatives to corporate control of the local economy (community-owned businesses, a community center, etc.), hostilities became directed at CDC members. Organizers were labeled "outsiders," "communists," and, perhaps worst of all in a Protestant area, "Catholics." Where the use of disempowering symbols failed to stop the CDC, violent intimidation was used.

As local residents participated in the relatively benign work of improving garbage pickup and organizing a craft cooperative, many participants experienced a political awakening. As this happened, they began to move in more aggressive directions, attempting to establish independent housing and community-based economic development projects. But to do so required land, and it was at that point that difficulties arose because the corporation owned virtually all the land in the town. As the CDC pushed the corporation for land, violence and intimidation erupted: "Twenty-two bullets were put through the community worker's home, the office of the health and development group was burned down, and an alternative school destroyed by fire" (Gaventa 1980, 214). Although much of the land that the CDC wanted from the coal company was unused, they refused to sell it for the purposes of developing local industry.

Genuine community rooted in the culture and social interactions of the people is seen by corporate managers as hostile to business. But the more progressive corporate managers, schooled in the new participatory management techniques, have come to understand the powerful influence that appeals to communal longings can have on controlling the workforce. One of the leaders in the use of such techniques is General Motors (Peters and Waterman 1982). Interestingly, although GM was one of the first companies to embrace such a management approach, its decisions affecting the external communities in which it operated seldom took into consideration the impact on local communities.

Beginning in the 1970s and continuing well into the 1980s, America experienced a considerable deindustrialization. One after another, factories producing steel, automobiles, electronics, and a wide range of other manufactured goods closed across the Northeast and Midwest. At the same time a new service industry, primarily non-union and lower pay, expanded. In the 1990s even this new industry became victim to downsizing as corporations cut staff and overhead, increased workloads for those who remained, and contracted out for labor. Corporate profits soared.

The impact of these trends on local communities was devastating. Employees either lost their jobs outright or were told that they had to relocate if they wished to continue with the company. This not only devastated workers financially and psychologically, but it destroyed many local communities. Tax revenues declined at the same time that the demand for public services increased as unemployed workers turned to government services for help. Verging on bankruptcy, local governments increased property taxes for those who remained, thus increasing their financial burden and helping to increase attitudes of alienation toward government: "In the wake of disinvestment, people are being forced in ever larger numbers to abandon their communities, seeking not so much greener pastures elsewhere, as ones that are not as economically parched as those they are forced to leave. In the course of this process, they are forfeiting something quite precious—their sense of security and their desire for community" (Bluestone 1982, 40).

One dramatic, though not unusual, example of corporate decision-making undermining community in an urban area took place in a Detroit neighborhood called Poletown in the early 1980s. Even while garnering huge profits, the leaders of General Motors decided behind closed corporate doors to shut down many of its older auto factories and build new, modern ones that would make extensive use of robots to replace workers. In an attempt to keep GM in Detroit, Mayor Coleman Young along with the overwhelming support of the Detroit City Council, made a deal with GM executives to raze some 1,176 homes, sixteen churches, two schools, 145 businesses, and one hospital in the Poletown neighborhood to make room for a new Cadillac plant. In an area covering 465 acres, more than 3,400 people were thrown out of their homes. Interestingly, the design for the new plant was a standardized corporate design followed by all new GM plants. It was to be surrounded by green spaces and large, open parking lots. Even though modification in the design to reduce the size of the green spaces and construct a parking garage would have saved many of the homes, GM refused to make such a modification.

Following the "quick take" procedures in a recently passed law by the state of Michigan, the city of Detroit moved rapidly to condemn private homes and businesses, paying owners what the city determined was fair market value, and razed the neighborhood. Although people in the community attempted to organize to fight the plan, their efforts were in vain. In a dramatic attempt to stop destruction of their neighborhood, a group of mainly elderly women staged an occupation of the neighborhood Catholic Church, Immaculate Conception, which ended when they were forcibly removed by a SWAT team and the church was demolished. With the demolition of the church, the opposition was broken and the project continued to completion.

The Poletown neighborhood was a poor, but not destitute, community composed of 30–50 percent Polish people, 5–10 percent Albanians from Yugoslavia, and a smattering of Ukrainian, Filipino, black, and southern white people. The neighborhood was successfully integrated, so much so that researchers at the University of Michigan cited it as one of the most continuously racially integrated areas in the state. By all accounts there was a strong sense of community in Poletown: "The community was still recognized as one in which there were strong emotional attachments, affordable housing, exceptionally good access to public transportation, and good health care" (Wylie 1989, 26). Many merchants lived above their stores, and many stores acted as active third places where neighbors met and socialized. A Poletown Area Revitalization Task Force was active, and the area was protected by a neighborhood-run C.B. radio patrol. In the late 1970s area merchants formed the Poletown Development Corporation to help support local business. Church participation, primarily Catholic, was active, with the neighborhood being served by six local churches. In many instances residents were born in the neighborhood and lived their entire lives there—some in the very same house. Nonetheless, the power of GM and the commitment of Mayor Young to keep GM in Detroit at all costs led to the ironic development to destroy one neighborhood in order to keep corporate jobs in Detroit (Bukowczyk 1984).

The dominant form of business today is corporate. Because of that, the leaders of business are no longer influenced by local community concerns, interests, or needs. Instead, decisions within the corporation are made solely on the basis of how those decisions affect the corporation and the corporate bottom line. This point, sadly, is neither startling nor new. In their study of Yankee City in the 1930s and 1940s, Warner and Low note the same phenomenon:

> The essential point to remember for the leaders of industry and finance is that they were subject to local control (1) because they were subject to local sentiments which motivated them "to take care of their own people," and (2) they were under the powerful influence of the numerous organizations to which they belonged and of their personal contacts with local citizens, which directly related them to influence from every part of the city. The advent of big-city capitalism shattered this closely woven network of personal relations, loyalties, and obligations. (1968, 34)

In Appalachia, in Detroit, and throughout America corporate leaders have made decisions that have maximized profit for their companies while, at the same time, devastating local communities. Perhaps not fully understanding their own complicity in the undermining of community they nonetheless have noted its demise and, seeing an opportunity to manipulate workers even more effectively than before, have adopted participatory management techniques. It is to the workplace itself that we must now turn to see the full impact of business on the promotion of counterfeit community.

Corporate Work

Industrialization has had the impact of separating the work sphere from the sphere of personal life. Workers changed from being farmers who worked their own land and craftsmen and shop owners who worked and lived in their own shops to become hourly wage employees who sold their labor and worked in places often far removed from their homes and neighborhoods. The gap between one's work life and one's private life has become so severe today that workers are often forced to make a choice between being successful in one's career or being satisfied in other parts of one's life. One influential management book put it this way:

> We have found that the majority of passionate activists who hammer away at the old boundaries have given up family vacations, little league games, birthday dinners, evenings, weekends and lunch hours, gardening, reading, movies, and most other pastimes. . . . We are frequently asked if it is possible to "have it all"—a full and satisfying personal life and a full and satisfying hard-working professional one. Our answer is: no. The price of excellence is time, energy, attention, and focus. (Peters and Austin 1985, 495–496)

Thus, the second dimension regarding the relationship of corporate business to the community relates to the conflicting demands placed upon American workers. In many instances workers are devoting more time and energy to the workplace at the cost of their personal and civic lives. Ironically, many workers are willingly embracing work as the more meaningful dimension of their lives.

In their influential and popular book *In Search of Excellence*, Peters and Waterman are quite frank about how and why American business can be successful by adopting the new participatory approach to management: "We desperately need meaning in our lives and will sacrifice a great deal to institutions that will provide meaning for us" (1982, 56). With the erosion of genuine community in America (often caused by business itself) and the increasing difficulties people are having maintaining healthy family relationships, individuals are particularly susceptible to overtures from the workplace to provide them with connectedness: "As broken homes become more common—and as the sense of belonging to a geographical community grows less and less secure in an age of mobility—the corporate world has created a sense of 'neighborhood,' of 'feminine culture,' of family at work" (Hochschild 1997, 55).

But it is not enough to merely note the increasing tendency in the corporate world to appeal to workers by appealing to their desire to belong. One must also understand the role the corporate business world has had in the destruction of genuine community itself. When we understand that corporations have seen genuine community as hostile to their own existence and have overtly and covertly taken actions to destroy community, an entirely different light is shed on the new participatory workplace management techniques. Seen from this vantage point, corporations become one of the major causes of the destruction of genuine community and, at the same time, one of the major promoters and beneficiaries of its counterfeit cousin.

Approaching the same phenomenon from a slightly different, yet complementary, perspective, Schaef and Fassel (1988) argue that the corporation now provides an environment that "addicts" people to work because it provides them with things they long for but are not present in their private or public lives: "Some organizations promise things people longed for in their families and never did get, like recognition, approval, the development of social skills, and caring" (Schaef and Fassel 1988, 120). This sense of connectedness is provided by the mission of the corporation:

> When organizations function as the addictive substance, it is in their interest to keep promoting the vision of the mission, because as long as the employees are hooked by it, they are unlikely to turn their awareness to the present discrepancies. . . . The mission is a powerful source of identification for workers. It is a type of philosophical orientation that appeals to their values. Through the mission they find a link between themselves and the organization. (Schaef and Fassel 1988, 125)

Thus, the purpose of the new participatory management approach is not really to promote the growth of the worker; rather it becomes yet another technique to manipulate and exploit the worker for the benefit of management and ownership. Instead of fulfilling the promise of individual growth and creativity, in reality what happens is that individuals subordinate themselves to rules, procedures, and established norms in a system designed to control the workers: "Membership is conditioned upon not being oneself and following one's own path. The . . . lesson learned is to keep attuned outside oneself and to be constantly vigilant about those things one needs to do to stay in the company's good graces and win approval" (Schaef and Fassel 1988, 121).

THE PALAVER OF COMMUNITY
IN THE BUSINESS WORLD

Perhaps the most blatant attempt to obtain employees' support is by getting them to believe that they are all linked together. This is attempted through devices known as "mission statements." Mission statements are often distributed throughout the corporation, often found posted throughout the business, and often referred to by management as their guiding principles. The primary objective of a mission statement is internal to the organization itself—to build morale among employees and to improve leadership effectiveness (Klemm, Sanderson, and Luffman 1991). Through the use of mostly pious platitudes, the objective is to create commitment to the organization on the part of the employees by continually bombarding them with the values of the organization: "People are searching for meaning and for an opportunity to transcend the ordinariness of day-to-day existence. Values give meaning. Living up to one's values or joining a group of people successfully following those values helps an individual feel a sense of transcendence. In those circumstances work becomes more fulfilling because it is filled with greater purpose" (Campbell and Yeung 1991, 17). It is the mission statement that first attempts to link employees to certain values articulated by a company and then gets them to adopt those values as their own.

Mission statements are written exclusively by either management or ownership (in many instances they are written solely by the CEO). Although the objective is to obtain compliance of employees, they are not generally included in the process of developing them. Instead, they are told that they will be treated with "respect, openness, and honesty," or that they will be encouraged "to be active and responsible citizens," or that the employees, "whose creativity and commitment to winning through teamwork is the key to our competitiveness," will be rewarded. Although the actual statements tend to be vague, they are designed to help create a corporate culture that is supportive of management: "If the mission can link the employees' values with the company's values then each individual employee will find a sense of mission" (Klemm, Sanderson, and Luffman 1991, 78).

Although mission statements often appear banal, effective mission statements are written to appeal to customers and employees on the basis of what the company actually does. Mission statements tend to emphasize those elements that are lacking in one's everyday life. Thus, they offer us honesty, openness, security, fairness, a sense of importance, and, of course, community. By identifying with the organization, one can be a part of a group of individuals similarly committed to delivering, not a service, but social responsibility.

PARTICIPATORY MANAGEMENT APPROACHES

Throughout corporate America the participatory model of management is becoming accepted as the superior management approach that distinguishes excellent companies from the mediocre. Inspired by Douglas McGregor's seminal statement of his famous "Theory Y" approach to management, delivered at the Fifth Anniversary Convocation of MIT's Alfred P.

Sloan School of Management in April 1957, a wide range of approaches to management that emphasize the human dimension of organizational management have been developed over the last four decades. Although each approach differs in some particular area or emphasis from the others, they all contain certain common elements: an emphasis on the active participation by all workers; a concern with individual dignity, worth, and growth of each worker; an attempt to fuse individual worker needs with organizational goals; an emphasis on openness and working-through of differences in the workplace; and an environment of trust, feedback, and human relationships (McGregor 1985).

In recent years a massive body of literature has developed that describes each of the new participatory management approaches. They go by a variety of names: Total Quality Management (TQM), quality circles, quality teams, Z-Theory, T-groups, management by objective, brainstorming, managerial grids, intrapreneurship, demassing, excellence, or managing by walking around (MBWA). Whatever the specific name of the particular approach, the goals of all contain common assumptions and beliefs. All of these approaches emphasize that workers should be treated in such a way as to increase their participation in making decisions about their immediate workplace. Systems are developed to encourage workers to cooperate and work in teams, good performance is recognized and rewarded, managers are encouraged to be facilitators rather than bosses, workers are granted rights to redress grievances, etc. Yet the underlying objective is not worker satisfaction in and of itself; it is improving profitability. In reference to the TQM approach, George and Weimerskirch are quick to point out that the real objective is profitability: "The pursuit of quality excellence does not come at the expense of financial excellence. Rather, financial results are another way of measuring the effectiveness of the system. The difference is that the goal of the new model is not profits, it is customer satisfaction, with the understanding that profits will improve as quality improves" (1994, 7). Even the most blatant approach to introducing community into the workplace, M. Scott Peck's Community Building Workshop (CBW), contends that the benefits for the corporation are an increase in productivity: "Community in the workplace and organizational civility will succeed because it is *cost-effective*" (Peck 1993, 366).

With all these approaches, the fundamental issues of power are ignored or not considered appropriate. Yet, in any organization, regardless of whether it is organized hierarchically or cooperatively, power is present. Power is inherently present in all forms of human interaction. Ignoring power does not make it disappear. The new participatory approaches deal with power in one of two ways: they either ignore the issue altogether, or they imply that power is inherently corrupt and should be avoided at all costs. By far the most common ways of dealing with the issue of power are to simply ignore it or to frame it so narrowly (e.g., worker empowerment) that it focuses only on how workers do their jobs. By doing so it is possible to ignore the more fundamental political issues about the overall direction of the company, issues of ownership, and issues regarding profitability. No matter how participatory the corporation claims to be, the most important decisions are made by management with little or no participation from workers. Instead, workers are given greater flexibility to do the jobs that are already narrowly defined by management. While this appears to be an improvement over the old scientific management techniques that viewed workers as cogs in a machine, in fact it merely creates the illusion of worker control. Real power remains in the hands of management.

It is beyond the scope of this work to examine in detail each of the particular participatory management approaches, but a closer look at a few will illustrate these points. One approach that brought together many ideas advanced in participatory management approaches was "excellence" as first described by Tom Peters and Robert Waterman in the hugely popular book *In Search of Excellence* (1982). Peters, far more than Waterman, turned excellence into a crusade. The initial book has sold more than five million copies, and Peters has followed it up with five other books (one co-authored with Austin) and hundreds of seminars he teaches around the world.

Although Peters has been attacked for being faddish and his ideas have been criticized for being contradictory (e.g., two-thirds of the companies identified as excellent in 1982 are now out of the running and Peters now says "there are no excellent companies"), more significant for our purposes are the ideas he initially advocated. The entire approach is summarized in eight attributes the authors identify in their initial work: (1) a bias for action; (2) closeness to the customer; (3) fostering autonomy and entrepreneurship; (4) productivity through people; (5) value driven companies; (6) "stick to the knitting"—do what you do best; (7) keep a simple form and a lean staff; and (8) keep control but be as decentralized as possible. The forty-three companies studied possessed all of these characteristics.

But the underlying significance of the excellence orientation is not found in any list of attributes a company may possess or in any kind of strategy that might be employed. Indeed, it is to be found in the assumptions the approach makes about how to motivate workers. Peters and Waterman spend considerable time discussing human nature and their belief that in order to motivate workers companies must adopt management approaches that are based upon a realistic view of human behavior. One (though not the only) motivational device is to create an environment in which workers identify the organization as an institution that can fulfill their own personal needs. When this is accomplished, workers see the company as a valued source of personal satisfaction and are willing to work for its success. This may be done by decentralizing the workplace environment (e.g., teams) and by creating a feeling that the company is like an extended family: "By offering meaning as well as money, [companies] give their employee a mission as well as a sense of feeling great. Every man becomes a pioneer, an experimenter, a leader. The institution provides guiding belief and creates a sense of excitement, a sense of being a part of the best" (Peters and Waterman 1982, 323).

The overall tenet of the excellence orientation (as well as the wide variety of quality approaches) begins with the belief that workers want to be a part of something that is meaningful and that meaning in people's lives is more and more difficult to come by. When an institution creates a workplace atmosphere that emphasizes and rewards excellence, workers are apt to believe that they may find meaning in the workplace. An effective way of creating such an atmosphere is through the use of groups or teams, whereby workers come to feel a sense of connectedness and where the values of the organization are inculcated by peers rather than bosses. The yearning for connectedness, not present in our everyday lives, is thus the primary reason workers will respond positively to such appeals. Yet, the range of decisions that falls within the scope of the worker groups is narrow, limited primarily to how workers organize their jobs. Consequently, we have the rather odd phenomenon that, on the one hand, corporations are one of the principle causes for the destruction of communities through plant closings, the undermining of locally owned and operated business, and similar activities, while, on the other hand, the same corporations are advocating a more participatory form of workplace involvement to re-create the feelings of connectedness destroyed by the loss of community in their neighborhoods.

Although most participatory management approaches avoid the explicit use of the concept of community—preferring instead concepts such as family, teams, or work groups—at least one approach has as its stated objective the building of community in the workplace. Founded in 1984 the Foundation for Community Encouragement (FCE) runs three-day Community Building Workshops (CBWs) with the intent of changing the culture of businesses. Organized primarily by M. Scott Peck, the CBW is a social-psychological approach designed to teach workers the principles of community.

Having conducted hundreds of workshops, FCE staff members claim that they know how to create community in a matter of only two days: "It generally takes no more than two days to build a group into a functioning community—even in an organization where the members have been at one another's throats for years" (Peck 1993, 286). CBWs go through four stages in order to build community: pseudocommunity, chaos, emptiness, and community. Pseudocommunity is filled with generalizations; people are polite, inauthentic, and mannerly. From this stage where individual differences are covered up, the group is pushed to the next stage, chaos, where the attempt is made to obliterate individual difference. Members try to convert, heal, or fix each other. This stage of unpleasantness is transformed into the third stage, emptiness, when the members purge themselves of their prejudices, their expectations, their simplistic beliefs, and their personal hatred and terrors. In effect, at this stage people bare their souls to each other. At some point during this stage, community is created when "a member will speak of something particularly poignant and authentic. Instead of retreating from it, the group now sits in silence, absorbing it. Then a second member will quietly say something equally authentic. . . . The silence returns, and out of it, a third member will speak with eloquent appropriateness. Community has been born" (Peck 1993, 275). Peck, of course, admits that while it is a relatively easy task to create community, it is far more difficult to sustain it: "You don't just build community; you rebuild it and rebuild it and rebuild it for as long as you have reason to continue to be together" (Peck 1993, 339).

CBWs were not originally designed for the workplace. Instead, they began as workshops for anywhere from 30 to 400 individuals who may or may not have known each other prior to the workshop. They attended for "spiritual education." The principles learned in these workshops were then extended to business organizations under the sponsorship of the FCE. In his book Peck documents the use of the CBWs to a variety of organizations, even including prisons.

The Community Building Workshops are merely one of the latest management techniques that exploit workers' longings to be connected to others. Certainly the assertion that community can be created among people who may not even know each other in a matter of only two days must strike scholars of community as patently absurd. Still, the popularity of such workshops and the effects they have on participants is revealing. The urges for community are an important motivating force, perhaps more so today than ever before. At the same time, that desire for connectedness may be easily manipulated by those with the skills to do so.

COUNTERFEIT COMMUNITY IN THE WORKPLACE

Attempts to elicit feelings of community from workers illustrate vividly how the nature of genuine community conflicts with the corporate sector. This conflict occurs because of two fundamental aspects related to the character of corporate business: (1) the profit motive; and (2) the private character of corporate decision-making.

While it is a truism to say that the primary objective of a business is to make a profit, corporate business has distorted the profit motive by orienting business toward not just profit, but toward the maximization of profit. In prior years, business, even corporate business, encountered at least some modest checks on its power. An organized labor union movement, local farm organizations, and a substantial number of elected politicians whose political support was independent of business all functioned to moderate corporate influence. Today, however, organized labor is in disarray, agriculture has been taken over by corporate farming, and elected politicians have been increasingly dependent on business for campaign contributions. Checks on corporate power are virtually non-existent.

At the same time that the social and political forces that could check corporate power have declined in influence, corporations have taken steps to consolidate their own power. In the last two decades corporate mergers and takeovers have increased dramatically. Profits have soared as corporations have downsized, reduced inventories, and replaced full-time employees with temps or robots. It is no longer acceptable for corporations to make a profit; instead they attempt to maximize profit using whatever techniques possible.

The desire to maximize profit has pushed corporate management to make virtually all decisions with concern about the bottom line. Issues of justice, equality, and diversity—issues important in genuine communities—will only be addressed if they can be shown to be directly relevant to the pursuit of profit. The intense desire to maximize profit has led to gross income inequalities within the corporation and, consequently, life within the corporate environment will not achieve economic justice or equality. The reason for the inequalities within the corporation occur because of what Frank and Cook (1995) call "winner-take-all markets."

Winner-take-all markets occur in areas where payoffs are determined by relative rather than absolute performance and where "rewards tend to be concentrated in the hands of a few top performers, with small differences in talent or effort often giving rise to enormous differences in incomes" (Frank and Cook 1995, 24). This is exactly the situation that exists in corporate America, and it has led to vast income inequalities within companies that vie for top executives. The prevailing belief within the corporate business community is that obtaining the best CEO can easily result in tens of millions of additional profits each year. Operating on the basis of this belief, CEO compensation has skyrocketed as corporations compete with each other to get the very best. Taking a sample of two hundred of the largest U.S. corporations, one researcher estimated the average CEO pay at around $2.8 million per year (Crystal 1991). This represents about 120 times the pay of an average manufacturing worker and about 150 times the pay of an average worker in both the manufacturing and service industries. While a $2.8 million salary may sound staggering, in fact, CEOs at the top twenty corporations all made more than $10 million annually in 1993, with Michael Eisner of Disney leading the way with $203 million.

The cultural norms that have developed in recent years in corporate America have come to justify vast income disparities even though the difference in talent and ability among the actors is minimal. As long as the norms supporting these income inequalities continue to exist, justice within the corporation is not possible. No matter what variation of participatory management approach might be used, without fundamental revision of the reward structure, attempts to develop community within the business world will remain counterfeit.

The second characteristic of participatory management approaches that leads toward counterfeit community relates to the private character of corporations. Although one might argue that the distinction between the public and private is culturally defined, it has been well established that business in America should, whenever possible, be owned and operated by private individuals. In a capitalist system this means that business ownership is held by a few—those with capital.

When organizations are considered private, many commonly accepted norms applied to public institutions are not relevant. Perhaps the most fundamental publicly accepted principle that finds little or no adherence in the private realm is that decisions should be made on the basis of democratic principles. It is ultimately the assumption that business is private that allows management to organize the workplace in whatever fashion they like.

Perhaps the most telling aspect of participatory management approaches is the limited sphere in which worker participation is allowed to occur. Fundamental financial decisions for the corporation, the ability to hire or fire employees, the wage structure for the entire company, and similar decision-making arenas are excluded from realistic worker participation. At best, workers may make recommendations in some of those areas, but in the areas most crucial for the well-being of the organization private norms of decision-making govern. Participatory management is restricted to merely how jobs are organized to produce the product or deliver the service. Because of the limited scope of decision-making power, participatory management techniques create the illusion of worker empowerment rather than producing a real shift to worker control of the workplace.

Genuine community power is, at least theoretically, equally shared among all members. In actual operation, of course, some individuals will have greater influence than others, but differences occur as a result of leadership abilities or status positions earned through participation in the community. This is not the case in the business world. While leadership abilities cannot be discounted as a source of influence, more important is the position the person holds within the management framework. All members of the corporation are not assumed to be equal; managers, primarily because of the positions they occupy, possess greater influence than non-managers, and CEOs, selected not by all the members of the company but rather by the board of directors, make the most important decisions.

Participatory management approaches are designed to convey the sense of belonging, even community, without involving workers in the most important decisions for the organization. Consequently, they manipulate and exploit workers' desires to belong and create a false sense of community spirit.

CONCLUSION

It is not merely coincidence that the decline in genuine community in America parallels the growth in popularity of participatory approaches to management in the workplace. The faddish approaches advocating greater worker involvement are effective only to the extent that feelings for connectedness are not satisfied elsewhere in one's life. As genuine community erodes, the attachment to one's neighborhood becomes less and less a source of identification. Suburban development and the creation of gated communities have physically isolated neighbors from each other, and the counterfeit communities that have been constructed to simulate genuine communities have failed to provide an enduring sense of meaning for their participants.

Participatory management techniques have exploited this physical and psychological isolation by offering workers an arena in which meaning may be rediscovered—the workplace. But ultimately the workplace is just as counterfeit and exploitive of feelings of community as are other aspects of our lives. While designing mission statements that claim that they are good citizens, corporations have undermined the economic viability of local economies through their expansionistic and competitive practices. Where participatory management practices have been implemented in the workplace, the scope of participation has been severely limited. Workers are allowed a say in determining how to best do their jobs but are rarely given a realistic opportunity to chart the overall direction of the business itself. Without real involvement in making the most important decisions, participation becomes yet another management technique to control them. Because these approaches are built upon an exploitive foundation, they seldom result in long-lasting improvements in either quality or innovation and instead produce a Borg-like work atmosphere in which loyalty to the company becomes the test of effectiveness.

6
Political Community

... the most potent part of [Reagan's] appeal was his evocation of communal values—of family and neighborhood, religion and patriotism. What Reagan stirred was a yearning for a way of life that seems to be receding in recent times.

—*Michael Sandel (1988, 21)*

On July 16, 1992, then-candidate Bill Clinton accepted the Democratic presidential nomination in Madison Square Garden in New York City. In his acceptance speech he sketched out his vision of a "New Covenant" he wished to establish between government and the American people. In describing that covenant, Clinton appealed to the American people through the concept of community seven times. America was in trouble, he said. We had a sluggish economy; people were unemployed and felt that government wasn't listening to them. The solution, he claimed, was community: "We offer our people a new choice based on old values. We offer opportunity. We demand responsibility. We will build an American community again."

Hearkening to images of President Kennedy's challenge for a renewed sense of citizenship more than thirty years earlier, Clinton blended citizenship with basic American values and oblique references to religion:

In the end, my fellow Americans, the New Covenant simply asks us all to be Americans again. Old-fashioned Americans for a new time. Opportunity. Responsibility. Community. . . . We can renew our faith in each other and in ourselves. We can restore our sense of unity and community. As the Scripture says, our eyes have not yet imagined what we can build.

As if to underscore the community emphasis of his acceptance speech, Clinton and his vice presidential nominee, Al Gore, immediately embarked on a six-day, 1000-mile bus tour that wove its way through eight states (117 electoral votes) from New York to St. Louis. Each stop on the tour was theatrically staged and scripted to symbolically link the candidates with old-fashioned images of community. Except for St. Louis, the stops were in small towns and the crowds were purposively modest—large enough to show enthusiasm, but small enough to remind us that community is small, informal, and friendly.

Often using the town meeting format that Clinton perfected, Bill Clinton and Al Gore, wearing plaid shirts, would sit on a bale of hay and, after a brief, canned speech, respond to questions from the audience. Over and over, images and references to community emerged. In Clinton's final speech on the trip in St. Louis he once again appealed to the yearning for community. "We want to restore to this country a genuine sense of community and caring, to say we're all in this together," he intoned.

The use of the concept of community is not new to American politics. What is new is the frequency of its use (which seems inversely related to its decline) and the hollowness of its meaning. Most politicians have developed their own community appeals, their own spins on the community theme. Bob Dole, in announcing his presidential candidacy in 1995, challenged America to follow him to recreate a "community of values," and Lamar Alexander called for a "Rising Shining America" where "the decisions about how to help the poor are made locally, by communities, charity, and voluntary organizations." It was not that long ago that Senator Joseph Biden, during his brief presidential candidacy, created an image of America as a "seamless web of caring and community," and Walter Mondale attempted to rally support by describing America as "a community, a family, where we care for each other, knit together by a bond of love."

In point of fact, these politicians had few plans to revitalize American communities. Some had ideas about how they wanted to improve the economy, some probably had specific ideas about abortion policy, and fewer had concrete proposals to improve the environment or to aid starving Third World nations; but none had proposals about how to encourage genuine community in America. While most critical observers of American culture realize that community is deteriorating, it is not an issue that lends itself well to glib political solutions. Still, expressing concern over the demise of community and making vague references to its reconstruction "plays well in Peoria" because it touches upon the aspects of our everyday lives that ring most true: community life in America is deteriorating. The appeal to community in its various guises is blatantly an exercise in palaver—propaganda designed to guile and charm the electorate but offer nothing of substance to solve the problem.

In the presidential campaign of 1988, Michael Dukakis attempted to win political support not with specific policy proposals designed to strengthen community, but by merely telling the electorate how he felt: "Dedication to work, to family, to community, to neighborhood; those are the values I believe in. They're the values I care about and the values you care about." Stymied for over a year by a Republican Congress and with little hope of passing bold policy initiatives, President Clinton fell back on the rhetoric of community in his 1996 State of the Union speech, referring to community almost twenty times in a little over an hour as he talked about family, education, crime, and the environment: "We have to go forward, to the era of working together—as a community, as a team, as one America, with all of us reaching across the lines that divide us, the divisions, the rancor." Few policy proposals were forthcoming.

If all it amounted to was manipulative political propaganda, we could undermine it by merely exposing it. We could show how campaigns are driven by public relations gimmicks, how campaign managers use focus groups to identify issues and candidate images they will use, and how the clever sound bite drives solid public policy proposals from the political dialogue. We could show how campaign managers discovered the resonant quality of the concept of community and how public relations experts marketed it. This will not be enough, however, because the problem goes deeper than that.

This chapter will show how the underlying assumptions of our political system and its defining parameters mitigate against and limit the possibility that community can be created through the use of "normal" politics. Thus, politicians' use of the concept of community tends to be manipulative, and initiatives to build community are inherently simulacra. The assumptions and operation of the political system create political dispositions that are anti-communitarian. If we accept the fundamental assumptions upon which the political system was founded—namely, that humans are motivated and guided by rational calculation based upon self-interest, that toleration and respect for individual rights are predominate values, and that the government should be neutral toward moral issues—genuine community becomes problematic. In such a system the citizen "uses the gift of choice to multiply his options in and to transform the material conditions of the world, but never to transform himself or to create a world of mutuality with his fellow humans" (Barber 1984, 22). While the dynamics of the human condition might illustrate the desire and need for humans to live in some form of association, the structure and operation of the American political system are based upon an alternative conception: that humans are self-interested and likely to oppress each other given the opportunity.

One of the basic reasons it is so difficult to create and sustain community in America is because genuine community runs counter to the form of elite democracy that has been developed. In this situation we are left either trying to create forms of community that struggle to survive in an alien culture or, more likely in recent years, forms of counterfeit political community.

The problem is difficult to see because the supporters of our political system have been so successful that alternatives are not only not taken seriously, but are never even considered legitimate. For most, different ways of orienting ourselves toward politics cannot even be imagined. Consensus on the political system is so widespread and so intensely held that alternatives appear "un-American." After describing to a class of college students the vision of genuine community I have explored in this book, I asked them for their reactions. After the usual pregnant silence, one student tentatively offered his reaction: "Isn't that communism?"

Still, American politics is neither monolithic nor unidimensional. Although assumptions hostile to the creation of genuine community dominate, there also exists a second language of politics more consonant with community. It goes by various names: Jeffersonian democracy, popular democracy, republicanism, participatory democracy, or, in the words of Benjamin Barber, "thick democracy." This thicker, richer version of democracy has, from time to time, predominated in American political history; but certainly since the middle of the twentieth century the thinner version of elite democracy prevails. Although what follows may appear obvious, elite democracy must be described first to show more clearly how the fundamental nature of the system makes it difficult to construct and maintain community.

ELITE DEMOCRACY

The United States is a democracy; of that, there is agreement throughout the world. We are, in fact, the world's preeminent democracy. But the exact nature of our peculiar form of democracy, although widely accepted, is seldom explicitly articulated. In reality the American political system in design and operation is fundamentally elitist. It is a system in which political elites "acquire the power to decide by means of a competitive struggle for the people's vote" (Schumpeter 1976, 269). The primary focus is on elections, and citizens consider voting to be one of the most important citizenship activities.

Although there are high levels of alienation reported among the citizenry today, voting is nonetheless considered an important responsibility on the part of citizens, even alienated citizens. But the manner in which citizens respond to voting further reflects the fundamentally elitist nature of the political system. The role of citizens in the electoral system is relatively passive. At best, they should pay attention to the campaigns, listen to what the candidates say, pay attention to the issues, and follow the news. Citizens are, in effect, spectators watching (usually on television) elites battle in the public arena. The passive role of the citizens is further reflected in other parts of the political system as well. The judicial system is controlled by highly trained elites (judges, attorneys, court administrators) who "process" citizens who may only go to court if damage has occurred directly to them or their property. As policy is administered by government bureaucrats, citizens are viewed as "clients" who have problems that need expert advice and assistance. Civic responsibility on the part of the citizen does not prevail; nowhere are citizens empowered; nowhere is there an attempt to construct genuine community.

Although one might be tempted to conclude that the elitist nature of the political system can be traced to recent technological approaches to campaigning or to the growth of massive, bureaucratized government programs, in fact, these developments have occurred within a constitutional framework that is elitist at its core. In the Constitution of 1787 distrust of the common citizen was so great that only one national office was to be directly elected by the people—Representative to the House. Senators were to be chosen by state legislatures, the president was to be selected by an elite group of members of an electoral college, and court justices were appointed.

This distrust of the average citizen is clearly articulated by James Madison, one of the principle architects of the Constitution and its primary author. In the classic "Federalist No. 10," one of many papers written in support of the new Constitution, he writes:

A zeal for different opinions concerning religion, concerning government, and many other points, as well of speculation as of practice; an attachment to different leaders ambitiously contending for pre-eminence and power; or to persons of other descriptions whose fortunes have been interesting to the human passions, have, in turn, divided mankind into parties, inflamed them with mutual animosity, and rendered them much more disposed to vex and oppress each other than to cooperate for their common good. So strong is this propensity of mankind to fall into mutual animosities that where no substantial occasion presents itself the most frivolous and fanciful distinctions have been sufficient to kindle their unfriendly passions and excite their most violent conflicts. (1961, 79)

The Founding Fathers started with the belief that human nature is evil and that the average citizen was governed more directly by those natural appetites. The more sophisticated elites, so it was implied, were educated and trained in a different fashion.

Given this viewpoint, popular democracy becomes problematic:

> A common passion or interest will, in almost every case, be felt by a majority of the whole; a communication and concert results from the form of government itself; and there is nothing to check the inducements to sacrifice the weaker party or an obnoxious individual. Hence it is that such democracies have ever been spectacles of turbulence and contention; have ever been found incompatible with personal security or the rights of property; and have in general been as short in their lives as they have been violent in their deaths. ("Federalist No. 10" 1961, 81)

Assuming those rather gloomy beliefs about humans, how then does one construct a viable government? The Founding Fathers arrived at two provisions: one, to create a system of checks and balances to prevent any single power base from dominating, and two, to ensure that elites would be included in key positions in the governmental apparatus. The system of checks and balances that pits ambition against ambition is recognized by anyone with even a passing familiarity with American politics. Each of the three branches of government is assigned areas where it has sole responsibility, but all three also share power in other areas. None has enough independent power to dominate.

The second provision was to assure that elites would play an important part in government. This was to be accomplished by creating the Senate in such a fashion that it would be a "temperate and respectable body of citizens" ("Federalist No. 63" 1961, 384), removing the selection of a president from the average citizens and giving it to people who "will be most likely to possess the information and discernment requisite to so complicated an investigation" ("Federalist No. 68" 1961, 412), and giving the court the power of judicial review so that it could be "an essential safeguard against the effects of occasional ill humans in the society" ("Federalist No. 78" 1961, 470).

In point of fact, one of the fundamental assumptions of the Constitution is distrustfulness of the common citizen. Consequently, an entire political structure was developed that effectively placed what were viewed as more reasonable, more refined, and wiser political elites in key governmental positions. While some changes have occurred over the years (we now directly elect senators for example), the characteristics of those serving in national office are not accurate reflections of the population in general: "By almost any measure, senators and representatives constitute an economic and social elite. They are well educated. They come from a small number of prestigious occupations. Many of them possess or amass material wealth. At least a third of all senators are millionaires" (Davidson and Oleszek 1996, 122).

One other assumption embedded in our Constitution deserves mention. While Madison was concerned about the urge for the average citizen to "vex and oppress" others, he further speculated on the reasons for such behavior. The problem with popular government was that humans divided into factions "united and actuated by some common impulse of passion, or of interest, adverse to the rights of other citizens" ("Federalist No. 10" 1961, 78). The major reason for these factions was, according to Madison, "the various and unequal distribution of property" ("Federalist, No. 10" 1961, 79). Thus, the cause for people to oppress had to do with the pursuit of their own material self-interest. Unlike Karl Marx, Madison does not look to the solution by attempting to redistribute property because he considers that fatal to liberty. Instead, he allows for self-interested behavior (even encourages it) and attempts to control the effects through checks and balances.

All this makes perfect sense if we follow Madison's logic and his frame of reference. But if we consider alternatives omitted from Madison's argument, we can see why community can only be counterfeit if based upon the political assumptions embedded in the Constitution.

While the fifty-five men slaved away all summer in Philadelphia forging a new constitution, the author of the Declaration of Independence, Thomas Jefferson, was in Paris, receiving occasional reports about what they were framing. Although Jefferson agreed with many provisions that strengthened the government's ability to conduct commerce, he differed quite fundamentally from Madison about the common citizen. In a letter to Madison after the convention had taken place, Jefferson expressed his faith in the common man and his ability, through civic education, to overcome self-interest: "It is my principle that the will of the Majority should always prevail. . . . Above all things I hope education of the common people will be attended to; convinced that on their good sense we may rely with the most security for the preservation of a degree of liberty" (quoted in Peterson 1975, 432). Jefferson, having participated in the revolution, is in the tradition of popular democracy which posits that an active, engaged citizenry is essential for a democratic polity.

If political community is created, it must emerge out of the interactions of the common people and cannot be imposed from on top or protected by elites. As Benjamin Barber says, "Citizenship and community are two aspects of a single political reality: men can only overcome their insufficiency and legitimize their dependency by forging a common consciousness" (Barber 1984, 216–17). Community is dependent upon a sense of political obligation and a feeling of solidarity. But the notion of the self that emerges from elite democracy prevents individuals from identifying any elements of obligation that go beyond self-interest. Thus, communal obligation makes no sense unless it is directly attached to promotion of the self.

Over 200 years after the creation of the Constitution we continue to feel the effects of structures created on the basis of assumptions inherently hostile to community. It is in those structures, still operating today, where the values underlying our public philosophy play themselves out. But partially because of the compelling desire for connectedness, politicians have attempted to develop procedures and methods that appear to satisfy those needs, even while using institutions hostile to genuine community.

The difficulties of creating community are partially due to the assumptions of self-interest that have shaped our political structures, but there also exists a complementary and mutually supporting view of humans—individualism. To some extent self-interest represents the seamy side of individualism with its implications of material greed, its limited view of responsibility, and its narrow vision of political activism. But individualism has another side that is more positive and emphasizes the rights of individuals and the ability of people to realize their human potentialities through free choice. As its self-interest sibling, the more positive dimension of individualism can be explicitly traced to the eighteenth-century English philosophers Thomas Hobbes, John Locke, and Adam Smith. Each in his own way contributed to the growing body of political thought that influenced our own revolutionary leaders who questioned the authority of the monarchy and claimed that human beings possessed inalienable rights to life, liberty, and property.

Basing arguments on assumptions that humans naturally possessed "right reason," the individualism that emerged made it possible for revolutions against arbitrary authority and repressive monarchies to occur. Through the use of reason humans could determine the legitimate limits of state authority, and where the state overstepped its bounds, humans had the right to rebel.

Within the ethos of individualism, politics is narrowly defined and the state's authority is limited. Political activity occurs only if one sees that one's self-interest can be advanced through such activity. Real meaning is created by individuals working in the private arena—in the workplace, the family, or through religious service. It is the private realm that is to be protected from political incursion.

Working within the parameters of individualism, community becomes problematic. At best, community can be defined as the sum of the pursuit of everyone's self-interest; at worst, it becomes a private system devoid of politics altogether. In either case, it is counterfeit because it lacks the richness, complexity, and inclusiveness of genuine community.

CRITIQUE OF ELITE DEMOCRACY

There have been, of course, a host of critics of elite democracy over the years, starting with the Anti-Federalists who vigorously opposed adoption

of the Constitution and emerging from time to time in grassroots movements throughout history. Over the first 150 years supporters of a grassroots, popular democracy focused their efforts on local politics and, regardless of the assumptions found in the national constitutional
framework, were able to forge political community to at least a limited extent. This was possible because the size and scope of the national government was small compared with today.

While many communities flourished during this time, we should resist
the temptation to become too nostalgic about them. In reality most communities also fell short of our ideal. Two of the more substantial difficulties
they experienced were their exclusive character and their tendency to repress differences. Communities tended to be ethnically based or geograph-
ically isolated and looked with skepticism on "outsiders." Those within the
communities who differed in significant ways (e.g., gay men, Lesbians,
blacks in white communities) were shunned and oppressed. Women in all
such narrowly defined communities were assigned to supportive roles and
ran into difficulty if they became too aggressive and attempted to enter
and compete in the "men's world" of business or politics. Community became the refuge for prejudice and intolerance.

The expansion of the national government can be explained at least
in part as an attempt to break the patterns of repression and oppression
by extending to the oppressed the individualistic protections guaranteed
in the Bill of Rights. Beginning with FDR's New Deal and extending
through Truman's Fair Deal, LBJ's Great Society, the civil rights movement, the women's movement, and into the welfare state that exists
today, government programs and activities have intervened in local communities to protect individual rights and promote toleration. These efforts were at least partially successful and, by no means, should be discounted.

Unfortunately, these interventions were not guided or informed by a
vision of local civic virtue. By overemphasizing individual rights, notions of
communal obligations were de-emphasized. This dilemma was recognized
even at the time when national government intervention was in its infancy.
The response, effective then at obtaining political support, was to recon-
ceptualize community, shifting its focus from localities to the national
level. FDR, for example, argued for "extending to our national life, the old
principle of the local community, and encouraged Americans to think of
themselves as neighbors bound in national community" (Sandel 1988, 22).
Lyndon Johnson, while embarking on his Great Society, intoned a similar
theme, "America as a family, its people bound together by common ties of
confidence and affection" (Sandel 1988, 22).

This shift in focus to the national level, although it has resulted in
eliminating many forms of prejudice and intolerance, has helped under-

mine genuine community, which is inherently local in character. What's more, it established assumptions and political parameters that make most attempts to create community counterfeit. In this new political environment both Democrats, who talk about a "national community," and Republicans, who attack the welfare state and tout private property and the free market, have failed to develop a public philosophy that values and promotes genuine community. Instead, both parties have made use of community palaver to achieve short-term political advantage, and neither has seriously addressed the difficult task of building community.

A further dilemma for the creation of community inherent in elite democratic assumptions may be traced to Madison's conception of private property. Returning once again to Madison's classic "Federalist No. 10" he tells us that the fundamental causes of factions are found in "the various and unequal distribution of property" (1961, 79). This belief, discussed by Madison more than 200 years ago is commonly accepted as truth today. Daly and Cobb refer to this as *Homo economicus,* the concept of the human being as bent on optimizing utility or satisfaction through the consumption of unlimited commodities (1989, 159). According to this perspective, all calculations are made entirely by the individual without regard to others—extreme individualism. *Homo economicus* has no need for fairness or benevolence, or for the preservation of human life, or any other moral concern. Society is nothing more than individuals interacting in order for each to maximize his or her own wealth. There is no concept of a collective good, no community.

One of the fascinating things about this viewpoint is that, although it represents a fundamental belief upon which our political structure is founded, it is an almost totally inaccurate characterization of human behavior. Experiments done by economists to test the *Homo economicus* perspective invariably find that humans in fact contribute substantial resources to promote the overall good of the group even when it means less wealth for themselves (Rhoads 1985). Likewise, political scientists find that in instances where voters correctly perceive their own interests, what candidates are saying, and how candidate positions affect their self-interest they often vote against their own narrow self-interest, if they believe it will benefit society as a whole (Feldman 1982).

The dilemma we are presented with is that the assumptions upon which our political system is founded and upon which the political structures exist are not just erroneous, but also hostile to the creation of community. Whatever policies designed to create community that emerge tend to reflect the value assumptions hostile to communal life embedded in the institutions that must implement those policies. Inevitably, counterfeit political community emerges. A few examples will illustrate the point.

COUNTERFEIT POLITICAL COMMUNITY

In this section we will examine three aspects of counterfeit political community in America: town meetings, Fourth of July celebrations, and political campaigns. By no means do these exhaust the possible examples of counterfeit political community in America; they represent instead only a thin slice of the problem.

While there are numerous examples of politicians explicitly using the concept of community in a manipulative fashion, there are even more instances of the manipulation of the citizenry by creating the false impression that grassroots participation occurs, that it is valued, and that politicians listen to and are responsive to their constituents. We will take a look at town meetings and campaigns as examples of how a false sense of political participation is created. Although rituals are important aspects of genuine community, the rituals that have evolved in America exude a hollowness because of their disconnectedness from community. Perhaps no ritual should be more sacred than that which honors the establishment of the community itself—the Fourth of July. But even this ritualistic celebration of political community has become disconnected from genuine community and, because of that, has become counterfeit.

The Counterfeit Town Meeting

Members of Congress have discovered that an important way to obtain electoral support is to participate in activities that make it appear as if they are listening and responding to the problems of their constituents. The overall approach to obtain political support by dealing with constituent problems is called "constituent service." One interesting technique that is used by many Representatives is the town meeting. The town meeting effectively combines listening to constituent complaints while imitating the format of New England town meetings. New England town meetings, where they still exist, are a style of genuine community, where citizens discuss and debate issues that they are concerned about, where decisions are made by the entire community, where representatives are chosen to implement the decisions, and where the impact of those decisions is reviewed. Town meetings run by members of Congress, of course, are much different.

One of the interesting aspects of the entire town meeting phenomenon is that probably 99 percent of the entire electorate has never even seen a genuine town meeting. Town meetings have mostly been limited to small towns in some New England states. In the entire state of Massachusetts, for example, only slightly more than 300 towns hold annual town meetings, and many of those are representative town meetings. Thus, without even venturing into an examination of the specifics of how Representatives operate their own versions, we must realize that they are simulacra, imitations of things that, except in very rare instances, do not exist. Even further, however, we will see how, because of the elitist nature of the meetings, they fail to provide for genuine participation and fail to provide an arena in which people may develop connectedness and caring for their fellow citizens.

At a specified and publicized time and place, the Representative appears to listen to and address the concerns of the citizens who come. The time, the place, and the format are all arranged by the member of Congress's staff and is determined not by the needs and schedules of the constituents, but by the scheduling demands of the Representative. As is common practice for important people, the Representative tends to arrive fashionably late, makes a brief opening statement often referring to something he or she has done in Congress, and then lets his or her constituents queue behind microphones to voice their concerns. The meetings are often standing-room-only and usually populated by angry citizens complaining about a variety of things from the loud neighbor next door to foreign policy toward Cuba.

The citizens attending seldom know each other prior to the meeting, and unless there is a concerted attempt by some particular group to influence the Representative on a particular issue, most citizens arrive with their own agendas. Rather than talking with each other and trying to persuade each other (as would occur in a genuine town meeting), the participants address the member of Congress who, with a look of concern, tries to address the issue and makes sure his or her aide takes down the person's name and address so they may write a follow-up letter. The focus is on creating the image of a one-to-one relationship between the citizen and the Representative, not on creating a sense of connectedness among the citizens themselves.

In genuine town meetings participants often develop a sense of empowerment. As one researcher of Massachusetts town meetings concluded, "Townsmen [sic] appear to be convinced they can make decisions themselves as good as, or superior to, decisions that could be made by a body of elected representatives" (Zimmerman 1967, 87). This is seldom the case for participants in counterfeit town meetings where concerns are aired, notes are taken, and no decisions are made. At best, citizens go away from such meetings mollified but seldom empowered.

The counterfeit town meeting is elite democracy at its finest, responding to constituents within the context of what appears to be community, but is actually counterfeit. The appearance of a communal format, the programmed responses, the public nature of the event are all designed to give the appearance of community. Not surprisingly given the people's desire for community, this tactic works. While few citizens obtain complete satisfaction from the meeting, most go away believing that at least he or she listened, and many go away feeling sorry for the Representative because of the abuse he or she had to endure. A week or two later the citizens will usually receive letters thanking them for their participation and indicating that the Representative was "looking into the matter." The letters are, of course, signed by the member of Congress and, consequently, in some patriotic households are enshrined among other family memorabilia.

Although the town meeting format has been found to be successful at expanding and solidifying political support (on average each person who attends talks to between eight and ten other citizens about the meeting), it does not represent meaningful participation. The focus of these counterfeit town meetings is on the Representative, not on the citizenry. Such meetings tend to bring out those whose self-interest is most compelling on whatever issues are salient to them. Citizens are there to tell the Representative about their problem, not enlist the support of their neighbors; they are there to get someone in a position of authority to listen to them, not deal with the problems themselves.

Because these meetings are Representative-focused, citizens do not go away from them with any sort of connectedness to each other or to the area they live in. Each citizen goes to the microphone, asks his or her question, receives a polite response, and leaves the meeting as disconnected from others in the room as when they arrived.

In some instances the Representative may actually be able to do something to help solve the citizen's problem, but the success or failure to get one's grievance redressed is not the point. Because virtually all issues are self-interested in nature and because there is no interaction among those present, there is never an instance where citizens debate and discuss with each other and arrive at a common understanding about their community. At no point do they have to struggle with how their own self-interest may conflict with others' self-interest; at no point are they placed in a situation where they must recognize the underlying values of their community and how those values can be reconciled with their own.

A final observation about counterfeit town meetings relates to the notion of justice. On the face of it, town meetings would appear consistent with our notion of justice that should be present in genuine community: the meetings are open to all citizens, anyone may speak, the Representative will listen and respond. However, these meetings must be viewed in the broader context in which they occur. Although Representatives are interested in obtaining votes and because of that will listen to the citizenry at town meetings, the constituents who have far greater influence are those who have made substantial campaign contributions. Large campaign contributions assure more exclusive and more extensive access to the Representative where they may present their case in greater detail. This occurs outside of the format of the town meeting. In fact, town meetings tend to attract those citizens who do not have the kind of access money can buy. Instead of counteracting the influence of money, town meetings further underscore its unequal influence. If you can't afford a contribution large enough to guarantee a private audience with the Representative, one of your only avenues is a few minutes at the town meeting.

Town meetings, as used by Representatives, are distorted imitations of the idealized version of direct democracy practiced by a handful of New England towns. In their actual operation they are counterfeit because they exploit citizens' desires to be a part of a political community rather than building upon their concerns by offering a viable communal format. Built upon self-interest and discouraging a format that might allow citizens to interact with each other, debate, discuss, and share ideas, the counterfeit town meeting exploits the individualism so common in society for the personal political gain of the Representative.

The Fourth of July: Counterfeit Community Ritual

Public rituals may perform numerous and varied functions. They may express "the values, attitudes, theories, interpretations, potential actions, and expectations of individuals in a community" (Nieburg 1973, 17). They may legitimize authority, integrate marginal groups, form consensus, mobilize support for social actions, provide reassurance through displays of force, moderate conflict, clarify reality paradigms, and even shift paradigmatic views (Nieburg 1973). In genuine communities (as described in chapter 2), rituals should provide linkages for individuals and the communities in which they live, testing and confirming their interrelated roles and interdependencies. In addition, community rituals should reflect in operation what they symbolically assert—they should be organized and run in a democratic, participatory fashion.

In America there is, perhaps, no more fundamental a ritual than the Fourth of July. In theory it seeks to honor those brave men and women who participated in the ultimate political act that resulted in the creation of the nation: revolution. With the deaths of both Thomas Jefferson and John Adams on the fiftieth anniversary of the signing of the Declaration of Independence, the Fourth became a solemn, almost sacred day. Today it is celebrated as a day of relaxation with parades, picnics, and fireworks; "everyone has a good time, fellowship is all and the place fairly levitates with patriotism" (Greenfield 1991, 68).

But the very nature of public rituals is that they may be altered and adapted to serve purposes other than those originally intended. Such is the case of the Fourth of July. The Declaration of Independence, today considered a brilliant symbol of political freedom, was initially celebrated not as a statement of political rights but as an important document representing a break from England (Bodnar 1992). Early nineteenth-century Fourth of July celebrations commonly included a day filled with morning parades, long-winded speeches in the afternoon, and dinners for the entire community in the evening. Based upon an examination of hundreds of the Fourth of July orations from 1815 to 1860, Somkin (1967) finds a reconceptualization of the meaning of America to embrace the idea of America as a virtuous society destined for prosperity. This did not occur, however, without objection from the likes of Sam Adams, Thomas Jefferson, Ralph Waldo Emerson, Walt Whitman, and Wendell Phillips whose vision of America was far more political, participatory, and communal.

In times of war the Fourth of July was used to rally support for the troops and integrate "questionable" ethnic groups into the war effort (particularly German-Americans during World War I). For example, at the urging of President Wilson, Indianapolis officials declared July 4, 1918, as Americanization Day and included German-Americans in the parade as the "Friends of German Democracy," carrying only an American flag (Bodnar 1992). More recently, the 1991 yellow ribbon Fourth of July welcomed back the troops from the Gulf War in an orgiastic display of militaristic patriotism.

The present meaning of the Fourth of July seems, interestingly, disconnected from even the slightest notions of liberty or revolution. In an admittedly non-scientific sampling of the opinions of young Americans, *New York Times* reporter David Herszenhorn found that many young people did not even know why the Fourth of July was a holiday. As one nineteen-year-old New Yorker put it: "I know it means something so I'm going to show respect. It's like going to someone's funeral, you don't know who they are, but you show respect" (1995, 35). Still, while the meaning may not be obvious to some who observe only the trappings of the celebration such as parades and fireworks, the interpretations of the Fourth of July today may be easily discerned.

The Fourth of July has become a public ritual that promotes consumerism, the legitimization of elite democracy, and exploits our feelings to be connected. As such, it is yet another example of counterfeit community, in this case in ritual form. The days of closing one's business to observe the holiday are gone, and many businesses view the holiday as one of the busiest shopping periods of the summer. Stores are replete with "Blow Out" clearance sales on furniture, electronic equipment, clothing, and the like. To lure customers, businesses often blatantly appeal to the patriotism associated with the day by linking themselves or their products to the holiday spirit. A few years back, for example, Kmart collected funds for the Star-Spangled Banner Movement to construct a

monument to Francis Scott Key, and Kraft Foods developed a new flavor
of ice cream called American Glory. Indeed, a $220 million fireworks in-
dustry has emerged to service the needs of individuals and towns who put
on fireworks displays. As one observer sarcastically put it, "[The Fourth of
July is] part of the American Revolutionary spirit, the noise of politics
meeting the chaos of commerce" (Kerber 1993, 1). What sacredness the
Fourth ever possessed has given way to its use as yet another angle to sell
products.

As noted, the nature and character of the Fourth of July have changed
over the years in response to the needs of those in authority positions. In
an ironic historical twist the Fourth—which is set aside to honor, among
others, radical Thomas Jefferson (primary author of the Declaration and
well known for his statement that every generation should have its own revolution)—has become a conservative ritual designed to support established authority. Looking more broadly at a variety of commemorative activities including the Fourth of July, John Bodnar concludes: The "activity
examined here almost always stressed the desirability of maintaining the
social order and existing structures, the needs to avoid disorder or dramatic change, the dominance of citizen duties over citizen rights, and the
need to privilege national over local and personal interests. Accounts of
fundamental change such as the Revolution . . . were usually reinterpreted
in ways that fostered patriotism and made them seem inevitable and desirable" (1992, 246).

Symbolic representations of the Revolution as reflected in Fourth of
July celebrations have become ritualistic simulacra. At the time of the Revolution public allegiance was far more closely associated with the individual states than with the nation, and public distrust of any centralized authority was widespread. But contemporary celebrations employ national
symbols and national themes of patriotism, programs, and the recognition
of pluralistic interests under the protection of a strong government. While
localized interests often are present, the dominant symbols and interpretations usually define the tone of the day. In doing so, the Fourth of July celebration tends to encourage historical memory of an interpretation of the
Revolution that never existed.

Within this context of the nationalization of historical memory (which
occurs not just on the Fourth of July), our feelings of connectedness become redirected away from local communities and toward national patriotism and national loyalty. This is done on the basis of a metaphor of a national community. But national communities can, at best, be metaphorical
and, more likely, are counterfeit. Genuine community, because of the
needs for social interaction, must be local. In the words of Wendell Berry,
"community is a locally understood interdependence of local people, local
culture, local economy, and local nature" (1993, 120).

Political Campaigns

Political campaigns could be ideal environments in which to bring communities together, to involve citizens in a common enterprise, to create the spirit of community, and to legitimize political authority. American campaigns have been a curious mixture of theater, the serious consideration of important issues, community festivities, and dirty tricks. With only a modest amount of imagination, it is possible to envision campaigns as playing an important role in community-building and governance. To the extent that citizens (especially at the local level) actively participate in the identification of issues, the selection of candidates, and the choice of policy proposals, elections could provide important mechanisms that peacefully resolve conflicts, protect the rights of minorities, and still forge a communal identity based upon shared values. The entire electoral process offers the possibility of a civic ritual in which citizens participate to govern themselves and define their public personae, both individually and communally, where "competing interests not only press their own demands but come forward with general programs for the common good" (Bellah et al. 1991, 130–31).

Although containing divisive elements as citizens align themselves behind one party or candidate or the other, campaigns also bring people together within the parties and, at election time, the entire community. Ideally, campaigns and elections demonstrate that important differences of opinion can and should exist within a community but that the community may continue to survive and even thrive. Conflict need not be fatally divisive, and politics does not have to be inconsistent with community.

To function as a community-building activity requires that politics involve substantial portions of the citizenry in a meaningful fashion. To do so means not just that the candidates and parties address relevant issues (though they should), but also that citizens be intensely involved in the definition and conduct of the campaigns themselves. In other words, politics in genuine communities should be truly participatory. Why is this necessary?

Active participation in democratic politics helps to form political and moral character. The idea is not new. John Stuart Mill made a persuasive case for active participation, arguing that we may judge political institutions on "the degree in which they promote the general mental advancement of the community, including under that phrase advancement intellect, in virtue, and in practical activity and efficiency" (Mill 1910, 195). But perhaps even more important than individual growth is the fact that participatory democratic politics creates and broadens a vision of community that extends beyond the mere aggregation of particular interests. In the complex political process that takes place in participatory democratic politics, individual citizens are transformed, and in the process, they also participate in transforming the community.

One of the major difficulties with American politics is its elitist nature, which prevents the kind of participatory engagement necessary for the construction and maintenance of community. A brief look at campaigns will reveal their elitist character and show how the yearning for community and connectedness is exploited for narrow political purposes.

In operation very few citizens actively participate in electoral campaigns. In the 1988 presidential election year only 3.3 percent of the citizenry volunteered to work in a political campaign, 8.7 percent contributed money to a campaign, and 28.9 percent attempted to influence how others voted (Rosenstone and Hansen 1993). In the 1992 presidential election (one that saw an increase in voter turnout) an estimated 55.2 percent of the voting age population actually voted (Abramson et al. 1995). Participation rates in elections at lower levels are substantially lower in every category of participation.

What's more, the attitudes of the American people about politics, electoral campaigns, politicians, and political parties are decidedly negative. Substantial majorities of citizens don't believe they can trust public officials and don't believe that participation will make a difference. In 1988 over two-thirds of the electorate disagreed with the statement "elections make the government pay attention to what the people think" (Rosenstone and Hansen 1993, 149). Citizens' attachments to political parties have weakened over the last forty years, and there is less and less of an interest about which party wins the election. The American electorate is overwhelmingly alienated.

It would seem that the American people don't like what they see happening in electoral politics and are consequently electing not to participate. Some observers are concluding exactly that (Teixeira 1992). But it is not that simple. In fact, although alienation is occurring across all social and racial groupings, actual participation has a decidedly class bias to it. As one moves from the working class to the middle class to the upper class, we see a marked increase in participation in all forms of electoral politics (Abramson et al. 1995). This occurs regardless of attitudes of alienation—attitudes are not necessarily related to behavior when it comes to participation in American politics.

While it may seem almost obvious that participation in politics has a class bias to it because of the superior resources of the middle and upper classes (time, money, organizational skills, knowledge, etc.), things become a bit more muddled when we consider that this class bias does *not* exist in other industrialized nations. In fact, the relationship between class and participation, so prevalent in the United States, is so absent from politics in other similar nations that it is seldom examined at all. Why does this occur only in the United States?

The most persuasive argument to explain this participation puzzle focuses on the behavior of candidates and the nature of American political parties and reveals their characteristic elite nature. A complete presentation of the explanation is beyond the scope of this book, but its outline can be presented fairly easily.

In some instances (e.g., voting turnout) class bias exists because of the unusually onerous voter registration requirements, which create more formidable obstacles for the working class than the middle class who are more accustomed to dealing with bureaucracy. To note only one dimension of this problem, in the United States it is the responsibility of the citizen to register to vote, but in all European nations it is the responsibility of the government to find citizens and make sure they are registered. When citizens in the United States are registered, they tend to vote in numbers comparable to European nations.

But this is only part of the explanation. Perhaps more significant is the fact that political parties have failed in their responsibility to mobilize the electorate instead of concentrating their efforts on persuasion and manipulation. Because policies advocated and ultimately adopted reflect the involvement of those who participate, mobilization of the electorate represents a threat to the elite interests that control the electoral system:

> Politicians can serve either the active or the inactive. The active contribute directly to their goals: They pressure, they contribute, they vote. The inactive offer only potential, the *possibility* that they might someday rise up against rulers who neglect them. Only the rare politician would pass up the blandishments of the active to champion the cause of those who never take part. (Rosenstone and Hansen 1993, 247)

The bias we find in the campaign process is, therefore, intentional, designed to include some and exclude others. It is supported by an ideology of elite democracy that distrusts the common citizen and claims that only elites can be trusted to make wise, non-self-interested decisions. This pattern of full participation for some and limited participation for others runs counter to the vision of community articulated in chapter 2 and prevents the formation of genuine community.

Within this context of elite politics, candidates attempt to persuade and manipulate the electorate through the use of symbols, sound bytes, negative campaigning, and buzz words. One tried and true campaign theme that has been used particularly well by candidates has been the theme of community. The candidate is usually presented as coming out of a particular community where he or she learned the basic American values of hard work, fair play, and an understanding of the little guy. The community, whether it is Hope, Arkansas, Russell, Kansas, Eureka, Illinois, or Brooklyn, New York, is portrayed as small, friendly, supportive, and nurturing. From there, the candidate attempts to link other citizens in other parts of the state or nation to that warm community image by metaphorically suggesting that America itself is a community. It is here, when selling America as a community and linking their own histories with that image, that political palaver is particularly effective.

A brief examination of the uses of the theme of community in some recent election campaigns shows a modest partisan difference. For the Republicans, the images of community are presented as local community autonomy freed from the restraints of a bureaucratic federal government. For the Democrats, the vision of community is a national community in which business, government, and labor work together to solve problems. What unites both visions is the simple fact that both images are simulacra. In reality local communities have never been free of federal involvement (in many cases they sought such involvement). On the other hand, while business, government, and labor have under unusual circumstances appeared to cooperate, in fact, the interests of each are very much in conflict.

One of the masters of palaver, Ronald Reagan, embraced the vision of community in his presidential campaigns: The Republican party is "ready to build a new consensus with all those across the land who share a community of values embodied in these words: family, work, neighborhood, peace and freedom" ("Acceptance Speeches" 1981, 36B). His vice president and successor, George Bush, maintained the community theme in his own presidential campaign. Accepting the Republican nomination for president in 1988, Bush extended the theme: "We are a nation of communities, of thousands and tens of thousands of ethnic, religions, social, business, labor unions, neighborhoods, regional and other organizations—all of them varied, voluntary and unique" ("Republican Acceptance Speeches" 1989, 42A). The Republican community palaver as used in recent presidential campaigns argues essentially that the federal government must be reduced in size so that individuals may voluntarily work to improve their communities. As Reagan put it, "Let us pledge to restore, in our time, the American spirit of voluntary service, of cooperation, of private and community initiative; a spirit that flows like a deep and mighty river through the history of our nation" ("Acceptance Speeches" 1981, 37B).

The history of the Reagan–Bush years was that the erosion of community continued unabated and volunteerism proved to be far too modest a solution to solve fundamental communal problems. Using Republican reasoning, however, the failure to improve community stems from still too much government interference and an erosion of the private moral character of Americans.

The Democrats' version of the community theme is more metaphorical than the Republican theme, but equally as counterfeit. It extends back through Lyndon Johnson's Great Society where he saw "America as a family, its people bound together by common ties of confidence and affection," to FDR who argued for "extending to our national life, the old principle of the local community" whereby Americans treated each other as neighbors. Michael Dukakis used a similar vision: "It is the idea of community. . . . It is the idea that we are in this together; that regardless of who we are or where we come from or how much money we have—each of us counts. And that by working together to create opportunity and a good life for all—all of us are enriched—not just in economic terms, but as citizens and as human beings" ("Democratic Acceptance Speeches" 1989, 84A).

To be sure, both partisan versions of community may be criticized for being far too metaphorical and for ignoring the significance of the role of the structure of our modern economy in undermining community. But the characteristic that makes campaigns counterfeit is their inherently elitist character. Campaigns are not seen as a *process* by which community may be enriched and extended as citizens participate in discussions of issues; rather, they have become a means by which elites may use shallow images (including those of community) to manipulate voters to obtain short-term political advantage.

In a genuine community, discussions and debates about the nature of the community—its values, its problems, its successes, its direction—must take place. The institution most appropriate for this activity is the political campaign, for it combines seriousness with the detachment of support for a party and a candidate. This is done in a ritualistic fashion whereby a conclusion (admittedly temporary) is arrived at and accepted. In the process of conducting the campaign, community can be enriched. American campaigns—national, state, and local—fail in this regard.

CONCLUSION

The vision of democracy that represents the dominant political paradigm (elite democracy) is not the only form, nor is it even the only vision of democracy that has helped to shape American history. Standing in stark contrast to elite democracy is a vision of politics referred to in various contexts as republicanism, participatory democracy, popular democracy, or "thick democracy" (as opposed to "thin" democracy which is the elite version). For the purpose of discussion I will refer to this alternative vision of democracy as republicanism (not to be confused with the Republican

Party). It represents a second language of democracy and has formed the ideological basis of numerous political movements throughout history including the Populist Movement, the civil rights movement, the student movements of the 1960s, and the Revolution itself. While its roots extend back to the likes of Machiavelli and Aristotle, the American patron saint of republicanism is Thomas Jefferson.

Republicanism, as compared to elite democracy, embraces a communitarian view of politics and, if practiced, would lead us in the direction of genuine community. One of the central tenets of republicanism is connection rather than autonomy. The self is not an independent creation; rather it is shaped and formed in the context of a community of relationships. Self-knowledge is not independently arrived at; instead, it is a result of community. Jefferson put it this way: "Self-interest, or rather self-love, or *egoism*, has been more plausibly substituted as the basis of morality. But I consider our relations with others as constituting the boundaries of morality" (quoted in Sherry 1986, 548). The most fully developed citizen is one who possesses civic virtue, and that virtue is created by active participation in a genuine community. Participation in the life of the community, in democratic politics, is transformational. Not only does it create virtuous citizens, but in the conflict of particular, private interests and the transformation of those interests into communal interests, it encourages and creates citizens on the basis of commonality and equality.

Republican democracy offers the hope of altering the cynicism, passivity, and negativity so common in elite democracy. In discussing strong democracy, Barber makes the case: "For the first time the possibilities of transforming private into public, dependency into interdependency, conflict into cooperation, license into self-legislation, need into love, and bondage into citizenship are placed in a context of participation" (1984, 119–20).

Such a transformational effect obviously requires participation. The passive notions of representation inherent in elite democracy must be replaced with self-government whereby citizens participate in the ongoing process (debate, deliberation, decision, and action) of creating a political community. Thus, politics is necessary for the creation and sustenance of genuine community: "Community grows out of participation and at the same time makes participation possible; civic activity educates individuals how to think publicly as citizens even as citizenship informs civic activity with the required sense of publicness and justice" (Barber 1984, 152).

Freedom and rights, so central to elite democracy, become reformulated in republican democracy. Under elite democracy, freedom is defended on the grounds of allowing individuals to develop their own individual faculties; but for republican democracy, the focus shifts to the expression and development of one's individual faculties within the context of community. In elite democracy the assumption is that individuals are mostly free to do as they wish so long as they do not impinge on the freedom of others. In practice, of course, the actual amount of freedom is far more circumscribed. But in republican democracy, the expression of freedom takes place in the community. Since one's conception of oneself is forged with a community, one is obliged to actively participate within that context to enable all to create an environment in which all may realize their own, unique faculties. This is not meant to imply blind obedience to community norms, rather cooperation with others to create a rich, full, inclusive community in which all members, not just some, may experience fulfillment.

7

Religion

Religion is always primarily a communal, as distinct from a societal institution. Its operation is always essentially local. The basic commonality that religion purveys—reassurance about salvation—must be
available wherever its agents operate.

—*Bryan Wilson (1976, 89)*

Religion offers the possibility of adding to and enhancing genuine
community by encouraging relationships, promoting social justice,
and acting as a force for integration of the community. It can do
this in three ways: spiritually, symbolically, and sociologically. One of the
first observers of the development of American democracy, Alexis de Tocqueville, carefully observed the relationship of spirituality and politics and contended that it "is the road to knowledge, and the observance of the divine
laws leads men to civil freedom" (Tocqueville 1964, 25). Tocqueville made
this observation while commenting upon the New England Puritan culture, which developed lofty notions of democratic citizenship that extended to all members of the community. Tocqueville speculated, as have
others, that religion offers the possibility of moderating unrestrained self-
interest as a motivation for political activity, and transforming naked self-
interest into "self-interest rightly understood," or "enlightened self-interest" (Tocqueville 1964). He was not referring to "civil religion"; rather he
was observing the relationship between religion and politics as religion laid
the moral basis for democratic community. It is not so much that religion
provides a moral basis that allows individuals to transcend their own narrow self-interest as it is that religion is based upon, and engenders, an underlying hope in the perfectibility of humanity. Without faith in humanity,
politics becomes nothing more than an anarchistic battle of self-interest.

The second way that religion can build and shape community is
through the use of religious symbolism. To a large extent, religion is in-

volved with the construction of meaning around important issues such as authority, justice, and moral responsibility. Although many religious symbols have originated from deep within the fundamental core of their religions, many of those symbols have come to take on meaning for nonbelievers. For example, one need not be a Christian to recognize the meaning of suffering, overwhelming love, and the possibility of human transformation embodied within the symbol of the cross and the story of the crucifixion and resurrection of Jesus. Religious symbolism alone does not perform these functions because it may just as easily be turned in directions antithetical to community or toward the shaping of counterfeit community. Nonetheless, the promise of constructing community through the use of religious symbolism remains a potent resource.

The third way that religion may enhance community is sociological. When religion becomes organized into churches and subsequently into congregations, those congregations may perform community-building functions for the members of the congregation as well as for the broader community. The range of functions may vary depending upon the degree to which secularization has affected the church. It is the promise of religion that it may, through its congregations, be involved in the political, economic, educational, and social dimensions of the lives of its members. By maintaining the tension between the broader, more secular culture and the loftier communal goals derived from religious beliefs, the congregation as a social institution helps integrate its members into the community.

Religion also offers the possibility of moral leadership for the community. Ironically, this can occur only if such leadership occurs publicly, but not in the political realm. If and when moral leadership overlaps with political leadership, the need for social cohesion runs the risk of being confused with the desire for political unanimity. Moral leadership should be free to engage in social and political discussion but must be separate from political leadership in order to avoid the imposition of any particular perspective on the community.

We see many of these dimensions of community-building in operation in St. Nick's parish on the southwest side of Chicago as described by Ehrenhalt (1995). Although composed of Irish, Polish, Germans, Italians, and Lithuanians (not necessarily ethnic groups disposed to cooperation), the neighborhood Catholic Church acted as a strong integrating force. Not only did the St. Nicholas of Tolentine Church draw in thousands each Sunday to the three morning masses, but special organizations and societies sponsored by the church further connected members to both the church and to the immediate community. For men, the Holy Name Society acted as a sort of social fraternity where they played cards, attended sporting events together, participated in dinners and breakfasts, hosted famous Catholic notables, and marched in holiday parades. For women, the Altar and Rosary Society was primarily work-oriented, helping out with church tasks, but it also provided an important social outlet. In addition, the church ran the neighborhood elementary school and hosted discussion groups on issues as wide-ranging as poverty, segregation, and the spread of nuclear weapons.

In addition to a host of social groups and activities, the parish priests did not shy away from moral instruction of their flock. The priests took strong, clear, and forceful positions against "sin" and made it clear that one must have a solid set of moral principles in order to be a responsible parent, neighbor, and citizen. This was not simply religious instruction; it was also political instruction. Church members were told by the priests, in no uncertain terms, that it was their responsibility to help others and to work together to improve their community.

As illustrated in St. Nick's parish, religion offers the possibility of forging a sense of community in the congregations themselves, as well as building community in the immediate neighborhoods. It does so by encouraging a strong sense of justice that transcends self-interest and by supporting institutions that connect members of the community to each other in complex ways.

Religion in America is, of course, a large, complex, and multifaceted topic. The variety of religious denominations, sects, cults, and movements is massive. Within the boundaries of the United States, there are practicing Episcopalians, Presbyterians, Methodists, Lutherans, Baptists, Pentecostals, Adventists, Mormons, Christian Scientists, Unitarians, Catholics, Jews, Buddhists, Muslims, Scientologists, Quakers, Amish, Wiccans, and followers of thousands of other religions, sects, and cults. Even within any particular denomination, congregations divide along lines of ideology, race, ethnicity, and social class. Some are fundamentalist while others are liberal, some are followers of a charismatic leader while others reject any form of leadership whatsoever, some are rigidly hierarchical while others are amazingly democratic, and some have built spectacular churches while others meet in living rooms and basements.

Given such variety it is extremely difficult to attempt to draw any generalizations that would embrace the entirety of the topic of religion in America. Instead of attempting to do so, I will first examine a few changes that have occurred in America that have influenced virtually all religions as they relate to community. These changes are primarily social and economic and have affected how congregations (especially congregations in mainstream churches) relate to their local communities. Second, I will briefly examine the cult phenomenon as an extreme example of counterfeit community. Cults dramatically illustrate how longing for connectedness can be exploited and how community can be distorted. Although cults are admittedly on the extreme, many other religious denominations and organizations use similar techniques and distort community in a related, if more moderate, fashion.

CONGREGATIONS

An examination of religious community must inevitably lead to a consideration of congregations. All major faiths conceive of religion as fundamentally a collective endeavor. Religion has, of course, been concerned with the lives of individuals, but more significantly it has encouraged worshipping together, maintaining ongoing organizations, and promoting social renewal. It has traditionally sought to achieve these objectives through the functioning of local congregations. As one scholar puts it:

> The congregation is typically the level of social organization at which religious commitment is conceived of as being most influential. If it does not affect the lives of individuals by drawing them into an intimate community, encouraging them to worship, and providing them and their children with instruction, religion is unlikely to be of any lasting personal or social significance. (Wuthnow 1994, 40)

It is in the congregations where we should be able to see the spiritual, symbolic, and sociological character of community become manifest or to see its false brother, counterfeit community.

Since the end of World War II, the social life of congregations has changed in ways that undermine the creation of genuine community. Although the forces that caused these changes may ultimately be traced to more fundamental changes that occurred in American society, the response of religious leadership was not to counteract social change; rather it was to accommodate and reformulate their churches to accept and adapt to the new social environment. Two changes in particular led to the undermining of genuine community and the replacement of it with counterfeit community.

First is the increasing emphasis placed on the individual. Although individualism has always played an important role in American society, it intensified after World War II. The postwar economic boom was driven by getting individuals to find meaning in life through the consumption of products. Families were encouraged to leave the cities and buy new homes in the suburbs; the husband developed a love relationship with his automobile; the wife was presented with new home appliances that were supposed to make homemaking more enjoyable; and the children were shown love by being showered with gifts. The ethic that we are all separate individuals who must make it on our own began to flourish. In the 1980s and 1990s, individualism was pushed to an even greater extreme as greed became not only acceptable but even laudable and children were taught that the most important thing in life was to be "happy" and that happiness was obtained by being wealthy. The emphasis on individualism had an impact on religion as many mainline churches initially failed to respond to the heightened feelings of individualism and, subsequently, saw a decline in membership. Bellah et al. captured the essence of how far individualism has gone in challenging traditional religion in their interview with Sheila Larson, a young nurse whose religious beliefs are presented by the authors as representative of many in America. When interviewed about her religion, she said the following: "I believe in God. I'm not a religious fanatic. I can't remember the last time I went to church. My faith has carried me a long way. It's Sheilaism. Just my own little voice" (quoted in Bellah et al. 1985, 221). For those not willing to go quite as far as Sheila, the compromise position is to "shop" for the congregation that suits one best.

With the shopping model firmly in mind, individuals often "shop" for the congregation that most clearly addresses their needs and interests. Remaining in adulthood with the religion in which one was born and brought up is becoming a thing of the past. Doing so is not being a smart consumer. Instead, people seek out the religion in which they feel most comfortable. George Barna, who owns and operates a church marketing business, describes his own search for the right church after a recent move:

> When my wife and I moved to California, we searched for a church that would be right for us. We searched and searched and searched. We were tired of churches that seemed like they had thrown everything together an hour before the service began. Our goal was to find a church where the worship and teaching was taken so seriously that preparation was evident, personal growth was possible, and commitment to service was appealing. (Barna 1988, 93)

The second change in post–World War II America that has had a dramatic effect on religion has been the massive flight to the suburbs by the economically advantaged. The suburbanization of America's urban areas has been well documented, as have many of the economic, social, and political consequences of this flight (Jackson 1985). Less well understood has been the effect of this population shift on religious congregations.

Many congregations followed the flight of their members and physically moved to those same suburbs. In addition, new congregations emerged to address the needs of the new suburbanites. In the process, congregations became disconnected from the organic relationships that made them such vital contributors of community.

The new religious style that developed addressed the needs for community and connectedness in only the most superficial fashion. Deprived of the kind of physical connectedness so important for genuine community, suburban congregations have come to offer counterfeit community as the only alternative they see possible.

Both of these trends—individualism and suburbanization—will be examined in greater detail as they have affected the inner life of religious congregations and the relationships of congregations with the community.

Individualism

It is ironic that, although religion is overwhelmingly practiced within a congregational framework, the values underlying almost all religious beliefs in America are individualistic. Consequently, it is not unusual to find people who consider themselves very religious and yet have little or no difficulty switching denominations or attending no church at all. These beliefs are reflected in polling data. In a 1978 Gallup poll 80 percent of Americans agreed that "an individual should arrive at his or her own religious beliefs independent of any churches or synagogues." Obviously, beliefs such as these have significant consequences for the viability of congregational life, and specifically for congregations as they relate to community life.

While on the one hand individualism provides an underlying structure of values for Americans' involvement in religion, on the other hand, Americans are drawn to churches, at least in part, because of the desire to satisfy needs left unfulfilled by individualism—community and connectedness. Congregations still represent caring communities: people who care for each other and for others in society. It is this sense of caring and empathy that attracts even the most individualistic people, for even they feel a sense of responsibility to help others. Churches often represent the possibility of fulfilling those needs.

The result is to fill congregations with people who are not looking for moral or ethical guides for action but who seek a sense of empathy with others: "The ultimate meaning of the church is an expressive-individualistic one. Its value is as a loving community in which individuals can experience the joy of belonging" (Bellah et al. 1985, 230). In this sense religion becomes a form of therapy to attempt to deal with fulfillment of the self, and congregations become composed of a series of programs targeted at specific types of people experiencing particular social or psychological problems.

In her study of Presbyterian and Baptist sermons on Luke 15:11–32, Marsha Witten found that the language used today has shifted to accommodate the private, psychological orientation of people: "In speech about God, notions of the deity as sovereign of the collectivity are displaced by portraits of God as Significant Other, who provides comfort, counsel, and understanding for the individual's psychological concerns" (1993, 130–31). When sin is discussed, it is presented as violations of personal satisfaction or family values rather than as violations of community norms. Regardless of the success of the therapeutic approach at attracting members, it does so at the cost of maintaining already weakened communal relationships and failing to draw attention to the wider context of meaning traditionally provided by religion.

The Willow Creek Community Church, a megachurch in the Chicago suburbs, also uses the therapeutic approach in its messages and, in order to target its audience more precisely, has developed a wide range of programs addressed to singles, single parents, baby boomers, Generation Xers (called Busters), teens, the elderly, people experiencing crisis, and the like. Indeed, one of the four weekend services is specifically focused on dealing only with the problems experienced by Generation Xers (defined as those born between 1961 and 1981). To help even more in dealing with your problems, you don't actually have to attend church; you may instead purchase one of their books addressing your particular concern or, better yet, buy the video. Therapeutic assistance is everywhere, and you don't have to be burdened by the deeper and more disturbing elements religion has traditionally dealt with that might directly challenge the secular lifestyle of the members.

In the therapeutic approach there is considerable talk about community, but the version of community presented is far more counterfeit than genuine. As one church secretary interviewed by Bellah et al. put it: "Certainly all the things that we do involve caring about people in a loving manner, at least I hope we do. For the most part, I think this community is a safe place for a lot of people" (1985, 230). Community is not viewed as a rich and complex set of relationships formed over many years, but as an "empathetic sharing of feelings among therapeutically attuned selves" (Bellah et al. 1985, 232). These are counterfeit communities of psychological support for separate individual selves.

The point is not that in genuine communities people do not and should not develop a sense of empathy for others in the community. Rather, in genuine communities the feelings of fellowship and empathy are the by-products of a rich and complex network of social, economic, political, and cultural interactions whereby a sense of community identity is formed. It is as an active participant in the democratic community that one's private orientations are challenged and transformed and a sense of caring for the community and others in the community is developed. As Rousseau puts it: When a person enters civil society, his "faculties are so stimulated and developed, his ideas so extended, his feelings so ennobled, and his whole soul so uplifted" (Rousseau 1950, 18).

The feelings of empathy elicited in the therapeutic church often occur outside of any genuine communal context. Participants remain private, and consequently no transformation of either the individuals or the community occurs. The perspective of the Willow Creek Church is instructive on this point. Willow Creek relies heavily upon marketing to both project its image externally, and to shape what kinds of programs to offer internally. (The marketing model for churches will be discussed in greater detail later in this chapter). The assumption underlying the marketing approach to religion (embraced by so many churches today) avoids an emphasis on active participation. Rather than attempting to actively engage members of the congregation and transform them by doing so, the marketing model takes people where they are and merely provides them with products (programs) that address their psychological needs. To be sure, there is an attempt to bind people to the church through greater activity by offering a series of programs that dovetail into one another (there is even a seven-stage philosophy of spiritual growth), but the approach is entirely "soft sell" and participants may drop out at any time, no questions asked. Referring to Willow Creek, Shawchuck et al. say, "No one is pressured to remain a member, since this would go against the church's commitment not to apply pressure or embarrass anyone" (1992, 37). Instead of organizing the church to enhance and intensify the participation of its members, the suburban church is more concerned with customer satisfaction. A disturbed consumer is not likely to buy the product, or even likely to return. Lacking relationships that link the congregation to the community, the church's alternative is to satisfy the customer.

The secular force of individualism has been accommodated by most religions in America. Rather than attempting to oppose individualism, religion has accepted it and attempted to adapt to it. In doing so, it has altered its message and changed its congregational structures. Driven by membership concerns, American religion has turned to exploiting the dysfunctionalities associated with individualism rather than challenging the root causes of individualism itself. Instead of providing a broader vision for believers and becoming full partners in the difficult task of building genuine community, religion has embraced the therapeutic approach. While social, economic, and political capital are being drained from our communities, religion in America has responded by attempting to get believers to feel good about themselves or to improve their communication skills.

Suburbanization

One of the most significant changes in American society in the twentieth century has been the massive relocation of the middle class from the cities to the suburbs. Encouraged by the construction of low-cost single family homes, the availability of the family automobile, the improvement of road systems, new long-term, low-interest financing, and the encouragement of government, hundreds of thousands of people have left the inner cities for the suburban American Dream. The exodus from the cities began almost immediately after World War II and, with modest declines due to economic recessions or high interest rates, has continued to the present. These changes have had significant effects on religious congregations.

As the middle class began its exodus from the central cities to the suburbs, so too did many of the churches. But the congregations that developed in the suburbs found that old ways seemed out of place and ineffective at addressing the concerns of the new, more mobile populations that they wished to attract. Unlike congregations in the central city, the suburban churches drew not upon those families within walking distance to the church, but upon a far more mobile population that thought nothing of driving miles to attend church. In order to survive, church leaders thought they had to become more effective at appealing to the concerns of the new suburbanite.

Separated from neighborhoods, church members sought congregations that made them feel comfortable and provided for their psychological needs. Not only did the approach to religion change, but so too did the organizational orientation of the congregation. Significantly, the church moved toward developing a host of organizational activities and programs designed to serve and maintain the congregation. While there is an attempt to bring people together who share similar interests and concerns, perhaps the more significant function such organizations perform is to develop the loyalty of the participants to the congregation itself. It is necessary to obtain participation because genuine communal bonds have been severed in suburban America:

> Whether he ushers, cooks, raises funds, or recruits members, he contributes to the support of the organization and has a stake in its success. Even these essentially impersonal performances on behalf of the common goal generate loyalty to the organization and a consensus about the value of the local church. The organization, in other words, creates a network of interdependent activities and functions through which members develop loyalties to the organization. (Winter 1962, 106)

It is through this structure of the organizational church that members come to develop feelings of community and connectedness that they often mistake for those that occur in genuine community. This is possible precisely because of the lack of genuine community members feel in their own neighborhoods. Because the churches have become disconnected from communities, they must simulate the feelings of community and fellowship through the use of the organizational structure: "The organizational church appeared as a substitute form of community rather than a representation of an existing community. It filled the communal void created by urban mobility" (Winter 1962, 108).

The organizational church is most clearly illustrated in the megachurches that have sprung up in the suburbs of most major metropolitan areas. Once again, the Willow Creek Community Church serves as an excellent example. If nothing else, Willow Creek is a massive organization that generates a host of programs to try to connect the consumer to the organization. Ranging from Promiseland (toddler care), to Son City (male high school students), to Camp Paradise (a 250-acre camp in Michigan), to HEAL (a sexual addiction program), Willow Creek has developed more than ninety specialized programs to slowly draw the person further into developing a loyalty to the church. From the entertaining Sunday services geared toward "Unchurched Harry" (a profile developed from market research), the participant is encouraged to attend the more serious Wednesday night services and led from there toward becoming a full-fledged tithing member. Loyalty is developed by providing a range of programs to meet the psychological needs of the disconnected.

While exploiting the desire for community, the suburbanized, organizational megachurches fall short of genuine community in at least two significant ways. First, they are economically and racially homogeneous, and second, they have withdrawn from the local neighborhoods and have become private.

Racial discrimination today rarely takes overt forms. Jim Crow laws have been eliminated, racial covenants have been successfully challenged and overturned, and even the suggestion of racism often brings a flurry of investigative activity in most organizations. Still, racism exists. Unlike racism, classism has never been considered "real" discrimination because it is not based upon the natural characteristics of people and instead upon characteristics due to one's own control (the accumulation of wealth). In this way, class discrimination is acceptable (even though most wealthy people inherit their money).

The suburbanized church, without ever needing to overtly establish rules of exclusion, has established an organization that excludes racial minorities, the working class, and the poor. This is accomplished through the physical placement of the church, the marketing appeals the church makes, and the programs the church develops for its members. As an exclusive organization the church falls short of genuine community on this criterion alone.

Americans have come, more and more, to live in areas where those similar to them socially, economically, racially, and culturally live. The dominant housing patterns may best be described as "lifestyle enclaves"

(Bellah et al. 1985). These enclaves are segmented in two senses: "They involve only a segment of each individual, for they concern only private life, especially leisure and consumption. And they are segmented socially in that they include only those with a common lifestyle" (Bellah et al. 1985, 72).

Churches that serve these enclaves have adapted to the exclusive housing patterns rather than try to challenge them, break them down, and integrate people into inclusive communities. The underlying assumption of marketing, for example, relies upon the ability of the marketing expert to segment the target consumer in order to refine the message for maximum impact. The isolated individual, devoid of community connections, yet similar to his or her neighbor, is an attractive (and easy) target.

Congregations that exist within genuine communities tend to represent the religious interests of the community, even though many members of the community may not actually be members of the church. The church in these neighborhoods is embedded within the network of relationships of the community. But suburban churches have been stripped of their communal linkages and have instead attempted to replace them with programs that the organizational church develops. Similarly, the suburban church reflects the mobile character of its environment. Located in suburban settings, surrounded by greenbelts, artificial lakes, and massive parking lots, the suburban church consciously selects the mobile middle class as its target population. The physical location more often resembles a neatly groomed college campus than a church. The grounds are integrated into the overall marketing plan. Pastor Charles Sineath of the First United Methodist megachurch in Marietta, Georgia, commented upon the physical facilities this way: "Every blade of grass is an evangelist. People see the lawns and gardens before they see the inside of the building" (quoted in Shawchuck et al. 1992, 259).

RELIGIOUS PALAVER: CHURCH MARKETING

Many mainstream churches in America are facing declining memberships as a growing proportion of the population has become unchurched. Since 1965, mainstream Protestant denominations have experienced more than a 50 percent decline in membership, and surveys indicate that only a minority of adults consider the church to be "relevant for today." Running counter to this trend is the Catholic Church, which has experienced an increase of about one-sixth (primarily because of higher birthrates and immigration from Latin America). In addition, the more conservative evangelical, fundamentalist, and Pentecostal groups have experienced a similar increase. Still, a feeling of crisis pervades most churches in America today.

All churches, whether mainstream or not, have attempted to respond to this perceived crisis. After years of study by a host of special councils set up by almost all denominations, religion in America has turned to marketing techniques to address membership concerns. As one expert on church marketing says: "The successful marketing-oriented church, by identifying the key concerns of its desired publics, will design the types of programs, worships, preaching, counseling, and relationships that their constituents are seeking (product)" (Considine 1995, 22).

A clever marketing strategy to lure potential customers into the flock is to offer them what they yearn for, but lack in their everyday lives. One important dimension of this marketing strategy is to offer them a sense of connectedness, a feeling of community: "As one of the big aspects of the product of the church is the offering of relationships with others, it is logical that the best way to promote the church is through the development and growth of meaningful relationships with others" (Considine 1995, 21). Another religious marketing advisor assessed the current situation this way: "*Gemeinshaft* (community) is disappearing. As a result, persons are experiencing a growing need for meaningful association with others, for fellowship. . . . Congregations are in a most opportune position to meet the growing hunger for fellowship" (Shawchuck et al. 1992, 27).

Using this marketing approach, churches have promoted themselves as religious communities, moral communities, pilgrim communities, prayer communities, fellowships, communities of worship, spiritual communities, Christian communities, church communities, or communities of believers. In a world where community has eroded, churches have attempted to exploit our desire for community and connectedness rather than play a vital role in rebuilding community. Rather than attempting to counter the broader, more fundamental, social trends that have led to the erosion of community, churches have done what other social institutions have done: they have exploited our desire for community to achieve short-term gains, that is, they have resorted to palaver.

One of the most successful church marketing ventures is the Willow Creek Community megachurch in South Barrington, Illinois. Based upon a marketing survey conducted in 1975, Pastor Bill Hybels founded a highly successful evangelical operation. Applying sound principles of market segmentation, Willow Creek offers its clientele a wide range of programs for children, teenagers, singles, adults, and the elderly. Short courses covering topics such as parenting skills, marriage, and divorce are among the more than ninety different programs offered. The idea is to link people with those similar to them and thereby make them feel connected both to other, similar people and to the church.

Adjusting their Sunday services to the results revealed in their marketing surveys, Hybels avoids pulpits and robes (he preaches instead from a lectern in a business suit) and uses rock, jazz, folk, and Dixieland music as well as a theatrical troupe and an occasional modest-sized orchestra to entertain. There are no hymnals (the words to songs appear on huge video screens), and the messages are primarily therapeutic with only occasional references to the Bible. Sin is never mentioned, but improving communication skills is a frequent theme. As sociologist Stephen Warner has said of Willow Creek: "Hybels is preaching a very upbeat message. It's a salvationist message, but the idea is not so much being saved from the fires of hell. Rather, it's being saved from the meaninglessness and aimlessness in this life. It's more of a soft-sell" (quoted in Sullivan 1991, 44). Judging from membership and attendance figures—more than 6,000 "true believers" who are encouraged to tithe and attendance of about 15,000 for four weekend services—the soft sell works.

The modern marketing approach of religion today is to sell the church through the use of direct appeals to being part of a spiritual community or in a more indirect, soft sell fashion by promoting the church as a place where the development and growth of meaningful relationships with others takes place. This is the palaver of religious community.

COUNTERFEIT RELIGIOUS
COMMUNITY IN CONGREGATIONS

Where genuine community existed, the congregation played an important role. In such communities the congregation became a gathering of believers (no matter what the denomination) who represented the interests of the community. The social fabric of the congregation emerged not so much from the activities of the church as from the community. Religious activities functioned to enhance and enrich the community. In many instances it was difficult to determine if activities organized and endorsed by the church were more activities of the surrounding community or church activities. There was, in those situations, no need to fabricate a community since the congregation existed because there already was a community.

In addition to the important representation function that congregations have played for community, they have also been instrumental in helping to transform the consciousness of its members so that they may overcome narrow conceptions of self-interest. Churches operating within genuine communal contexts help produce moral leadership that encourages mutuality, civility, and cooperation, which, in turn, helps to build communal bonds. In effect, religion is able to counter the natural narrowing effects of localism by encouraging action based upon ethical standards far nobler than self-interest and individualism.

But as populations have shifted and as communities have eroded, religion in America has also become transformed. Fearing membership declines, congregations have changed their structures, their message, and their approach. Instead of attempting to transcend narrow individualism and consumerism, they have adapted to it, developing therapeutic rather than religious messages; instead of trying to counteract the forces that have undermined genuine community, they have created their own counterfeit versions disconnected from their own neighborhoods; and instead of acting as organizations that enhance the richness of the local community, they have focused on building loyalty to the congregation.

CULTS AS COUNTERFEIT COMMUNITIES

While most congregations struggle with building membership by attempting to market themselves effectively, other religious organizations, namely cults, have gone even further. Most mainstream church marketing attempts would be classified as "soft sell," but cult approaches are at the very least "hard sell," and most could more accurately be described as brainwashing.

At the core of the cult experience, and initially one of its most attractive features for potential converts, is the feeling of community they get from recruiters. Although the cult belief system is a strong reinforcing mechanism once a person is a member, one of the important early attractions the cult has for new recruits is the feeling of community that they experience (Balch 1980). "People end up joining cults when events lead them to search for a deeper sense of belonging and for something more meaningful in their lives," says Harrary (1994, 20). While there are a host of psychological characteristics associated with cult members that are often used to explain their involvement, many of their concerns are addressed through the sense of belonging and the feeling of love and acceptance they receive as a result of the communal experience.

Recruiters for cults are well trained to exploit the longing for connectedness that exists among potential members. Once the prospect is lured to the initial meeting with other members, a process known as "love-bombing" begins. The prospect is greeted warmly, complimented on some aspect of his or her appearance, and repeatedly told in a variety of ways how wonderful they are. In that meeting, positive experiences are shared by all. At the conclusion of the meeting, the prospect is invited to a free weekend at a retreat or camp. It is at this intensive weekend retreat where the longings for connectedness that the recruit feels are more fully exploited.

In the fully controlled environment of the retreat, the recruit is brainwashed into believing that meaning in life may only be obtained by becoming a member of the cult. Recruits are food- and sleep-deprived, allowed to talk only with members of the group, made to listen to repetitive lectures, and impressed with the loving and caring nature of the group. Cults attempt to separate the recruits from all outside relationships (especially family) and link them emotionally to the cult.

Once the recruit has joined, the entire dimension of the counterfeit community becomes visible. Cults are run in an authoritarian manner with the leader or leaders usually claiming some sort of divinity. Those who violate any particular rule are often dealt with harshly (public beatings and public humiliation are common), and the ideological/spiritual beliefs are further imposed. The cult leaders are said to possess the only truths, and all who are not members of the cult are purveyors of lies. The roles that members play in the community are sketched out, and everything the member does is choreographed by the leader.

Certainly cults represent the minority of approaches to religion in America today. Because of their secretive nature, no one knows exactly how many there are or how many people are actually members. Estimates range from 600 to over 3,000 cults in operation today. However, more relevant for our purposes is the initial appeal that cults use to entice prospective members: the exploitation of longings for community. Once the recruit demonstrates an interest in becoming a member, the religious beliefs are introduced more completely to further solidify their attachment to the group, but the initial attraction is the feeling of community. The universalistic values and symbols that characterize the religious beliefs add legitimacy to the new patterns of communal interaction: "Gratifying interpersonal relationships among devotees in a cult crystallize a legitimating 'plausibility structure' for the symbol system of the movement, which in turn provides a symbolic mystique which enhances the perceived 'loving' quality of the spiritual fellowship" (Robbins and Anthony 1982, 66). In genuine community, religion encourages and complicates interactions among the members of the community, and usually there are many members of the community who may not be members of that particular religion. But in cults the religion structures and defines the entire communal experience—community and religion become inseparable.

CONCLUSION

Religion in America has not only failed to stem the tide that has led to a deterioration of community, but it has adapted to it by accepting community's demise and attempting to survive by developing its own version of community, inherently counterfeit in nature. Instead of using the congregation as a building block for the maintenance of community, religion has accepted individualism as the dominant driving force in America and adapted by delivering therapeutic messages to its members in order to facilitate their ability to get along with each other as individuals. Instead of maintaining a presence in local neighborhoods and attempting to work with neighborhood organizations, congregations have turned toward the creation of the organizational church and attempted to provide a feeling of community by involving followers in "church work" to connect them to the church itself, rather than the local community. The result of these activities has been, at best, the expression of feelings of community among the members of the congregations while the congregations themselves remain disconnected from the neighborhoods of which they should be an organic part.

8
Cyberspace

For many people, the choice seems to be between a very good simulation of community and no community at all; that choice makes the virtual community look very attractive indeed.

—*Evan Schwartz (1995, 41)*

If you boot up your computer, log on to the Internet, and punch in the web site address www.ccon.org, you will arrive at the home page for the Sherwood Forest Community Project. On that home page you will see a report of the activities of the first fifteen cyberspace pioneers as they worked and interacted with each other on March 24, 1996, the founding day of existence of a new cyberspace community, Sherwood Forest Towne. As stated in the town charter, the project is designed "to create a viable community within this new medium of human interaction and to observe how this community will be built, grow and work." If you decide to become a citizen of the community-building project, you can create an avatar persona (a humanoid representation with a head and body that can move through a cyberspace environment) that can participate in discussions with other citizens; debate, discuss, and ultimately vote on community policies and laws; or visit avatar friends and neighbors in plazas, gardens, talking circles, or in the comfort of their own cyberhomes. Citizens of Sherwood Forest may select their own lots, apply for a building permit, build a house, and furnish it whatever way they wish. Whatever structures you build, you are encouraged by the building code to choose something "that you consider . . . beautiful and fitting the Sherwood Forest Towne theme: more like a medieval English community." Unlike many virtual communities that rely entirely upon verbal communication, in the 3D world of Sherwood Forest "property is paramount." There is one major community rule: "Be considerate to others and their land and property as you would wish them to be unto you."

The Sherwood Forest Community Project is an experimental project in community-building in cyberspace designed by a company called Contact Consortium, which describes itself on its web site as "an organization dedicated to studying, publicizing and enriching the Internet-hosted 3D worlds as a new space for human contact and culture." The initial participants were members of the consortium, but since its founding, participation has been opened to those from other walks of life.

Another form of cyberspace community is represented by a web site know as The WELL (Whole Earth 'Lectronic Link, www.well.com). Thousands of WELLites from around the world communicate with each other anytime during the day or night through Internet access links on a wide variety of topics. The WELL was first created in 1985 by Stewart Brand and Larry Brilliant and is co-owned by the Point Foundation and NETI. With its first computers and modem rack located in Sausalito, California, it now hosts more than 260 conferences on subjects as wide-ranging as pop culture, the Rocky Mountains, eroticism, or the best restaurants in Paris. In its welcome, the WELL describes itself in the following way:

> The WELL is an on-line gathering place like no other—remarkably uninhibited, intelligent, iconoclastic. For over eleven years, it's been a literate watering hole for thinkers from all walks of life, be they artists, journalists, programmers, educators or activists. These WELL members return to The WELL, in many cases daily, to engage in discussion, swap information, express their convictions and greet their friends in unique on-line environments known as Conferences.... Conferences are the heart of The WELL. A vibrant on-line community emerges from conversations in these members-only Conferences. Each Conference has a distinct flavor and crowd, and regulars check in frequently to offer expertise, debate ideas, play word games and indulge in banter and gossip.

Thousands, perhaps millions, of people are finding that community in real life (IRL) is becoming increasingly problematic, and they are turning to virtual reality (VR) to attempt to satisfy their longings for connectedness and community. The WELL, with its hundreds of conferences on a wide variety of topics; Sherwood Forest Towne, with its floating avatars and medieval cyberstructures; and thousands of other cyberspace environments claim to be building community.

One active WELL participant and articulate proponent of cyberspace communities, Howard Rheingold, provides us with numerous stories of on-line community in his book *The Virtual Community* (1993). He describes one emotional event that occurred during his participation in the Parenting Conference. While participating in that conference he tells the story of Jay Allison's fourteen-month-old daughter, Lillie, who for weeks hovered on the edge of death while Jay told his on-line friends, most of whom he had never physically met, about his fears and concerns: "I am sitting in the dark of my daughter's room. Her monitor lights blink at me. . . . Above the monitor is her portable suction unit. In the glow of the flashlight I'm writing by, it looks like the plastic guts of a science-class human model, the tubes coiled round the power supply, the reservoir, the pump" (reported in Rheingold 1993, 19). After his daughter recovered, Allison wrote the following in *Whole Earth Review* about his Internet experience:

> Before this time, my computer screen had never been a place to go for so-lace. Far from it. But there it was. Those nights sitting up late with my daughter, I'd go to my computer, dial up the WELL, and ramble. I wrote about what was happening that night or that year. I didn't know anyone I was "talking" to. I had never laid eyes on them. At 3:00 a.m. my "real" friends were asleep, so I turned to this foreign, invisible community for support. The WELL was always awake. (Allison 1992, 4)

The WELL is populated with "perns" (genderless pronouns used in place of he or she) who send each other "beams" (WELL units of positive energy) and "group hugs" through the use of words or emoticons. Emoticons are combinations of key strokes used to indicate an emotional state. Some are as follows (read sideways):

:-)   = smiley face; associated with good intentions.
;-)   = wink; sardonic humor.
:(= sadness.

The purpose of the use of emoticons is to project emotional states which would otherwise be conveyed through the use of verbal inflections or physical mannerisms.

In the early 1990s the WELL was sold to Bruce Katz, who developed an aggressive expansion plan to create "regional WELLs," or "McWELLS," which he hoped would increase the feeling of community in the areas where they were located. In turn, the regional WELLs would be linked together to form one huge "global WELL," a global virtual community. Clearly the feelings of community, of connectedness with others in cyberspace seem present. Katz sketched out his vision for The WELL in a conference discussion in which he was criticized after a series of system crashes and slowdowns: "We are a group of individuals that believe that the proper role of business is to build a just, humane and sustainable world. Working at the WELL is my way of carrying out this mission. I believe in this medium and what it can do to help empower social change from the grassroots level. At last a truly democratic medium."

Virtual communities are attempts to overcome the physical limits of genuine community. Not only is the physical nature of property replaced with electronic bits, but the character of social relationships is also dramatically altered. The primary ways in which interaction occurs on the Internet are either through the written word or through pictures. One need not live within any geographical area (all you need is a computer terminal, a modem, and a telephone line), and membership only requires that you are able to log on (and often pay a small fee). There are no secondary organizations such as families or churches, and those in virtual communities like to claim that the only rule they have is that anyone is free to say anything.

INTERNET PALAVER

"Community" is an extremely popular word on the Internet—so popular, in fact, that it has become the dominant metaphor when talking about Internet groups. If you were to go to one of the more popular search engines, Yahoo, and type in "community," more than 9,600 web sites would appear. On the Lycos search engine, apparently less discriminating, more than 20,000 web sites will be listed, and if you use Web Crawler, you will find more than 87,000 listings. Somewhere in their own descriptions of themselves, many organizations, groups, and individuals thought that the concept of community was critical to what they were doing on the Internet.

In the 126-word preamble to "The Bill of Rights and Responsibilities For Electronic Learners," developed by eleven academics in October 1993, the word "community" is used five times. In the three remaining pages of the document it appears twenty-two additional times. Netizens (people who frequent the Internet) are serious about using cyberspace to reconstruct community in America. Not only are there web sites, chat rooms, conferences, and MUDs (Multi-User Domains or Multi-User Dimensions, sometimes called Multi-User Dialogues, formerly called Multi-User Dungeons) which attempt to bring people together to experience feelings of connectedness, but there are also a host of amateur and professional sociologists documenting the phenomenon and offering community-building advice.

Claims of community are usually quite blatant on the Internet, so usually the home page of the particular web site will include a description of the nature of the community being constructed. They are described variously as virtual communities, on-line communities, electronic communities, global computer networks, cyberspace communities, sociable virtual environments, or virtual villages. Whatever the particular variant of community they are offering, they all have reduced the concept of community to its barest essential—communication—and then claimed that this is what community is really all about. The notion of community is dynamic, so the argument goes, and it must be adjusted to fit the times. Presently, millions of people are logging on to the Internet each day from computer terminals across the world. Many are searching for more than simply information; they are attempting to satisfy their desire for connectedness. In this context, cyberspace community, reduced merely to communication, is offered as "real" community. Evan Schwartz puts it quite bluntly, "For many people, the choice seems to be between a very good simulation of community and no community at all; that choice makes the virtual community look very attractive indeed" (1995, 41).

Personal testimonials from participants and the on-line analysts of virtual communities demonstrate convincingly that the feelings we associate with genuine community are present among many of the members. However, as we have seen, this is not unusual for many of the non-cyberspace forms of counterfeit community. By its very nature, counterfeit community offers superficial satisfaction of the desire for community; it allows people to express feelings of community but fails to provide the physical and social settings to fully satisfy those desires. Upon deeper reflection the feelings may seem to have more of a basis in hope than in actual experience. But "community" is not primarily a psychological term—community does not merely exist in one's head.

In his entertaining account of his first two years in cyberspace, John Seabrook does an excellent job of capturing the excitement associated with first communicating with unknown people on the Net and then, upon reflection, of showing the limitations of cyberspace to build community:

> In the beginning I felt that special lightness of hope and possibility that new communications technologies seem to be uniquely capable of inspiring, a kind of spiritual feeling, which surprised me, as I don't like going to church. By the end I no longer felt that way about the technology, and I wondered whether the feeling had been an illusion, and whether I and countless others had in fact been duped by capitalists into requiring ever better, ever more expensive technology to maintain our "religion." (1997, 14)

Although most attempts to build community on the Internet have occurred for social or psychological reasons, the commercial incentive is also clearly present. Creating and managing virtual communities are now new forms of entrepreneurialism: "Our view is that the profit motive will in fact create new forms of virtual communities whose strong commercial element will enhance and expand the basic requirements of community—trust and commitment to each other" (Hagel and Armstrong 1997, xi). Community on the Internet offers the possibility of making the shrewd investor and manager a fortune.

COMMUNITIES IN CYBERSPACE

The optimism for the possibility of creating community is probably greater on the Internet than in any aspect of society today. Throughout cyberspace are experiments in creating virtual community, ranging from the modest form of linking people through chat rooms, to constructing cybercities with avatars, to creating a series of regional cybercommunities to develop local community feelings that would be linked together on the Internet into one big global community (Katz's vision). Indeed, the community metaphor is so dominant that even the harshest critics talk about communities in cyberspace, even while criticizing them for not living up to the standards of genuine community.

There are literally thousands of experiments in community on the Internet. Most occur in either a form called a MUD or a conference. The first MUD, originally called a "Multi-User Dungeon," was developed in 1979 and was a spin-off of the popular Dungeons and Dragons game. Many of these games, or variations of them, exist today. In them participants can walk around, chat with other participants, attempt to slay monsters, solve puzzles and riddles, find money and treasure, and even create their own rooms or items. As your character successfully navigates the world, you develop experiences and skills that allow you to move up in status, hierarchy, and power. Those who are most influential are called either wizards or, in some games, gods. They have the power to change the game, discipline participants, and even expel them from the game (known as "toading").

In addition to these adventure MUDs, there are social MUDs. The first of this type, called a "TinyMUD," was developed in 1989 by a Carnegie Mellon graduate student by the name of James Aspnes. This form of MUD de-emphasized the adventure aspect of MUDs and introduced a stronger social dimension. More frequently referred to as MOOs (MUD, Object-Oriented), this type of MUD encourages a gathering of people. In it, people chat, tell jokes, create their own environments, discuss a variety of topics, and even have TinySex with each other. TinySex occurs as people type in messages with erotic content to each other, describing, often in considerable detail, a sex act of some sort.

Most MUDs are entirely text-based with participants typing in text from computer terminals. Some have the capability of using personalized avatars that can float throughout the cyberenvironment. Discussions start out in rooms where everyone in the room knows who else is there and can see what they say. In such cases discussions tend to be short, choppy, and fragmented. When this is the case, users may withdraw into a corner of the room for a more intimate conversation (or in some instances for TinySex), or they may exchange e-mail addresses and talk through another forum.

When participants join a MUD, they create virtual names for themselves as well as textual descriptions that others will see. Thus, it allows individuals to be people they are not in real life (IRL) and to possess characteristics they do not actually possess (in some cases even changing their gender). Some MUDs insist on anonymity; others require that participants use their real names; still others allow for multiple characters. Individuals may be members of numerous MUDs, portraying different characters in each. This can even be done simultaneously by boxing off parts of the computer screen (called windows) for each MUD.

MUDs are not the only areas where community-building takes place. Internet Relay Chat (IRC) is another widely used forum in which any user can open a chat area, invite guests, and talk as if they were in the same room. Most commercial on-line services, such as America Online, also host chat rooms for their customers.

Whether it is in MUDs, chat rooms, or conferences, millions of people throughout the world are claiming that they are creating community in cyberspace. People are finding emotional support on-line where they are denied it in real life; people who are rejected in everyday life are finding acceptance on the Internet; and people who feel isolated in real life are finding feelings of connectedness on-line. But is this genuine community?

COUNTERFEIT CYBERSPACE COMMUNITY

Regardless of all the hype about the prospects of community in cyberspace, virtual community is inherently counterfeit in nature. It falls short of genuine community in at least three respects: it is undemocratic; it is exclusive; and it is based upon superficial, secondary relationships rather than primary relationships. Each of these difficulties will be examined in the remainder of this chapter.

The Undemocratic Virtual Community

One of the claims of virtual community advocates is that the Internet offers possibilities to promote participatory democracy, an essential component of genuine community. Although enthusiasts sometimes vary in what they mean by this, they usually argue that the Internet is accessible to all (equality), that there is and should be no censorship of what is posted, and that it is a many-to-many medium (as opposed to the one-to-many media that dominate society today). These are all characteristics of the Internet itself and the way it is designed (or not designed as some would put it). Because of its technological nature, the Net is fundamentally a medium that democratizes and levels.

This argument, however, relies upon an extrapolation from the mechanical to the social that runs contrary to what actually happens when one is on-line. It substitutes the character of the technology for the nature of the human interactions that occur using the technology. Stephen Talbott makes the point cogently: "Given this substitution, a community is no longer . . . a group of people bound together by certain mutual concerns, interests, activities, and institutions. . . . Rather, a community becomes the mere 'instantiation' of a network diagram that shows the available technical means for interaction" (1995, 65–66).

For example, one of the cherished beliefs of Netizens is that censorship is not permissible. This tenet is partially an extension of the libertarian beliefs of many of the users, but it is also, to a large extent, merely a recognition of how the technology operates. Because the Internet is composed of thousands of computer nodes scattered throughout the world, any attempt to control a message at any particular site will only result in the message automatically rerouting itself until it reaches its final destination. Perhaps the only effective way to control information is by controlling it at the web site itself, but most virtual communities have few formal rules to limit what can be said. Although informal "netiquette" rules abound, no mechanisms exist to enforce them.

In actual operation, however, cyberspace community builders are notorious for harshly punishing participants who violate informal community norms. These punishments take the form of "flame wars." In his account of his experiences in cyberspace, John Seabrook experienced brutal attacks because he dared to write an article that portrayed Bill Gates in a favorable light. He was called an "asshole," a "toadying dipshit scumbag," and "a rank shithead," among other things. Freed from the restraints that face-to-face interaction imposes, people feel free to say whatever they like, no matter how vile and insulting.

Flame wars occur at some time in almost all Internet exchanges, and some become so deadly that the groups in which they occur are either devastated or they merely fall apart: "Sometimes I arrived at a dead site after a flame war had broken out; it was like walking through what had been a forest after a wild fire. I came across voices that were just howling at the world, rage and savagery pouring out through people's fingers and into the Net" (Seabrook 1995, 118). While flame wars are usually conducted by the most militant and extreme users, they have the effect of polarizing the dialogue rather than encouraging reasonableness and respect. Many newbies (newcomers to the Internet) are deceived into thinking that because rules are not written down, no rules exist, and anything goes. In actual operation, however, informal rules and norms permeate the Internet, although they may differ slightly from group to group. Seabrook writes, "The pressure to conform to the thread was strong. It was fed by the general desire to belong, to find a home on-line, as well as the desire to seem 'clued' to the others in the group" (Seabrook 1997, 197).

While Netizens pride themselves on their free speech attitudes, in fact most virtual communities are composed of members who are so similar to each other that little significant difference of opinion actually exists. Where differences often occur is when enthusiastic newcomers, excited about their newfound freedom, post material that violates the agreed-upon consensus of the group. This often results in flaming the newbie. It is not unusual to find these newbies withdrawing to become lurkers (participants who listen to the conversation of others but do not participate themselves) or getting out of the group altogether after they have been viciously attacked by the old-timers.

The real problems with flaming are not so much that they impose informal rules (even genuine communities have informal rules of operation), but that genuine conflicts are not dealt with in an open, civil manner in which the resolution of the conflict functions to strengthen the community. At best, flame war participants, after days of blasting each other, will simply agree to avoid the topic altogether. There is no resolution to the conflict, only an agreement to avoid it. Genuine communities, on the other hand, possess formal and informal procedures to resolve conflict whereby the rights of members are protected and where civil public dialogue is maintained.

Cybercommunities also create the illusion of publicness when genuine public control is lacking. Policies in genuine communities are made by all members of the community after a process of debate and discussion has taken place. While it may at first appear that the Internet, with its thousands of web sites and home pages, is a massive public marketplace of ideas and entertainment, it is more accurately described as a massively complex web of private spaces. Virtual community is private community, owned and operated not by the members, but by private owners and managers. This is made ever so clear in a recent book by Hagel and Armstrong (1997) who provide the Netizen entrepreneur with a practical guide of how to make money by creating virtual communities: "Virtual communities can tap into a number of potential fee-based revenue streams of the type that characterize on-line sites today" (Hagel and Armstrong 1997, 45). Owners of virtual communities may obtain revenue by charging subscription fees, usage fees, or member fees. Whatever fee structure is used, the point is that cybercommunities are private organizations increasingly managed to make a profit.

In order to maintain the myth of democracy, virtual community owners attempt to manage their site "organically." Rather than imposing rules on the community, owners/managers attempt to carefully manipulate the direction of the community into areas where profits can be maximized. Advice on the elimination of some virtual communities is a case in point: "Weeding should not be imposed on community members arbitrarily. It must not be perceived as heavy-handed. For example, one way to phase out stagnant or uneconomical areas of the community is to set a predetermined time limit on the life of all subcommunities or individual chat areas and to reevaluate their continuation at that time" (Hagel and Armstrong 1997, 157).

Many MUDs, even the social ones, often have users who are called wizards, in some MUDs, gods. Wizards are, in effect, the managers and often the owners of the MUDs. They often come from the ranks of the participants and, after having demonstrated mastery of the MUD, are dubbed wizards by other wizards. Wizards deal with technical and social problems in the MUD and possess powers that other participants do not have. For example, they are able to move about the MUD undetected and listen in on conversations. They also possess the power of "toading," expulsion from the MUD. If, in the determination of the wizard, a participant has become disruptive to the social environment, he or she may be turned into a "toad." In effect, to be toaded is to be banned from the MUD, virtual death. Given the libertarian character of most web sites, there are no formal rules that govern toading; there are thus no hearings, no right to confront one's accusers, no procedures of appeal. It is the authoritarian wisdom of the wizard that wins out.

Although many social MUDs have eliminated wizards because of their undemocratic nature, even in the social MUDs that claim to be most democratic, not all participants possess equal power. However, the issue is not so much that some may have more power than others, but that those invested with greater power are neither chosen in any sort of open, democratic fashion nor held accountable for their actions by the other participants. At best, power in the social MUD is a benign form of authoritarianism.

Democracy is not merely the free expression of ideas—it involves issues of ownership. Genuine communities are owned by everyone, yet no one in particular. Counterfeit communities, on the other hand, merely provide the appearance of democracy. On the fundamental issue of ownership they are owned and managed by the few in the interests of profiting the few; the members are merely consumers. In the case of cybercommunities the members are consumers of interactions, not citizens. Virtual communities are private and consequently subject to the private decisions made by their owners and managers.

Exclusivity

Cyberspace community activists claim that participation is open to all. This is because the technology makes no discrimination based on race, gender, ethnicity, social status, or any of the other characteristics commonly used to discriminate against people. The Internet, in all its variations, is a many-to-many medium in which freedom of expression for all is the dominant norm. Anyone with the appropriate technological equipment can participate in cyberspace community. One Netizen expresses the hope clearly: "I think networks of the future will be the most incredibly egalitarian technology ever invented. It will transform our entire societies. Imagine that homeless people or single parent children can 'interconnect' with anybody who is willing to talk to them in the *world*" (quoted in Talbott 1995, 65. From a contribution to the "irvc-l" list "irvc-l@byrd.mu.wvnet.edu," 9 October 1993).

But, once again Internet enthusiasts have extrapolated from the technological to the social without fully understanding the social and political context in which technology develops and is used. The image of homeless people throughout the world logging on to their computer terminals to chat with other homeless people (one would assume) strikes one as humorous if it were not so sadly politically naive. Putting aside the economic absurdity of the situation, the entire vision assumes that giving the socially isolated on-line access will somehow lead them toward re-integration into society merely because they can now talk to each other on the Internet. This vision fails to recognize why society has isolated and marginalized groups of people in the first place—reasons that chat rooms, MUDs, bulletin boards, and cyberspace communities fail to address.

The failure to understand the social context in which technology operates is further reflected in the gender differences already strikingly apparent on the Internet. By one estimate, 94 percent of the users are males (Spender 1995, xvi). Other estimates put the percentage of female Netizens higher, at around 36 percent (Evard 1996). Whatever the exact figures are, it seems clear that women are significantly underrepresented on the Internet. While the reasons for this are in need of greater study, one compelling argument is that women are socialized to be hesitant toward "technical objects" and instead are encouraged to focus more on human relationships: "It isn't that they can't do it, and it is not necessarily that they don't like the subject. What they turn away from is the image of the scientist or the computer hacker. It doesn't fit with their notions of themselves as women" (Spender 1995, 173).

It should also be noted that the Internet is not particularly welcoming to women. Those who are brave enough to log on to MUDs are often greeted with numerous "wanna fuck" messages from male members. Women who aggressively speak their minds run the risk of being flamed or even harassed. Stephanie Brail's story of harassment has become folklore among women of the Net. After posting a message defending another woman, she was viciously attacked by a man who not only called her names but also flooded her e-mail box with pornographic images. After weeks of this she began receiving strange messages from *alt.sex.bondage.* Upon investigating, she found out that he was sending messages to that web site and leaving her name and e-mail address. Unable to discover who the person was, she finally threatened to go to the police. His messages calmed down for a few months, but then she received a veiled threat of violence: "By this time I was incredibly paranoid. I made sure the doors to our bungalow were always locked; I practiced self-defense" (Brail 1996, 147). It was only after the harasser made a mistake and she was able to track him down that the harassment ended.

While Brail's experiences seem clearly to be unusual, they suggest a cyberspace environment that is, if not hostile to women, at least tolerant of harassment. In fact, during Brail's pleas with others to try to stop the harassment she was taken to task for trying to limit the free speech of the harasser.

As is illustrated in the case of women, rather than expanding access to individuals and groups who have been marginalized and thus moving us in a more inclusive direction, the Internet has merely reinforced the patterns of exclusion, marginalization, and oppression that already exist in society. The Internet continues to be a male, white, middle-class bastion: "Simply stated, the information crisis—denial of access and debased messages and images—deepens social inequality and intensify [sic] the general social crisis" (Schiller 1996, xvi). Technology alone is not sufficient enough to assure inclusivity. Creating an inclusive community requires more than simply another technological fix; it requires a shared vision that values and encourages diversity and a reorientation of political and economic power centers. The creation of a genuine, inclusive community is ultimately a human endeavor, not a technological advance.

Relationships: Superficial and Secondary

Virtual community is about relationships. Given that real places do not exist in cyberspace, that politics is denied any form of legitimacy, and that social institutions supportive of community (e.g., church, family) are not present, the only basis for claiming to be a community is that people develop relationships with each other. Those relationships are based almost entirely upon the written word, although some virtual communities are experimenting with avatars.

In genuine community, relationships are rich and complex; people interact with each other in numerous settings and, in doing so, they play multiple roles and perform a variety of functions for the community. People interact with each other as friends, neighbors, customers, antagonists, elected representatives and constituents, and the like. As a consequence, intricate webs of primary and secondary relationships are formed. Primary relationships are developed through primary experiences, active engagement with our world, with others in our environment, and with our physical environment itself: "Our actions change the environment, but they also change us. Experience goes hand in hand with action, and both can be improved and enlarged" (Reed 1996, 49). Some of these relationships have substantial permanency while others are more transitory; some are planned and structured while others are spontaneous. Furthermore, people in community are connected to a place that helps to define the community itself as they interact with and shape their own property and the property of others in the community. There is no simple form or pattern that community relationships take; rather they include all forms and, by doing so, encourage the full dimension of human development for each member. Still, for genuine community to exist, it must at the very minimum provide a rich environment in which primary relationships can thrive. Through this active engagement with our environment, meaning is created, both for the individual and for the community.

It is here where cyberspace community fails so significantly. Simulacra are distortions of reality, not reality itself, and because of that, our interactions in simulated environments are incomplete and less meaningful. Seeing a picture, even a moving picture drawn from a CD-ROM, of a rattlesnake coiled and poised to strike is not the same as overturning a rock on a hike in the woods and being confronted with the possibility of a venomous attack. Similarly, interacting with others through words or avatars on computer screens is not the same as meeting people face-to-face. Relationships on the Internet are "thinned," and the meaning of human relationship is undermined. A few examples drawn from the archives of Internet lore illustrate the point.

Much of the activity in MUDs and chat rooms is related to sex. Virtual sex (often referred to as TinySex) consists of two or more individuals going to the corner of a chat room and typing in descriptions of physical actions, emotional reactions, and verbal statements about their sexual encounter. These individuals will describe their physical bodies to each other, engage in a seduction of each other (usually very crude and direct), and proceed through a sexual encounter usually resulting in on-line orgasms. In her study of cyberspace experiences Sherry Turkle finds that "this activity is not only common but, for many people, it is the centerpiece of their on-line experience" (1995, 223).

Not only is TinySex a frequent activity of users, but it is not uncommon that participants often distort descriptions of themselves, so much so that they often develop on-line personae that take on the opposite gender than what they are. Most frequently, this occurs in the form of men becoming women. In the MUD Habitat, for example, there is a real-life membership ratio of four men to every woman, but inside the MUD fantasy world the ratio is only three male characters to each female.

While this electronic cross-dressing may seem playful (and Turkle even suggests that it has the possibility, if approached from a healthy, flexible view of oneself, of developing a fuller sense of identity), it is based upon

deception. In fact, cases of deception have led to profound shock and out-
rage when one of the virtual lovers found out that he (usually a he) was not
having TinySex with a woman but with another man. Even where the users
are not cross-dressing, the descriptions the users provide of themselves are
often far more flattering than is the case in real life (IRL).

When experiencing primary relationships, an individual is free to scru-
tinize the relationships as carefully as he or she likes to uncover new information. But in secondary relationships, such as occur on the Internet,
scrutiny is extremely difficult. Primary experience requires that we use all
our senses to attempt to determine the intention of others and how one
thing leads to another (causality). On-line experiences severely restrict our
abilities to perceive and make it difficult to establish meaning in relationships. In the process of interacting through primary relationships, individuals, as they agree and disagree, may come to a deeper, broader understanding of each other. It is in this respect that community enhances the
individual's identity and, in the process, creates a deeper meaning of the
importance of community life: "Communities are made by activities that
broaden and deepen real sharing. Real sharing is not the matching of
ideals—whether spontaneous, forced, coaxed, or inculcated. Real sharing
is acting and experiencing together" (Reed 1996, 115).

One of the most meaningful human relationships is physical love.
Whether that relationship occurs between members of the opposite sex or
the same sex, physical love creates a trusting bond between humans that allows both in the relationship to grow, while at the same time creating a
new, meaningful relationship that encompasses both partners. It is formed
not just on the basis of words, but on feelings and actions. At its core is
trust of the other person. Physical love is dependent upon the full range of
human perceptions people bring to bear on the relationship. As practiced
on the Internet, TinySex cheapens and undermines this critically important relationship since it is based entirely upon words, often involves deception, and reduces love to sex (virtual sex at that).

Indicative of the extent to which on-line interaction limits our ability
to perceive is the case of the on-line robot (bot), Julia, and her amorous
adventures. Julia is a computer program developed by Michael Mauldin of
Carnegie Mellon University. Julia roams from MUD to MUD imitating a
human female who loves to talk about hockey and flirt. When asked, she
will provide a physical description of herself. For a while she was five-feet
one-inch tall, weighing 123 pounds, with frizzy blonde hair, but the physical description has been known to change from time to time. She is programmed to simulate human typing, typographical errors and all. When
she gets confused by questions she changes the subject, usually to hockey.
Possessing only the ability to communicate through writing, Julia the bot
elicits seductions from a host of male personae and tries to befriend female

personae. Many on-line users, after talking with her extensively, are convinced she is a real, though somewhat boring, person. Many males have attempted TinySex with her and have come away either disappointed or angry after discovering the person they were trying to seduce was actually a computer program.

On-line relationships are based on limited perceptions. Even if deception was eliminated (as The WELL attempts to do by insisting that participants use their real names), the possibilities of genuine community are limited because of the inability of individuals to fully perceive their environments. Words alone are not sufficient to build bonds of trust or to resolve significant conflicts. Caring about people on-line resembles crying at movies more than cherishing people you see and interact with every day. Flame wars drive away from the virtual community those who express real difference, and those left are either passive lurkers or on-line users whose beliefs match. Yet genuine community is not so much based on a matching of beliefs as a sharing of experiences and a working out of ways in which individuals can cooperate with each other: "In a real community of people who are trying to join their actions and experiences one sees shared exploration and performance, the attempts to locate meaning and values that can be made to *work together*. Note that working together does not mean that the values match" (Reed 1996, 115).

CONCLUSION

This analysis should not be seen as an indictment of the Internet. In fact, there are many aspects of the Internet that may prove to be quite beneficial. The amount of information now readily available is impressive; the speed of communication has increased dramatically; access to information for people with disabilities has improved; and the interactive capabilities and potential of the Internet on balance seem beneficial. But attempts to create community through Internet interaction distorts the meaning of community to such a degree that the concept loses its texture and meaningfulness. With the assertions that community can be constructed in cyberspace, we have developed simulacra so counterfeit in character that, if accepted, would almost totally change the meaning of community altogether.

Still, attempts to create communities in cyberspace should not be ignored. They reveal much about ourselves and much about the state of genuine community in America. Like the proverbial canary in the mine shaft, virtual communities may be seen as a warning signal about the state of genuine community. Even though there is no physical space and no primary interactions among people, the desire to be connected with others who have something in common seems compelling—so much so that people are willing to embrace obvious counterfeit versions of community and convince themselves that it is perhaps the best that can be done today. But playing with community on the Internet is far too safe. People do not have to deal with the things that make them uncomfortable, with the inevitability of being forced to make choices in the midst of ambiguity, or with having to deal with problems that appear unsolvable. Instead, in virtual communities one may simply log off. Commitment is minimal. What's more, a person can be a member of a community in cyberspace and still maintain isolation. Alone in front of the computer screen, a person never needs to become a public person and experience both the joy and the agony of doing so.

Virtual communities are constructed almost entirely on nothing but the psychological needs of the members. Consequently, they are such a thin and distorted version of genuine community that they cannot sustain community. When difficult problems arise that threaten one's involvement in the cyberspace community, it is far too easy to either avoid or withdraw. The community thus fails to provide a genuine and lasting group of relationships. This temporariness is a fundamental characteristic of the structure of cyberspace communities and makes it inevitable that communities on the Internet will be counterfeit.

9

Popular Solutions

Experience with the antecedents of current initiatives provides some
guideposts to what has worked—and even lessons about mistakes to
avoid.

—*Lisbeth Schorr (1997, 308)*

The prior six chapters have examined how counterfeit claims of
community are used throughout society in order to manipulate and
exploit our longings for connectedness. In each area examined, the
palaver of community occurs within the context of someone attempting to
obtain advantage. As such, they are more akin to particularized marketing
appeals than coherent ideological perspectives on community.

In recent years there has been growing interest across the ideological
spectrum in renewing a sense of community in America. Conservatives, lib-
erals, radicals of both left and right, fundamentalist religious leaders, moderate clergy, and community activists have all called for a renewing of communal bonds. However, while all are in agreement that community needs
to be reinvigorated, there is substantial disagreement about what the problem is, what should be done, or how it should be accomplished.

FOUR POPULAR PERSPECTIVES

In this chapter I will discuss a few of the more popular perspectives on how
to rebuild community. In particular, this chapter will examine the traditionalist, the communitarian, the libertarian, and the community organizing perspectives. While there are disagreements among those who might
be identified with any single perspective, there is still enough agreement
within the perspectives to consider them distinct. As will be seen, none of
the perspectives go far enough in addressing some of the fundamental issues required to achieve genuine community. Some fail to accurately iden-

tify the problem, some focus too much on the symptoms of the problems without addressing the underlying causal factors, most ignore the effect of corporations on communities, and all fail to recognize the existence of counterfeit community.

The Traditionalist Perspective

For adherents to the traditionalist perspective, the primary problem in America today is the loss of virtue among its citizenry. High crime rates, drug abuse, teen pregnancy, divorce, and even poverty may all be traced to a common cause: an absence of virtue. Virtue is at the core of these dysfunctional behaviors because virtue provides us with standards that tell us what is right and wrong. Our society has taken the wrong path by emphasizing individual choice, toleration, and pluralism because it has led to a belief that "anything goes."

To address the problem we must resuscitate virtue by returning to a firm set of moral principles. Those principles can only be found in the traditions of the past and the wisdom of our ancestors as manifest in our religious teachings and time-tested customs. Rather than participating in social experimentation to correct present-day injustices, we should expend greater effort to preserve what is good. Traditionalists would like to reform the individual and, through the individual, reform society. Community can only be restored by creating virtuous citizens.

Because community can only be created by developing virtue among citizens, we must focus on how virtue is formed. For traditionalists the only effective way of creating virtuous citizens is through the guiding principles of religion: "One cannot pursue virtue unless he sees himself as serving a higher good. There must be some source of standards above us, giving us rules to live by which we cannot change or discard at our whim. Otherwise everything is permissible—even the rule of promise-keeping would be out of order and no longer a rule" (Frohnen 1996, 16). The traditionalist perspective claims that community must be divinely inspired by a Creator. Religion provides the guiding principles for the ordering of community and society. It is not clear that there must be a particular form of religion, but advocates consistently draw upon Christian heritage for examples and guidance.

Sociologically, the fundamental building block of community is marriage between a man and a woman. Other family relationships (homosexual unions for example) are not considered legitimate and are considered from the traditionalist perspective to be inconsistent with God's principles. Together the man and woman create a family, or household, and a grouping of households in turn becomes the basis of community: "Successful households are the natural reservoir of liberty. They aim at autonomy or independence, enabling their members to resist oppression, survive economic, social, and political turbulence, and renew the world after troubles have passed" (Carlson 1994, 295).

The household unit, although cooperatively intertwined with others (often in a covenant), should function autonomously in terms of providing food, clothing, and shelter for its members. It celebrates human achievement and encourages self-sufficiency of its members. The central function of the family is the education of children, and in order to accomplish that task there must be a clearly defined authority structure in which all family members defer to the wisdom of the elders. Within the private family, children learn values and skills and develop virtuous character, which will be used to construct community. The family is the cradle of liberty, the central institution for the education of children, and the basis for community itself. It must be autonomous and private in order to perform such functions. When the family becomes politicized, social pathologies such as suicide, crime, abuse, and dependency follow.

When families voluntarily intermingle, they create community. It is in community where the rough edges of family life are tempered and where commerce among households occurs. When dysfunctional behavior occurs in the family, the community has a right and even an obligation to intervene. Public actions are guided not so much by formal laws as they are by custom and convention: "When deviance from community norms occurs, informal and non-aggressive measures such as shunning are normally effective in restoring order and bringing the wayward back into harmony with the community" (Carlson 1994, 299).

From the traditionalist vantage point, social inequalities have always existed and always will exist. Poverty, for example, is an inevitable feature of human existence. Creating government programs to eliminate poverty is a mistake, not just because they don't work, but also because they make the teaching of virtue irrelevant. If government bureaucracies assume the responsibility of correcting social ills, it is no longer important for religious leaders to emphasize religious duty, such as being one's brother's keeper: "Religion motivated charity work and gave it its early character. Charity workers sought to emulate Christ (or follow the dictates of the Torah) by serving others and teaching them proper faith and morals" (Frohnen 1996, 225).

The traditionalist perspective of community has at its core two essential features: the belief in some divinity as the source of life and the critical importance of the family as the basis of all social relationships. It is from these two premises that community is ordered and that individuals obtain the kind of character needed to build community.

Certainly the heavy reliance on religion as the exclusive basis for morality and the building of virtuous character seems not only impractical in a pluralistic society as we have in America, but it is also inaccurate as a description of the way virtue is created. If God is the basis of moral standards, one must legitimately ask, "Whose God?" What's more, what is to be done with the non-believers or those who believe in a different God?

But the traditional perspective also inaccurately describes how character is formed or how moral standards are developed. While belief in God may indeed lead to the acceptance of particular moral standards, similar (or different) moral standards may also be created by those who do not believe in a divinity. For example, Bernard Gert (1970) arrives at moral principles very similar to those advanced by most religions through the application of rationality.

Even more disturbing about the traditional perspective is its reductionist approach. Virtually all social evils may be reduced to the problem of character. In reality, social problems are far more complex than that. As we saw in chapter 5, the razing of the Poletown community in Detroit to build a Cadillac plant was the result of competing values between those who believe that economic growth is the most important value and those who value community to a greater extent. It would be a distortion to say that the advocates on either side lacked virtue. Similarly, it is far too simplistic to say that the problems with our political system are due to politicians who lack character. One must recognize that in most instances people on all sides of an issue possess virtue. Differences emerge not because of a lack of virtue but because of legitimate disagreements over values. Given that we have disagreements over competing values, what is needed is an effective forum in which value disputes may be peacefully resolved while building community. Our present-day institutions have been only modestly successful at resolving disputes and giving voice to community interests.

The Communitarian Perspective

The communitarian perspective grows out of a critique of liberal society and claims that Americans have focused too much on individualistic, self-centered forms of citizenship and ignored responsibility. According to this perspective, too many Americans are quick to claim rights but reluctant to assume responsibility: "Claiming rights without assuming responsibilities is unethical and illogical" (Etzioni 1993, 9). This has occurred because we have lost our moral compass—there is moral confusion bordering on anarchy. Because of our obsessive orientation toward rights, we are reluctant to accept any moral norms.

What communitarians hope will happen (and what they are working toward) is to reinvigorate a sense of community so that moral inclinations will be developed among community members. "Communities speak to us in moral voices," Etzioni says. "They lay claims on their members. Indeed, they are the most important sustaining source of moral voices other than the inner self" (1993, 31). For communitarians, the creation of moral individuals does not come from God, as traditionalists would claim. Instead, higher-order values come from an agreed-upon acceptance of fundamental values that have been a part of the American experience for many years. These core values include toleration, honesty, the importance of the peaceful resolution of conflicts, hard work, respect of others, frugality, and a belief in democracy. These values should be taught in school, in the family, and throughout society.

Communitarianism supports institutions such as families, education, and local organizations of all types. These institutions are the cornerstones of community. Families, particularly two-parent heterosexual families, should be encouraged and supported, and divorce should be made more difficult to obtain than it is presently. The community has an interest in maintaining strong, two-parent families, and it should make it difficult for them to be destroyed. The communitarian perspective believes that the family is an important force for the moral education of children: "It is important that parents who have satisfied their elementary economic needs invest themselves in their children by spending less time on their careers and consumeristic pursuits and more time with their youngsters" (Etzioni 1993, 88).

Likewise, schools should support the moral education of children by teaching the basic values that Americans share and creating an environment where good character is encouraged. A key to good character is self-discipline, which should be a central tenet of a child's education, but beyond that children should be exposed to a program of community service as a regular part of the curriculum.

Communitarians advocate a return to civic activism for citizens at the local as well as the national levels of politics. Etzioni and Galston's "Communitarian Platform" document obtained support from a variety of public officials and members of academia for local initiatives to support local communities, while Michael Lerner calls for a national community of compassion, love, and caring. Bellah argues for a new view of localism based on the Catholic social teaching known as the principle of subsidiarity, which suggests that higher-level associations should never replace what lower-level associations can do effectively. Whatever the level of focus, communitarians are in agreement that a common purpose for local communities and common tasks for the nation can be agreed upon and pursued through a renewed emphasis on citizenship activism: "Service to the community through action is a part of what it means to be a citizen" (Conner 1994, 313). It is through community service that citizens come to understand their own sense of responsibility and help to forge the common purpose of the community itself.

The communitarians, like the traditionalists, are concerned with a perceived deterioration of the moral standards of American citizens. In place of such standards they see selfishness—an appeal to rights without concern for responsibilities. But the basis of the moral standards communitarians want does not come from religion; instead, it is found in the historical tradition of the United States. Regardless of the origin of such values and regardless of what values are supposedly lacking, both the traditional and communitarian perspectives have located the causes of social problems in the value systems of individuals. Both perspectives fail to recognize the importance of social, economic, and political environments in which people must function.

This becomes even more problematic when communitarians focus on the family and the education system as the two primary agents that shape a child's value system. With little sensitivity to the economic situations in which families and schools function, the communitarian perspective attempts to reform these institutions through regulation. But the problems that families, schools, and other community-based organizations must deal with are more fundamental than that, and the communitarian perspective seems reluctant to deal with more basic causal factors.

The Libertarian Perspective

According to the libertarian perspective, the major problem in America today is the expansion of government. Government has become so large and so bureaucratic that it has created a culture of dependency. Virtually no human activity today is outside of the realm of politics. It is this pervasiveness of the political that has led to our problems: "America's reliance on politics as the solution to most every problem and alleged problem has turned envy into official public policy, stripped individuals and communities of their traditional social responsibilities, destroyed economic opportunities for the disadvantaged, promoted unjust foreign intervention, and undermined private moral and spiritual values" (Bandow 1994, 321). Our political institutions have become too strong, too powerful, too authoritarian, and in the process they have weakened communities.

With the growth of government comes the development of professional bureaucrats who view everything in society as problems to be solved by experts. Professionalism creates an expert-client relationship in which individuals are forced to become dependent upon the social welfare state: "When the capacity to define the problem becomes a professional prerogative, citizens no longer exist. The prerogative removes the citizen as problem-definer, much less problem-solver" (McKnight 1995, 48). The age of politics has failed and must be replaced by the libertarian vision of community.

While it may appear contradictory at first to talk about a libertarian version of community, a strain of community thinking does come from some moderate versions of libertarianism as well as some community organizing attempts with a libertarian bent. A libertarian community comprises groups of people who work together on a face-to-face basis to create a public life. It will be successful only if people in it are virtuous. People will need to work hard, be temperate, respect each other, and take responsibility for themselves as well as others in the community: "Every life in community is, by definition, interdependent—filled with trusting relationships and empowered by the collective wisdom of citizens in discourse" (McKnight 1995, 123). This is possible, but only if governmentalism is reduced to a bare minimum.

To create a moral community means that individuals and communities must be free. Virtue cannot exist without freedom because individuals and communities must be free in order to make moral decisions. By making people dependent upon government, we have taken away their freedom and denied them the ability to be moral individuals. Government's attempts at controlling behavior by passing laws and creating bureaucratic systems fails to address the ethical problems of today: "Forcibly preventing people from victimizing themselves does not automatically make them more virtuous, righteous, or good. The rest of us may feel better, but we should not confuse uplifting society's moral core with improving society's superficial appearance" (Bandow 1994, 328).

In order to create community in America, government must be dramatically reduced in size and scope, and private institutions must be strengthened. Values are central to community, and only local institutions such as the family, the church, and local community organizations can promulgate and enforce moral standards. Parents need to take responsibility for the moral education of their children, religious leaders need to speak out and be active in their communities, and local leaders need to exhibit morality in their own lives.

For libertarians virtually all social problems, whether communal or individual, can be traced to a single cause—the growth of government. Government has become so pervasive that it has intruded on all aspects of our lives and taken our freedom. Where government has not established programs, it has implemented a system of regulation and imposed standards. This perspective presents a view of freedom that, although widely held, is only partially accurate. Freedom, according to the libertarian perspective, is the absence of restraint. By viewing freedom as the absence of restraint (especially governmental restraint), libertarians fail to accommodate situations in which some individuals have more resources than others. Without government constraint and coercion, inequalities (both economic as well as political) could be expected to grow at even greater rates than is presently the case.

But another form of freedom also exists—a more positive view that contends that freedom is the ability to accomplish things. Seen in this light the expansion of government services could, if implemented properly, enhance rather than restrict one's freedom. This could happen if government programs would allow more people greater access to benefits than would otherwise be the case.

The libertarian viewpoint also seems unwilling to extend its position far enough. If the difficulty with government is bureaucracy—its turning citizens into clients and its ability to make citizens dependent—it would seem that the same concerns should be applied to the private sector. Certainly modern corporations have bureaucracies every bit as massive, convoluted, and unresponsive as do governments. Similarly, corporations have shown little reluctance about intruding into the personal lives of their employees. Yet libertarians have remained silent about corporate power. Because corporations have become influential in America today, care must be taken to make sure that their actions do not undermine community. Libertarians do not have such a concern.

The Community Organizing Perspective

The community organizing perspective focuses primarily on urban areas and has emerged from the learning experiences of those involved in community organizing activities. As such it is a practical perspective on community—how it can be built and how it can be maintained. As is true of all of the perspectives, it has developed as a result of a perceived crisis in America. As far back as the 1940s the guru of community organizing, Saul Alinsky, identified the crisis confronting America's urban neighborhoods: "These destructive forces are unemployment, deterioration, disease, and crime. From the havoc wrought by these forces issue distrust, bigotry, disorganization, and demoralization. Together they constitute significant indexes of a rapidly growing crisis of confusion in our democratic process" (Alinsky 1946, 69). Other than the addition of a few more modern vices, not much has changed since Alinsky first started organizing; his assessment of the problems in urban America ring true today.

Community organizing occurs primarily in neighborhoods that have experienced economic and social problems. The creation of community by mobilizing citizens and strengthening neighborhood organizations is seen as the solution to those problems: "Neighborhood associations' goals range from preserving and beautifying neighborhoods to securing better municipal services to keeping out 'undesirable people'—often drug dealers, hustlers, and the homeless" (Rabrenovic 1996, 3). Although in many instances the causes of the problems extend far beyond the control of neighborhoods (and cities for that matter), the community organizing perspective emphasizes the creative ability to solve problems by working with the limited resources available.

The most important resource in a community is the people, and organizing the people is the central focus of community. Although considerable differences exist among people in any neighborhood, the initial focus of community organizing should be a concrete, non-controversial goal—the installation of a traffic light, a health care center, elimination of a drug house. "Through mobilization and confrontation," Rabrenovic says, "participants gain a sense of togetherness that helps to establish unity and cohesion in the organizations in the neighborhood. Through such actions, long-lasting ties of mutual support are forged, and they help residents survive poverty" (1996, 202). Organization thus becomes an educative process, not to create virtue (which the people already possess) but to raise their consciousnesses about political issues and to show them how to use the democratic process to effect change.

The community organizing perspective makes no assumptions about the form or function of families, businesses, or churches. Rather, it attempts to make realistic assessments about the ability of any local organization to provide the resources necessary to cultivate and encourage local leadership wherever it may emerge in order to strengthen local communities.

The community organizing perspective is an interesting blend of the optimistic and the realistic. Its optimism is found in the underlying assumptions it makes about humans. Most community organizers work in inner-city neighborhoods that are experiencing significant social and economic problems. Yet community organizers consistently rely upon local people as the major resource to improve neighborhoods. In doing so they demonstrate a faith in the abilities of the average person.

At the same time the community organizing perspective is realistic, for it is based upon more than fifty years of experience of organizers working in a variety of settings. Thus, the belief in the essential goodness and abilities of local people to work together to solve local problems is not just idealistic; it is also a practical political strategy. People must be intimately involved in developing and implementing their own solutions to their own problems, and they have the ability to do so.

But the community organizing perspective is limited by the resources available from local sources. Where local governments lack resources themselves, little can be done to reverse the deterioration of neighborhoods no matter how well organized the neighborhood becomes. The more fundamental economic and political dynamics operating within cities may be more significant in determining success or failure of community organizing than the quality of the efforts themselves.

ANALYSIS

The four perspectives briefly presented above by no means exhaust the thinking about community and, indeed, they appear often by different names than have been assigned to them here. While the thinking about what community is and how it can be created is virtually endless, it is nonetheless helpful to see how each perspective links fundamental aspects of community together and the different emphases each places on trying to recreate community. Although any of the four represents an improvement over the versions of counterfeit community examined earlier, none addresses all our concerns. Overall, three major areas of concern remain. The first two relate to themes that recur in many writings about community—the decline in citizen virtue and the deterioration of the family. The third concern is notable because of its absence in the writings about community—the impact of corporate economic power on community. Each of these concerns will be addressed in order.

Morality

Three of the four perspectives (the traditionalist, the communitarian, and the libertarian) believe that an important element to reinvigorate community must be to create moral sensitivities in citizens, often called virtue or moral character. Moral training may occur in the family, church, school, or other social settings. Regardless of where it occurs, it is supposed to be the glue of community: it forms the basis for communal decisions and policies. Looking at the problem from the communitarian viewpoint, Etzioni wants "a climate that fosters finding agreed-upon positions that we can favor authoritatively" (1993, 25). The assessment is that significant segments of the population today simply do not possess moral standards at all. From the traditionalist point of view, Frohnen says: "In order to serve the common good one must have a proper moral character, the virtuous habits that cause one to put the needs of one's fellows above one's own wants and desires" (1996, 212). This can only be accomplished, so he argues, through religious instruction.

However, this viewpoint fails to recognize the reality of the problems communities are confronted with today. The problem is not that individuals lack a set of values; rather it is that even when basic values are held in common, life experiences shape our specific values so as to create differences in their applications. Furthermore, even holding certain values does not mean that they can be acted upon. The social, economic, and political environments often dictate behavior more than do values. African Americans growing up in the inner city are likely to develop an entirely different view of social justice than suburban, middle-class whites. Although they may both agree that social justice is an important value, its specific meaning will be disputed. Given recent experiences that African Americans have had with police authority (e.g., the Rodney King beating, the Jonny Gammage death), they may also possess substantially different views of police authority although they also value law and order. The third generation

Scandinavian farmer in the Great Plains has life experiences and a different view of the proper role of government than does the white tenant
farmer in Alabama. Life experience often shapes the particular meaning of
abstract values.

William Ryan (1976) has argued that it is not so much that some Americans possess moral standards while others do not, or even that there are
significant differences in beliefs about fundamental values among Americans; rather it is that differences in behavior are the result of different economic and social circumstances. For example, both the poor and the middle class value education, but the life circumstances of the poor are such
that they are far less likely to attend quality elementary and secondary
schools than the middle class, and far less likely to be able to go to college
if they do graduate. The reasons have less to do with values that are held
and more to do with the politics of how education is financed (through
local property taxes) and the financial support systems readily available for
the middle class but more difficult to obtain for the poor. Ryan's argument
extends as well to issues in which those in economically or socially disadvantaged positions are commonly labeled immoral or amoral on the basis
of their actions.

There is much to be learned from the community organizing perspective on this issue. Effective community organizing begins with the belief in
the essential goodness of people: "[Organizers] regard with wonder the
fact that the masses of people, subjected to the kind of society in which
they have lived, should retain so much decency and dignity" (Alinsky 1946,
114). The community organizing perspective begins with an inherent trust
and respect for people. People in less-privileged circumstances believe and
value things everyone wants: quality education, health care, jobs, a decent
home. The only things that differ are the social situations:

> The organizer should at all times view each individual or group in terms
> of the total social situation of which they are a part. . . . He knows that in-
> dividuals and groups must make an adjustment to their social situation be-
> cause they have to live in it. He knows that the opinions, reactions, and be-
> havior of persons and groups will be to a large extent determined by what
> their own community thinks. (Alinsky 1946, 128–29)

The community organizing perspective also provides a constructive
approach to dealing with the issue of morality. The problem of morality is
inaccurately portrayed when the focus becomes the morality of particular
behaviors. Instead, such behaviors are indicators of a dysfunctional social
environment that needs support to be rebuilt. To focus on morality,
virtue, or character misses the point. Behavior becomes moral or immoral
only with respect to a broader community. What has happened in Amer-

ica is that we have lost our communities, not our values or our sense of morality.

I do not wish to imply that virtue and moral sensibilities are not important in building community; they are. But too often those who focus on such concerns lose sight of the interactive quality that should be at the heart of community. The creation of virtuous character cannot be thought of as distinct or separate from the social context in which it develops. The danger in focusing on the development of character is that we tend to consider only the most obvious social institutions primarily responsible for character development—mostly the family, but also the church and the school—and, by doing so, we fail to address the more fundamental issue, the total reconstruction of community.

Ultimately, community is based upon the belief that citizens, given resources and opportunities, will act responsibly. This is the fundamental assumption of community and the fundamental assumption of democracy. Community will not be created by imposing moral principles on people or attempting to coerce them into acting responsibly unless the groundwork for community has already been laid.

The Family

Of all the social institutions considered essential for the creation of community, the family is perhaps the most misunderstood. Over the years a myth of the traditional family composed of four basic aspects has developed: (1) the family is the basic building block of community and ultimately of society; (2) the family should be an autonomous, private social institution, a haven from the corrupting influences of the public arena; (3) the ideal is the nuclear family unit with clearly defined gender roles; and (4) the private family is the most important area where virtuous character is developed. This image of the family is not only historically inaccurate, but when used as the model for policies to rebuild community, it leads us astray by taking us further down the path toward counterfeit versions of community. This image of the nuclear family, however, lies at the heart of the traditionalist and libertarian perspectives and in some versions of the communitarian perspective.

As Stephanie Coontz and others have shown, the private nuclear family has little or no historical basis in fact (Coontz 1988, 1992; Kirk 1972; Laslett 1973; Skolnick 1981). Even at its height in 1950, no more than 60 percent of families fit that description. Prior to and following that year, the nuclear family was in the minority in terms of the type of family structures that existed. Beginning in the colonial era and extending throughout American history, families have taken on a variety of forms. High mortality rates throughout the eighteenth and nineteenth centuries meant that many children lost one or both parents before they came of age. For

African American families, slavery resulted in a total devastation of the nuclear family. Even in the twentieth century it was not unusual for parents in working-class families to be absent in pursuit of jobs elsewhere. As recently as 1991 only 15 percent of the families in America could be classified as nuclear in form.

In addition to the historical inaccuracy of the form of the nuclear family model, the assertion of the family's autonomy and private character is similarly inaccurate. From colonial times to the present, local communities, businesses, and government have consistently intervened in family life: "The nuclear family has never existed as an autonomous, private unit except where it was the synthetic creation of outside forces" (Coontz 1992, 145).

However, the problem of embracing the nuclear family as the ideal model for the construction of community is not merely one of historical inaccuracy. More profound is the concern that the nuclear family in fact provides an inadequate base for the construction of community. Proponents of the nuclear family serving as the basis of community argue that the family is the primary institution that provides values for children. One of the leaders of the communitarian movement, Amitai Etzioni, puts the case for the nuclear family this way: "Those who bring children into the world have a social obligation to attend to their moral education. Children have no inborn moral values, and unless these values are introduced, they will not become civil members of the community. The best way to educate most infants (up to at least two years) is through bonding with their parents" (1993, 88). The nuclear family is pictured as a safe haven for the children where, under the benevolent authority of the father and the nurturing guidance of the mother, children learn the importance of honesty, hard work, fairness, commitment, authority, responsibility, and the value of education. By teaching such values early in life, domestic violence, divorce, crime, drug abuse, teen pregnancy, and a host of other dysfunctional behaviors may be avoided.

This view, accepted by many, has little empirical support. Rather than the family being the incubator of civic values, research seems to indicate that the more private the family becomes, the more likely it is to become an environment of domestic abuse and violent conflict (Coontz 1992; Demos 1986). In such families women are far more likely to be oppressed, forced into narrow gender roles, and have their alternatives prematurely limited than in families more open to public interaction. In the nineteenth century a host of illnesses (e.g., "green sickness," "white sickness," compulsive laughing) exclusively identified with women who were restricted to the household became major concerns for the medical profession. Richard Sennett (1976) has argued that the increasing sense of privacy leads to our placing unrealistic expectations on the family. The nuclear family is supposed to satisfy a host of psychological needs, many of which it is ill-prepared to satisfy.

If the private nuclear family provides a poor basis for the construction of community, what type of family would be most appropriate to accomplish the task? In genuine community, families interact with other members of the community (other families and individuals) in multiple and complex ways. The family does not constitute an isolated private social institution. Instead, it is embedded within the web of social relationships that make up the community.

This is not to contend that families do not have private dimensions to them; they do. In reality families have both private as well as public dimensions, but the private aspects of the family are integrally linked to the public. In genuine community, children are raised not just by their parents but by the entire community. The family provides the children with intimacy, unconditional love, support, and nurturance, while the public moderates and tempers the potential that exists in the family for unrestrained egoism. Thus, the child learns community responsibility by participating in the interactive process between the family and the community. Likewise, the adult members of families interact with members of other families, both children and adults, and in the process help to shape the sense of community as well as defining and expressing themselves. In a sense the two arenas provide for different modes of expression, each checking the other, each dependent upon the other. The public realm would modify a person's natural incivility and the private realm would allow for forms of expression not allowed because of social conventions. In this way the family is an important social institution that involves people in the life of the community.

If the nuclear family is to exist in a community, it cannot maintain the extent of privacy generally associated with it. To ensure that healthy development of children and adults occurs, the nuclear family must be actively engaged in public activities. The critical feature for the family is not its structure, but the type and quality of relationships that exist both within the family and between the family and other individuals, families, and groups. Focusing merely on raising children, the nuclear family is not the key to raising well-functioning citizens. Werner and Smith's (1992) study of high-risk children in Hawaii shows that the critical feature for raising healthy children was the presence of a close relationship with at least one adult. That relationship could be a parent, a grandparent, an older sibling, a neighbor, a teacher, a minister, or even a youth worker. The critical feature was not family structure but the importance of a relationship with someone who cared for and nurtured the child. Also of interest was the finding that self-esteem and self-efficacy grew for the children who actively participated in service activities in their neighborhoods or communities.

One learns responsibility by being actively engaged in communal activities.

Certainly family is an important element of community, but family structure (traditional or non-traditional) is of less importance than how the family interacts with others. Genuine community can be created with a variety of different types of families. Of greater importance is that family members experience both private as well as public environments.

Economics

None of the four perspectives presented effectively addresses what must be one of the most crucial aspects for building community—its economic viability. For example, the "Communitarian Platform" originally drafted by Etzioni, with the assistance of Mary Ann Glendon and William Galston, contains considerable discussion about building moral character, about the family, school, politics, and even social justice. But other than a few brief references with respect to treating employees humanely in the workplace, there is virtually no mention of corporate power or corporate responsibility in doing its part to support community. Similarly, Alan Ehrenhalt's (1995) account of three communities in the Chicago area in the 1950s fails to adequately assess the impact of economic trends on community and instead concludes that we must somehow rebuild respect for authority and reinvigorate a culture that builds virtue in its citizens. The traditionalist perspective draws a sharp distinction between the public and the private on the issue of economics and considers the business world "out of bounds." By ignoring the impact that corporate forces have had on community, our focus becomes misdirected toward the personal.

The silence on the role of business in building community seems puzzling. Libertarians go to great lengths to criticize government bureaucracy for infringing upon our freedom, but they ignore corporate bureaucracy for going even further in regulating personal freedoms; traditionalists believe that God should guide the decisions of our politicians, but they make no mention of God's relationship to CEOs; communitarians talk about corporations creating humane workplaces but fail to recognize the impact more fundamental corporate decisions have on community; and community organizers, to their credit, recognize the devastating impact that corporate decisions have on communities but because of their narrow local focus have no particular suggestions about what should be done.

Consequently, each perspective in its own way fails to provide guidance about what the proper role of business should be in community, how and when private business decisions should legitimately be subject to public influence, and to what extent business should be responsible to the local communities in which they operate. This is a glaring omission.

One of the most significant forces affecting communities today is economics. To be viable social and political organizations, communities must be viable economically. To accomplish this, communities must be able to control some aspects of the local economy directly and other aspects indirectly. But to ignore the economic system altogether (as most writers about community do) is to detach one's perspective from reality. Although the community organizing perspective accurately assesses the difficulties communities face when corporations make decisions that devastate local communities, community organizers are at a loss to develop effective strategies to counter them because those decisions are made by actors quite distant from the neighborhoods affected.

CONCLUSION

Turning to other perspectives on community offers little guidance for addressing the problem of counterfeit community. Concerned with developing solutions to address particular social problems, the most popular perspectives on community fail to even recognize how claims of community are being used in American society. Rather than looking at the status of community in America, these perspectives only consider community as a means to achieve a desired end—the solution of the particular problems they have identified.

Yet Americans seem to be saying something else about community. The extent to which even the slightest hint of connectedness obtains popular support is striking. Americans want, or perhaps need, community. It is this longing that leads to their exploitation by those who pass off counterfeit community as the real thing, but it is the same longing that offers hope for the creation of genuine community.

10

Pathways to Genuine Community

During revolutionary moments, stable regimes are unexpectedly de-
mystified by the emergence of alternatives.

—*Henry Kariel (1977, 125)*

Counterfeit community is a pervasive phenomenon. As this book has
shown, its tentacles reach into virtually every corner of American society—into our neighborhoods, our public spaces, our workplaces,
our politics, our religion, and most recently into cyberspace. Perhaps because of its subtle and pervasive quality it has gone unrecognized as a
major aspect of our social landscape. In this concluding chapter I bring together many of the themes developed in the topical areas examined earlier
and end with suggestions to point us down the pathways toward genuine
community.

Through the identification of these themes I first attempt to more fully
explain what has happened to community in America or, perhaps more accurately, what the characteristic hallmarks of counterfeit community are.
Counterfeit community represents perhaps the most significant obstacle we
will encounter on the path toward genuine community. Second, this chapter offers some tentative explanations of why counterfeit community has become so dominant. Who have been the primary creators of counterfeit
community, the chapter asks, and why have they created it? Third, I identify
some techniques used to create and sustain the counterfeits. Finally, I identify some areas where community, at least tentatively, has developed, and I
offer some suggestions of where to begin the journey toward genuine community. The most effective check we can place on counterfeit community is
to develop genuine community, but even more than that, genuine community is the only thing that can satisfy our longings for connectedness.

WHAT IS COUNTERFEIT COMMUNITY?

As was explained at the beginning of this book, counterfeit community is composed of images, symbols, structures, and suggestions of association and connectedness that are false and exploitive. Based upon our examination of how it has become manifest throughout society, we are in a position to explain more fully what those images and structures are and how the dynamics of counterfeit community operate.

At the core of genuine community lies a complex web of relationships. Most fundamental are those that link the place in which community develops with the social interactions there. The communal interactions, in turn, lead to the second major linkage, the creation of feelings of connectedness (or a spirit of community). The more complex and intricate these relationships are, the healthier and more viable the community becomes.

Looking at the community in St. Nick's parish in Chicago as reported by Ehrenhalt, we can see how all of these linkages were present. The bungalow-style housing units were close to each other, and most were designed with front stoops where neighbors gathered on summer evenings. Front parlors also served as more formal meeting areas where guests were entertained. Children played with each other in the streets, the back alleys, or in the attics—all within close proximity of an adult. Neighborhood businesses within walking distance flourished as they were frequented by community residents. The local Catholic church, neighborhood bars, and the local bank where most people obtained their home mortgages were active third places. Most residents worked at one of the many candy factories or at Midway Airport, all within walking distance of their homes. The schools were locally run, and local high school sports, especially football, further linked people together. As a result of this complex web of relationships, people developed an emotional connectedness to the neighborhood and a feeling of community. This feeling was genuine because it resulted from a host of primary relationships among people in the neighborhood.

Counterfeit community undermines the web of relationships needed for genuine community, leaving our longings for connectedness isolated from social experience and vulnerable to exploitation. In each area where we have found counterfeit community, we can see how either the web of relationships or the character of the physical environments in which community occurs have been weakened or eliminated. Common Interest Developments (CIDs) begin by undermining our linkages to place. Planned communities such as Kendrick, Bear Creek, or The Landings destroy our relationship to place through standardization, sanitization, and segmentation. All housing must follow guidelines the developer has established so that property values for all may be maintained. Third places, as Oldenburg describes them, are seen as unsightly and only allowed if controlled and regulated by the community association of the CID; most are banned altogether. Neighborhoods are strictly segmented on the basis of the cost of one's house, and social interactions are encouraged only in strictly regulated and clearly designated areas (inside the home, on the patio, at the clubhouse, etc.), thus eliminating spontaneity in human association.

Practicing one's religion no longer entails strolling to the neighborhood church as occurred in St. Nick's parish or in Poletown. Instead, it means getting in the car and driving to church where the people with whom one interacts may only be seen on Sunday. Churches are no longer focused on the well-being of residents in particular neighborhoods and instead are focused on building their memberships through marketing appeals. Willow Creek Community Church may be located in South Barrington, Illinois, but its members come from across the Chicago suburban area. Located on a sprawling campus adjacent to farmland, it is disconnected from any particular neighborhood. Once severed from place, Willow Creek attempts to simulate community through the suggestion of a community of worshipers.

Although politics could provide a mechanism by which people could interact and forestall the erosion of community, it has failed to do so because of its elite character. Instead of encouraging people to interact, representative politics asks only that we pursue our self-interest and let someone else act for us. Politicians may then manipulate us through the use of symbols of community and platitudes about America as a national community. Where an activist form of politics could help to multiply and enhance community relationships, our elite form of democracy brings us together by manipulating our longings for community through the use of political symbols disconnected from the primary experiences of citizens.

Certainly one of the most significant factors that has destroyed the neighborhoods in which genuine community could exist has been the unfettered use of corporate decision-making. Corporate decisions designed solely to maximize profit have devastated local neighborhoods. In the case of Poletown, corporate power, with the approval and support of local politicians, completely destroyed a viable community by razing homes, churches, schools, businesses, and hospitals to construct a high-tech, robotized Cadillac plant. While not as blatant, other corporate decisions—to close factories, for example, or to undercut the prices of locally owned and operated small business—have further led to the demise of communities through the country. In place of genuine community based in neighborhoods, corporations have manipulated workers' longings for connectedness through the guise of participatory management techniques. Where once local business leaders who lived in the neighborhood felt a sense of responsibility to the people there, corporate leaders are now outside of the web of communal relationships and participate in the local community only symbolically. Corporations may contribute money to local organizations or adopt a local school, but those activities cannot replace being a full-time participant in the social fabric of the community.

Indicative of how far counterfeit community has extended itself is the attempt to construct community in cyberspace. It is here where the geographical space so critical for community has been totally obliterated and primary social relationships have been replaced with typing words into a computer terminal. Still, people want community so desperately that they are willing to pretend they have found it in chat rooms and MUDs and MOOs, even though they have no idea if the people they are talking with even exist.

Counterfeit community represents a serious obstacle in the way of genuine community. The first steps that must be taken are to recognize its existence and understand how it is used to exploit us. Based upon our examination of counterfeit community, we see that it survives by destroying the places where genuine community exists and undermining primary social relationships—the lifeblood of genuine community. Once the roots of genuine community are destroyed, people become vulnerable to manipulation; once genuine community has been weakened, citizens become willing victims to the lure of appeals for connectedness.

WHY DOES COUNTERFEIT COMMUNITY EXIST?

Counterfeit community is intentional: it does not naturally evolve, it is not accidental, it is not merely genuine community gone sour. From its very inception it is designed to manipulate people by appealing to their longings for community but never empowering them to actually achieve it. The forms it takes in various settings are the result of careful study and analysis of which communal appeals will work and which will not.

Housing developers know that when people buy houses they also want to become members of a community, and politicians have discovered through focus groups the resonant power of the concept of community. Housing developers thus use the concept to sell houses by conjuring up images of close-knit enclaves, while politicians combine community with patriotic appeals to obtain electoral support. Mall managers have created distracting environments that encourage us to discover our true selves by purchasing products, and restaurant owners simulate community to increase the purchase of food and beverages. The Cheers bar at Boston's Logan Airport, as well as other Cheers bars around the world, conjure up images of places "where everybody knows your name" in order to relieve anxieties and sell more beer. Religious leaders from mainstream religions, to heads of megachurches, to cult gurus use the appeal of community to increase membership and, by doing so, maintain their own positions. Corporate managers such as Fred Smith at Federal Express use participatory management techniques to make workers feel connected and happy and thereby increase productivity and, in turn, profits. The creation of structures that allow counterfeit community to become manifest and palaver appeals to be effective are designed by business and political elites to serve their purposes, not the purposes of the masses. Power and economic advantage are the goals; the creation of counterfeit community is the means by which those objectives are achieved.

In order for this strategy to be successful, however, the non-elites must be convinced that they themselves are not competent enough to control things themselves. Although America claims to be a democratic nation, in actual operation it is run by elites who claim to be acting in the interest of others. James Madison, the major architect of the Constitution, distrusted the common person and designed an intricate system of checks and balances and federalism to limit anyone's ability to act decisively. Although workers grumble and complain about management, most gladly defer to them and to so-called experts. Throughout our democratic society we are inundated with messages that those in positions of authority are experts and expertise must be deferred to. Doctors know best how to promote the health of people, lawyers and judges have the best visions of justice, professors possess the most knowledge, business managers know what is best for the company.

While expertise certainly has its place, many of the most important decisions are, in fact, not matters of expertise at all—they are matters of value. In the value realm all are equal in that all reasonable people can discuss, debate, and decide issues that involve value choices. Community is such a value choice.

Thus, counterfeit community exists, first, because elites have used it to achieve their purposes of obtaining advantage and, second, because non-elites have become convinced that they are not competent enough to make decisions themselves. Therefore, the prospect for genuine community lies not in elite behavior, but in the behavior of the non-elites.

THE ECONOMICS
OF COUNTERFEIT COMMUNITY

Throughout American society counterfeit community is created and marketed for the purpose of economic gain. In contrast to genuine community, counterfeit community is created by elites and imposed on those who wish to feel a sense of community. This process is accomplished through the use of palaver. By subtly conjuring up images of community and passing them off as the genuine article, economic elites obtain the acquiescence of those who desire community. This acquiescence is not without a price, and in most instances those costs are financial. A brief review of some of the "markets" where counterfeit community has been developed illustrates the point.

Perhaps the most obvious arena where we may see the economic motivation for counterfeit community comes in the area of housing. It is in our neighborhoods where we are most likely to expect to find community. For the most part the construction of housing in America occurs in the private sector, the economic arena. To be sure, government is involved in developing regulations and standards for housing construction and in zoning, but housing initiatives and actual construction are private, economic matters. Developers with access to capital have become the primary shapers of housing in America. Given the private character of housing construction, developers are motivated primarily by economic incentives—they attempt to maximize profit for themselves and their investors. Sensing that their buyers want to live in communities, housing developers use marketing strategies that appeal to those desires, yet they fail to develop the structures and encourage the types of social interactions necessary for genuine community to emerge.

Similarly, third places have been thought essential for the creation of community, for it is there where the informal social interactions fundamental for the formation of genuine community begin. But for economic elites, third places represent merely another arena where profit may be maximized. Utilizing a variety of tactics to undermine the economic viability of third places, corporations market newly sanitized imitations through the palaver of community. All the while the goal is consistent—the maximization of profit through the superficial use of appeals to community. Genuine third places are replaced by their counterfeit brethren.

No one should be surprised to find that the primary purpose of the workplace is to maximize profit. Yet here, as elsewhere, appeals to workers are phrased in terms of community in order to obtain their cooperation. By getting workers to think of themselves as part of a team, management can elicit concessions and obtain workers' support that would appear, at first blush, to be inconsistent with their own interests. Under the guise of suggestions of community, management has been able to increase profits far more than might otherwise be the case.

Even in the realm of religion it has been shown that church economics becomes the motivating factor for many programs. Under the pressure to maintain and expand their congregations, religious leaders have resorted to distorted appeals for community. By claiming to develop a feeling of community among members of the congregation, religious leaders link the members to the church and assure it of its economic existence. The stronger the attachment, the greater the economic benefits that are likely to follow, as churchgoers come to believe that participating in building their congregation is the same as practicing one's religion.

In the newest frontier, cyberspace, the claim of community initially seemed to be the furthest from being driven by economic gain. But recent developments indicate that even the most well-intentioned attempts to create community in cyberspace may, and probably will, become subject to the dictates of an economic logic that requires that profits be made whenever and wherever possible. As the numbers of on-line users attempting to form cyberspace communities continues to grow, web site managers will increasingly manage those sites with an eye toward profitability.

These examples point to a fundamental conflict between our acceptance of the belief that business should be allowed to maximize profit whenever and however possible (with only a few exceptions) and our longings for community. When business is allowed to freely pursue profit, those features necessary for the maintenance of genuine community are often destroyed. In their place we find counterfeits. Although genuine community requires a firm economic foundation, criteria other than the merely economic must prevail. Businesses that operate within communities must be profitable, but profit is not their only objective. In addition to making a profit, community businesses function to reinvest in the community itself, providing jobs, functioning as viable third places, adding to the complexity of the social relationships, and helping to define people's sense of place. Thus, businesses that operate within genuine communities become embedded within the web of relationships that define the community.

The process by which all relationships are integrated to form community is inherently political. It involves the conflict and resolution of a variety of differing interests and values in such a fashion that relationships are maintained and enhanced. In our dominant form of politics, political leaders informally collaborate with corporate elites to create a system of power relationships that allows business leaders to pursue their goals of profit maximization relatively unfettered. Rather than controlling, tempering, and integrating business into the community, politicians attempt to satisfy their constituents through the use of symbolic appeals. Thus, in counterfeit community politics comes to serve the interests of corporate business, whereas in genuine community, politics helps to integrate business into the community and, hence, serve all.

HOW IS COUNTERFEIT COMMUNITY CREATED?

The techniques used to create counterfeit community are many and varied: some are obvious, others are more difficult to discern, some are immediate causes while others, more subtle, are designed to create an environment conducive to its acceptance. Much of this book has already identified particular applications of community palaver. What I wish to do here is examine the more subtle factors that lay the groundwork for the acceptance of counterfeit community.

Most power in America is exercised subtly. Though it has happened from time to time, seldom are police called out to quell riots or put down disturbances. Where riots have occurred they have been curiously apolitical—rioters have burned down their own neighborhoods, businesses, and homes rather than those of authority figures. The tradition of military engagement has been mostly applied against foreign enemies rather than domestic political foes. Instead of controlling people through the direct use of force, the exercise of power is more commonly hidden from view. It manifests itself through a diffuse system of socialization agents that shape values, attitudes, and beliefs that are supportive of those in power. Also, in recent years, the socialization process has been adjusted, ever so slightly, so that attitudes and beliefs that have made counterfeit community acceptable have been emphasized to a greater degree than ever before. A few examples will illustrate the point.

In most cases corporate business interests run counter to genuine community. As we saw in chapter 5, most corporate decision-making neither wants to nor does take into consideration the economic impact of its decisions on local communities. The executives at General Motors had few qualms about razing Poletown to build a Cadillac plant and, in fact, claimed it was good for the city of Detroit. What was perhaps more startling than the razing of a viable neighborhood to benefit a private business, however, was that so few people (except Poletown residents themselves) spoke out against the decision. Only one city council member publicly opposed the plan, the Catholic Church remained silent (and even worked with GM), and most Detroit residents ignored the issue altogether. But the silence of the citizenry in this instance was not unusual; throughout America citizens are acquiescent and compliant, allowing communities to be destroyed and allowing injustice to continue. The more fundamental reasons for counterfeit community are therefore found in Americans' attitudes and beliefs that encourage passivity and allow corporate business to operate unchecked. To examine the underlying causes, we will need to examine how such attitudes are formed.

Perhaps more than ever before in our history, the agents of socialization (schools, churches, the media, etc.) have consistently promoted favorable attitudes about business and, at the same time, helped the growth of citizen passivity. The media, which itself has been corporatized, tends to focus on political corruption, yet seldom reports similar activities that more frequently occur in the world of business. Dominated by the medium of television, news stories tend to be presented in such a fashion that few viewers can truly understand what has happened and fewer still have any sense of what can be done or what they can do to help. Instead, the hidden message is to not worry because someone in authority will take care of the problem (Bennett 1988). Stories appear as sound bytes and are presented with little or no context or analysis, leaving the viewer with a feeling of confusion and helplessness.

Yet perhaps the more effective socialization agent promoting citizen passivity and acquiescence is the education system. In the last several decades in particular, schools have increased their emphasis on education as job preparation. It is not uncommon for school systems to begin to introduce occupationally related issues into the curriculum in junior high school and some as early as elementary school. By high school, many students are on career tracks in which formal job training has already begun. Survey after survey shows that parents overwhelmingly believe that the primary purpose of education is job preparation.

However, perhaps even more significant for producing passive citizens are the pedagogical approaches employed. Traditional approaches assume that the student is ignorant and the job of the teacher is to fill the student with knowledge—referred to as the banking approach by Paulo Freire (1970). The role of the student is to passively absorb the information that the teacher chooses to impart, usually through the lecture method: "In the banking concept of education, knowledge is a gift bestowed by those who consider themselves knowledgeable upon those whom they consider to know nothing" (Freire 1970, 58). The result of this educational approach is a passive citizen well prepared to adapt to the world as given, but poorly prepared to act in the world and shape the future: "Translated into practice, [the banking] concept is well suited to the purposes of the oppressors, whose tranquillity rests on how well men fit the world the oppressors have created, and how little they question it" (Freire 1970, 63).

Although the banking approach to education is still the most frequently used, many educators concerned about the consequences of such an approach are now using pedagogies that emphasize student interaction. These approaches attempt to build self-esteem, creativity, cooperation, and initiative. Although they are successful at achieving the character-building and group-formation objectives, they often fail to provide students with the information and mental rigor necessary for effective citizenship. By failing to incorporate a substantial amount of content and rigor into these promising pedagogical approaches we fail to prepare students for a life of active citizenship.

These trends in business, in the media, in education, and elsewhere are not accidental. A passive citizenry is ideally suited to the kind of elite democracy desired by politicians and corporate leaders. Citizen activity means citizen interference, and Madison's distrust of citizens is also held by present-day leaders. Thus, by controlling the socialization process, political and business leaders have been successful at shaping a passive citizenry that accepts, and even welcomes, corporate domination of the economy. These generalized beliefs create fertile ground for the growth of counterfeit community.

RESISTING COUNTERFEIT COMMUNITY

During the founding period of our nation, two visions of America were debated. The perspective that won out posited a strong national government with representatives insulated from the common people. It was distrustful of the masses, thinking they were incapable of self-governance and would only pursue their own narrow self-interests given the opportunity.

But not everyone agreed with that perspective, and others argued that citizens, given the opportunity, could overcome narrow self-interest to become public-spirited citizens capable of building democratic community. To realize those ambitions, however, requires citizens to actively interact with each other. It is only through participation in democratic organizations that citizens move beyond narrow self-interest and construct genuine community. Although a minority perspective, this alternative view has remained alive for more than two hundred years. It provides us with the theoretical basis for genuine community today.

To more fully understand this alternative and to see its power today, it is helpful to examine some specific examples of where genuine community has been approached. By doing so we may begin to identify the features important for the building of genuine community in America.

The first example comes not from any concerted effort by community activists to build community; rather it is an example that develops out of necessity. The example is that of the black church. The central institution in the black community, the church has given birth to other institutions such as banks, schools, insurance companies, and low-income housing; served as an arena for political activities; nurtured young musical, dramatic, and artistic talent; and satisfied the traditional concerns of worship and moral development. Indeed, the black church has been a central institution in the building of a sense of ethnic identity and community for its members. While buffeted by some of the same social forces that have led to adaptation and ultimately counterfeit community in mainstream churches, many black churches remain strong and viable institutions at the center of their communities.

The vast majority of black churches have deep roots in the revival, a major form of renewal for many Protestants. Revivals can last anywhere from one day to two weeks and often take on the flavor of huge religious and community celebrations. Touring evangelists known for their preaching skills often move from revival to revival converting those not yet in the church and reaffirming those who are. They symbolize not just religious renewal but also the unity of the black community.

In a more concrete sense the church building itself also plays a major role by providing a meeting place for community events; in effect, it serves as a community center. Lectures and meetings about civic problems, including political meetings, take place in the church along with the entire range of social and recreational activities. Black churches are multifunctional and multipurpose institutions (Frazier and Lincoln 1974), traditionally because blacks were excluded from white public buildings. The homes of African Americans were usually too small to have group meetings, and in most communities not enough money was available to build a community center. So the church became the logical place for groups to meet. What's more, in the South, religion represented the one institution that the white man respected and thus provided African Americans with a relatively safe environment in which meetings could take place without the fear of interference from whites. Although this meeting place function has declined because of the decline in overt discrimination, it nonetheless retains an important function in many communities.

The black church has not undergone the degree of privatization of white mainstream churches. Although secular organizations developed in local black communities, many maintained close ties to the church. Many of these groups relied upon black churches for meeting places, leadership, financial resources, publicity, and membership. What's more, many black churches, particularly those in urban areas, developed a range of additional economic institutions designed to assist African Americans financially: "Black churches and their allied institutions like the mutual aid societies, the quasi-religious fraternal lodges, and the benevolent and burial associations, which often met in the churches, helped to create the first major black financial institutions: the black-owned banks and the black life insurance companies" (Lincoln and Mamiya 1990, 244–45).

The black church has never been entirely successful as either an economic institution itself or as an organization responsible for encouraging industrial growth, but to a considerable extent, that was never its primary objective even when establishing apparently obvious economic organizations:

It was generally agreed among the black churches that the economic standing of the race was directly proportional to the level of educational and moral development. Hence they believed that improvement in the latter would result in a corresponding improvement in the former. Although many black economic enterprises had their beginnings in the black churches and although the churches themselves constituted major economic institutions, they never gave high institutional priority to black economic development. (Paris 1985, 69–70)

The ethos that so dominated the black church was composed of self-help, the importance of education, moral training, and civil rights. African Americans have come to believe that education and civil rights must be attained first before economic development can occur.

For this reason black churches have given a high priority to education. The vast majority of black churches regularly recognize students who have done well (often interrupting Sunday services to do so) and contribute to scholarship funds for young members of the congregation. In addition, many of the major black colleges and universities began by being housed in churches (e.g., Tuskegee Institution, Spelman College, Morehouse College). All of the primary black denominations have established their own set of colleges and seminaries. The emphasis on education is consistent with the self-help ethos, supporting the idea that one must improve one's own character before economic advancement is possible.

Although many civil rights leaders have come from black pulpits, the more accurate characterization of the black church regarding politics is ambiguity. Lincoln and Mamiya explain the ambiguity as a result of the dialectical tensions "between the survival and liberation traditions; between the process of cultural assimilation and the assertion and preservation of a unique African American cultural heritage; between accommodation to the American mainstream and being independent of it" (1990, 228). Members of the black church often also find themselves caught between a conservative evangelical tradition that encourages noninvolvement in politics and a liberal critique of racism in America that supports civil rights activism. While the relationship between the black church and politics may be ambiguous, that orientation nonetheless is an accurate reflection of the state of most local black communities as well. This sense of ambiguity makes it possible for an element of flexibility not possible with a more clearly defined viewpoint.

It is ironic that one of the reasons for the black church's success in maintaining and sustaining a sense of community has been racism. Racism has prevented most African Americans from obtaining a middle-class status, thus forcing the black community to rely heavily on the church to perform a multiplicity of functions. Even when African Americans have been able to obtain middle-class status, racism has restricted their movement, thus forcing the emerging black middle class to remain in contact with the black working class and poor (Wilson 1987). But the case of the black church raises a more complex issue that must be addressed.

Genuine community strives to be inclusive, to not make any *a priori* exclusions of individuals who may live within the geographical boundaries of the community. Exclusions from the community must be based upon some reasonable decision. One may argue that the black church has made unreasonable exclusions by not including non-blacks in the church. These are not exclusions based upon religious beliefs (which would be reasonable) but upon race. In an ideal world such an argument would be more persuasive than it is, but there are two reasons that this argument is not sound.

The first reason the black church should not be criticized for being exclusive is based upon history. Although a few churches with exclusively African American memberships were begun in the South before the Revolutionary War, the major rush of African Americans to establish their own churches began in 1787, the same year as the Constitutional Convention. It was not a result of African Americans wanting to exclude others from their churches, rather it was a result of white church leaders' inability to understand the religious practices of African Americans. The critical break of African Americans was led by Richard Allen and Absalom Jones, both of Philadelphia. The triggering event occurred when a church trustee attempted to haul Absalom Jones to his feet during prayer. After the prayer was over, all African Americans walked out and founded their own church, first aligned with the Quakers but later with the Episcopalians (Jordan 1968). This pattern of exclusion from white churches throughout the United States characterizes the fashion in which the black church was created and continued. The issue of white exclusion from the black church never existed; rather the black church was created as a result of African Americans being alienated from white churches.

Second, we need to look at the functions groups that make such exclusions perform and ask whether, given those functions, such exclusions are reasonable. For example, one of the functions of public spaces would be to encourage the interaction of members of the community. Given that function, exclusions from public spaces on the basis of race or ethnicity would be deemed unreasonable since it would violate the purpose of the public space. One of the important functions of the black church has been to encourage African Americans to develop self-respect and a deeper sense of group identity. This could not be accomplished in the broader community and could only be accomplished in safe organizations of people who have been disadvantaged. Although speaking specifically about women's organizations, Belenky, Bond, and Weinstock make the relevant point: "A subordinated people must have the experience of living in and creating a caring, generative community if they are to ever develop the vision and the skills necessary for transforming an unjust society" (1997, 163). If organizations attempting to address the concerns of a marginalized group were open to all, the dominant patterns of oppression in the broader society would prevail and the organization would be unable to accomplish its mission.

In an ideal society there would be serious difficulties with organizations that were exclusive, but in a society where groups of people are subordinated and marginalized on the basis of race, ethnicity, gender, or sexual orientation, organizations that allow members of those groups to develop a consciousness and leadership abilities are essential.

Finally, the experience of the black church demonstrates the importance of what Lisbeth Schorr (1997) calls "synergy": the idea that the building of community can be accomplished only by combining all the elements we know are associated with community in order to accomplish the task. Attempts to rebuild communities by focusing on a single form of intervention such as poverty, housing, education reform, or the improvement of social services will fail if they remain isolated. It is only by combining physical and economic development and social and education reform into a complex web of relationships that community may be built.

To a large extent this synergistic approach is illustrated in the black church, because it serves not only religious functions, but economic, social, physical, educational, and even political purposes. It provides an arena in which the entirety of the African American experience can be addressed. In doing so it brings people together not around particular goals of strengthening the family, improving housing, or reforming education; rather, it brings together people interested in improving the entire community. Working to improve the community naturally results in working on particular goals or specific projects, but those projects have been effective in shaping genuine community because they are part of a broader, integrated vision of community.

While the characteristics of community that emerge from the black church have resulted from the need for people to survive constraints externally imposed on them because of racism, the patterns of genuine community arising today in other areas tend to be intentional. With the need to deal with critical problems such as high crime rates, deteriorating families, a lack of housing, poor education, and the like, the attempt to bring people together to solve these problems has, in some cases, resulted in genuine community. One such example has occurred in the city of Newark.

In the late 1960s a group of Newark community activists gathered to create an organization called the New Community Corporation (NCC). Initially the focus of the NCC was to construct low-income housing, but the vision was broader than merely building houses. Guided by a notion of how people needed to be connected with each other, the NCC began an ambitious building program in the mid-1970s that arranged apartments in such a fashion that each unit was built around a common courtyard with the kitchens designed so that parents could watch their children at play. Over the years, more than 2,500 new or refurbished apartments have been built, housing some 6,500 residents.

But the NCC realized that housing was only one of many community needs and that a range of services was needed to, in effect, construct a community from the bottom up. The NCC "operates transitional housing along with an array of social services for homeless families, teen mothers, victims of domestic violence, and abused or neglected children awaiting permanent placement. It runs a credit union, a scholarship fund, and after-school, summer, and teen-parent programs. NCC also provides day care services for more than six hundred children" (Schorr 1997, 349).

The NCC is also a major employer of local residents, employing more than 1,000 people as a security force, carpenters, plumbers, painters, and maintenance workers to care for the properties it manages. Encouraging people to better themselves, it operates an extensive job training and placement service and attempts to help people develop the skills necessary to move from low-paying to higher-paying positions.

Probably the most innovative aspect of the NCC has been the creation and operation of the Pathmark Shopping Center. While most businesses fled Newark following the 1967 riots, the NCC was successful at working out an arrangement to build the shopping center, which opened in 1990. It employs 325 workers, and more than 50,000 shoppers come to the Pathmark each week. The income generated far exceeds other shopping centers of comparable sizes as neighborhood residents frequent it on a regular basis because of its connections to the community. Over two-thirds of the Pathmark profits are returned to the NCC, which reinvests them in the job training and housing programs. Thus, even businesses that are not locally owned must return a substantial portion of their profits back into the community.

Although some of the NCC leaders are motivated by religion (several important leaders are Catholic priests), the community vision transcends religion. In fact, most people who make up the NCC are not Catholic. Instead, the NCC is driven by a strong sense of social justice: "Grounded on religious teachings of social justice, NCC can adopt and shift as opportunities present themselves without fear of losing its way. Its social justice goals keep it focused" (Schorr 1997, 352).

The NCC illustrates how the building of genuine community can be intentional if guided by a dynamic vision of social justice. Motivated by such concerns, community leaders can effectively hold business responsible and require that they reinvest locally. By creating a genuine community, business can be restructured to both make a profit and contribute to the maintenance of the community. Social justice provides a set of guidelines for making decisions within the context of the community while, at the same time, remaining flexible and open to new possibilities that might present themselves.

TOWARD GENUINE COMMUNITY

The most effective way to lessen the impact of counterfeit community is to build pathways toward genuine community. How then do we construct genuine community? At the outset we should recognize the difficulty. For the most part those who hold political and economic power will initially have little interest in creating genuine community. While they may indicate symbolic support for communal initiatives, they are far more likely to provide active support for counterfeit versions of community. Some will simply oppose any attempts to create genuine community, concluding that such efforts will reduce their own power and influence. The strategy that must be adopted then is to force elites to support community building initiatives (or at least not oppose them). The specific strategies for how and when to do this must be decided by local groups, but we should not assume that either local elites or national elites would be active supporters of community initiatives.

At the same time, it would be inaccurate to describe those in positions of power and influence as having universally similar attitudes and beliefs, let alone similar interests. This is especially true in America where so much diversity produces multiple power bases. At the very least, those who wish to build genuine community must attempt to identify like-minded leaders within their own communities and cultivate and support them.

We should also not expect political elites at any level to create packages of government programs that attempt to reinvigorate community. Although the communitarian perspective offers a number of worthy suggestions, the movement that it spawned smacks of elitism. Rather than focusing on policies that would empower local communities to develop their own reforms, the movement advocates changes such as campaign finance reform, gun control, and moral education in schools. Regardless of the merits of any of the particular reforms suggested, the point is that distant academic and political elites cannot effectively rebuild community by adopting policies distant from the communities they wish to change. Symbolic of this elitist orientation are reports that Etzioni's book *The Spirit of Community* appears on President Clinton's desk "from time to time" (no doubt depending on what group Clinton is meeting with or what policy he is supporting). If a true communitarian movement originates in local communities and develops into a national movement, we may well be able to use the national government to help, but lacking a truly local base we must be skeptical of such initiatives.

While it would be tempting to develop a laundry list of proposals to build community, such an approach would be a mistake for at least two reasons. First, every community is unique. Different communities have different types of people who are members, different needs, different leadership skills and resources, and different problems. Communities must be allowed to develop a sense of place and connectedness without being forced into predefined molds. Second, the development of a spirit of community is a result of the interactions of members as they discuss and debate issues, attempt to solve problems, participate in conversations for no particular purpose, or join in community celebrations and rituals. More important than the outcome of particular activities is the process of interacting itself. Through these primary interactions, people define themselves and their community and create a meaningful sense of connection with others.

This said, there are a number of paths that could lead us further in the right direction. Based upon our analysis it seems clear that one of the key elements for genuine community is public space. Whenever and wherever possible, public spaces should be created, enhanced, and protected. The specific nature or character of those areas will, of course, have to be determined by the members of the community itself. They might include the creation or maintenance of a neighborhood park, the establishment of a community center, the closing of a street on summer Sundays to create a common recreational area, or simply the linking of the backyards of neighbors to create a common area.

While private property allows individuals an avenue for personal expression, public space provides an arena in which the character of the community may be forged and displayed. As members of the community interact, they project public images of themselves they wish others to see. This allows for the expression of dimensions of one's personality not seen in the private arena of the family. The cumulative effect of these interactions creates a sense of community. The more and varied the types of public spaces, the more interesting and complex is the community, and the more interesting the people become as they must be constantly aware of their environment and must develop multiple dimensions of their personalities in order to successfully navigate the diversity.

The second critical feature for genuine community is the quality of the social interactions that occur. Community members should give thought to ways in which interactions among members of the community (either all the members or some of them) can be increased. Such interactions should range from the informal to the highly structured, from the serious to the playful, from the secular to the religious. Interactions could range from small groups of people to celebrations of the entire community.

Communities experience a growth process. Social interactions often begin informally, sometimes spontaneously. As people become acquainted, their interactions may become regularized and may also expand to include others. As community members interact and share experiences, a sense of connectedness to a place may begin to develop. When this occurs, people will identify themselves as being from a particular area (often called by the name of some physical characteristic in the area—a road, river, building, etc.). As we move down the path toward genuine community, the informal interactions will continue, but they will be supplemented and enhanced by more formal patterns of interaction—thus structures or institutions are created.

Initiatives to create and maintain public space and to enhance primary social interaction can only come about if there is an awareness of the importance of community. The first step in constructing genuine community therefore is to increase one's consciousness about its character, its importance, and the nature of counterfeits. Hopefully this book is a step in this direction. Before one can act to create or maintain public spaces, for example, a person must know the importance of such areas for the development of community.

Consciousness-raising has a long history in the United States, often as the initial step for social and political movements. For example, the second wave of the feminist movement initially began with small groups of women gathering and talking with each other about their experiences. As each group member shared personal experiences she thought were unique to her, the women began to see, in fact, that their experiences were actually quite similar. When this realization occurs, one begins to see the political nature of one's private life. If similar events happen to women in similar situations, the problems are no long individualistic; rather they are gender-based and socially constructed. Out of these groups arose a movement that took on national dimensions.

Likewise, for many years black churches brought African Americans together to discuss what it meant to be black in America and what each person's response to racism was. As African Americans talked with each other they began to understand more fully how racism was used to separate them and prevent them from realizing their own political power. Many civil rights leaders emerged from that form of personal reflection. Certainly sexism and racism are still with us today, but from those modest consciousness-raising groups, larger movements sprang up to improve, at least in some fashion, the status of women and African Americans. Perhaps more importantly, however, each person involved in such groups came to see himself or herself in a different light—as part of a broader movement to improve society. While it is possible to cognitively know the difference between genuine and counterfeit community, a more complete understanding is possible only through experience. By actually participating in the web of relationships of genuine community, a person can sense the shallowness of counterfeit community. What is thus needed at the outset is something akin to consciousness-raising groups for community.

In conjunction with this, educators need to take seriously the early goals of public education—to educate citizens for democracy. To do this requires changing not merely the focus of what is taught in the classroom but also the pedagogical approaches used. Education for citizenship entails a different approach to education and requires that schools be less concerned about preparing students for jobs and more concerned about supporting innovative teaching approaches that encourage student activity and involvement while maintaining rigor and content. The objective of education should be first and foremost to empower students to function as competent and effective citizens. It is not merely skill development that should be taught; the entire educational paradigm needs to be shifted in order to liberate rather than oppress students. This involves more than simply moving from a lecture style of teaching to a discussion style; it means examining assumptions about the roles of students and teachers and authority in the classroom, the importance of rigor and content, the nature of knowledge, and the function of education in a democracy. Teachers should assist students in working cooperatively in the classroom and in linking the school with the community while maintaining a rigorous program of study. While this may seem overwhelming, in fact, teachers have traditionally been given considerable flexibility in organizing their classrooms as they wish under the principle of academic freedom.

Although the power of corporations may seem overwhelming when compared with the modest seeds of a community movement, there are nonetheless things that can be done to support locally owned and locally operated business. As one's consciousness about the importance of community grows, the importance of local business to the neighborhoods will become apparent. Local business should be supported whenever possible through patronization and by opposing the incursion of corporate business into viable neighborhoods.

Major social and political movements in the United States have historically followed one of two paths to move from a local or regional base to become national in scope. They have either created their own organizations (e.g., the feminist movement), or they have taken control of existing political parties (e.g., the Populist Movement of the 1890s). If and when a genuine community-based movement begins to move from the consciousness-raising stage to the action stage, it may find itself in a position to make a decision about what organizational strategy to pursue. Even lacking a substantial movement, community organizers may wish to carefully consider the capture of local political parties as a strategy to push their agenda.

Political parties have historically been neighborhood-based organizations. In the days of political machines citizens were actively and meaningfully linked to the machine that dominated the city (usually a city although there were some in rural areas as well). But today political machines have vanished from the political landscape to be replaced by thin representative structures with little or no civic involvement. A well-organized movement of community-minded citizens could relatively easily take control of one or both political parties at the local level and push for policies to help communities develop. The advantage of working through the political party is that the movement would have immediate access to elected officials.

Once a critical mass of community-minded people were in positions of influence, it would be possible to implement a far more broad-ranging program of community development. It would be premature at this point to attempt to describe what that agenda might look like, but one could envision policies being developed that would support local initiatives to build communities and control the forces that undermine them.

CONCLUSION

Creating genuine community in America will not be an easy task. The forces that have undermined community have been long in the making and have become "givens" in American culture. Recreating community is not as simple as improving the moral character of the citizenry, placing additional burdens on the education system, or manipulating family policy to support nuclear families. The only hope of creating genuine community lies in the desire of Americans for community. Much can be done locally, but to extend the model will require a community-based movement.

Before we can initiate such change, however, we must become aware of the false claims of community in our midst. These counterfeit attempts function to deflect us from our goal. They offer the hope of community only to exploit us. Our reactions all too often are then to withdraw and conclude that community is neither possible nor desirable.

Yet our longing for community—to be connected to others in some meaningful fashion—persists. It is this longing that represents the hope for the creation of genuine community. It is both our weakness and our strength; it is what makes us vulnerable to counterfeit claims of community and it is what provides us with a vision of something greater. If community is to be created, it will be the result of millions of citizens discussing and debating in thousands of public places throughout the country, for the prospect of community in America lies in its people.

Certainly an objective assessment of the prospects is not bright. Those who control the greatest amount of political and economic power seem set on the pathways that lead toward counterfeit versions of community. If measured by the objective standards of reviving community throughout America, it seems that the most likely outcome would be failure. Nonetheless, throughout history Americans have shown a willingness to fight worthy battles regardless of the odds. This is not to say that justice will win out; it often has not. But something deep within the American spirit periodically calls out to us to band together to create a deeper meaning of what it means to be Americans. This longing for connectedness must be focused on the local community and sustained and nourished there if genuine community is ever to be achieved.

References

Abrams, Charles. 1955. *Forbidden Neighbors*. New York: Harper & Brothers.

Abramson, Paul R., John H. Aldrich, and David W. Rohde. 1995. *Change and Continuity in the 1992 Elections*. Washington, D.C.: CQ Press.

"Acceptance Speeches: Reagan: 'Time to Recapture our Destiny'," 1981. *Congressional Quarterly Almanac 1980*. Washington, D.C.: Congressional Quarterly Press, pp. 36B–39B.

Allison, Jay. 1992. "Vigil." *Whole Earth Review* 75: 4.

Alinsky, Saul D. 1946. *Reveille for Radicals*. Chicago: University of Chicago Press.

Altman, Irwin, and Setha M. Low, eds. 1992. *Place Attachment*. New York: Plenum Publishing.

Balch, Robert. 1980. "Looking Behind the Scenes in a Religious Cult: Implications for the Study of Conversion." *Sociological Analysis* 41: 137–43.

Bandow, Doug. 1994. "Libertarian: Building Civil Society Through Virtue and Freedom," in *Building a Community of Citizens: Civil Society in the 21st Century*, ed. Don E. Eberly. Lanham, Md.: The Commonwealth Foundation.

Barber, Benjamin R. 1984. *Strong Democracy: Participatory Politics for a New Age*. Berkeley: University of California Press.

————. 1992. *An Aristocracy of Everyone: The Politics of Education and the Future of America*. New York: Ballantine Books.

Barber, James David. 1992. *The Presidential Character: Predicting Performance in the White House*. 4th ed. Englewood Cliffs, N.J.: Prentice-Hall.

Barna, George. 1988. *Marketing the Church*. Colorado Springs: Navpress.

————. 1992. *Church Marketing: Breaking Ground for the Harvest*. Ventura, Calif.: Regal Books.

Barton, Stephen E., and Carol J. Silverman. 1987. *Common Interest Homeowners' Association Management Study*. Sacramento: California Department of Real Estate.

Baudrillard, Jean. 1983. *Simulations*. New York: Semiorext(e), Inc.

————. 1994. *Simulacra and Simulation*. Translated by Sheila Faria Glaser. Ann Arbor: The University of Michigan Press.

Beales, Ross W., Jr. 1991. "The Preindustrial Family (1600–1815)," in *American Families*, ed. Joseph M. Hawes and Elizabeth I. Nybakken. New York: Greenwood Press, pp. 35–82.

Belenky, Mary Field, Lynne A. Bond, and Jacqueline S. Weinstock. 1997. *A Tradition That Has No Name: Nurturing the Development of People, Families, and Communities.* New York: BasicBooks.

Bellah, Robert N., Richard Madsen, William M. Sullivan, Ann Swidler, and Steven M. Tipton. 1985. *Habits of the Heart.* New York: Perennial Press.

———. 1991. *The Good Society.* New York: Vintage Books.

Beniger, James R. 1987. "Personalization of Mass Media and the Growth of Pseudo-Community." *Communication Research* 14: 352–71.

Bennett, W. Lance. 1988. *News: The Politics of Illusion.* 2nd ed. New York: Longman.

Berle, Adolph A., Jr. 1954. *The 20th Century Capitalist Revolution.* New York: Harcourt Brace.

Bernard, Jessie. 1973. *The Sociology of Community.* Glenview, Ill.: Scott, Foresman.

Berry, Christopher J. 1989. *The Idea of a Democratic Community.* New York: St. Martin's Press.

Berry, Wendell. 1993. *Sex, Economy, Freedom & Community.* New York: Pantheon Books.

Bluestone, Barry. 1982. "Deindustrialization and the Abandonment of Community," in *Community and Capital in Conflict: Plant Closings and Job Loss,* ed. John C. Raines, Leonora E. Berson, and David McI. Gracie. Philadelphia: Temple University Press, pp. 38–61.

Bodnar, John E. 1992. *Remaking America: Public Memory, Commemoration, and Patriotism in the Twentieth Century.* Princeton, N.J.: Princeton University Press.

Boyer, M. Christine. 1992. "Cities for Sale: Merchandising History at Street Seaport," in *Variations on a Theme Park,* ed. Michael Sorkin. New York: Hill and Wang, pp. 181–204.

Brail, Stephanie. 1996. "The Price of Admission: Harassment and Free Speech in the Wild, Wild West," in *Wired_Women: Gender and New Realities in Cyberspace,* ed. Lynn Cherny and Elizabeth Reba Weise. Seattle: Seal Press, pp. 141–57.

Bukowczyk, John J. 1984. "The Decline and Fall of a Detroit Neighborhood: Poletown vs. G. M. and the City of Detroit." *Washington and Lee Law Review* 41: 49–76.

Campbell, Andrew, and Sally Yeung. 1991. "Creating a Sense of Mission." *Long Range Planning* 24: 10–20.

Carlson, Allan C. 1994. "Traditionalist: Strengthening the Bonds of Civil Society," in *Building a Community of Citizens: Civil Society in the 21st Century,* ed. Don E. Eberly. Lanham, Md.: The Commonwealth Foundation.

Caudill, Harry M. 1973. *My Land Is Dying.* New York: E. P. Dutton & Company.

Cochran, Clarke E. 1989. "The Thin Theory of Community: The Communitarians and their Critics." *Political Studies* 32: 422–35.

Coles, Robert. 1980. "Civility and Psychology." *Daedalus* 109: 133–41.

Combs, James E., and Dan Nimmo. 1993. *The New Propaganda: The Dictatorship of Palaver in Contemporary Politics.* New York: Longman.

Conner, Roger L. 1994. "Communitarian: A New Balance between Rights and Responsibilities," in *Building a Community of Citizens: Civil Society in the 21st Century,* ed. Don E. Eberly. Lanham, Md.: The Commonwealth Foundation.

Considine, John J. 1995. *Marketing Your Church: Concepts and Strategies.* Kansas City: Sheed and Ward.

Cooley, Charles Horton. 1929. *Social Organization: A Study of the Larger Mind.* New York: Charles Scribner's Sons.

Coontz, Stephanie. 1992. *The Way We Never Were: American Families and the Nostalgia Trap.* New York: BasicBooks.

———. 1988. *The Social Origins of Private Life: A History of American Families 1600–1900.* London: Verso.

Crystal, Graef. 1991. *In Search of Excess: The Overcompensation of American Executives.* New York: W. W. Norton.

Daly, Herman E., and John B. Cobb. 1989. *For the Common Good: Redirecting the Economy Toward Community, the Environment, and a Sustainable Future.* Boston: Beacon Press.

Davidson, Roger H., and Walter J. Oleszek. 1996. *Congress and Its Members.* 5th ed. Washington, D.C.: CQ Press.

Day, Graham, and Jonathan Murdoch. 1993. "Locality and Community." *The Sociological Review* 41: 82–111.

Dean, John P. 1947. "Only Caucasian: A Study of Race Covenants." *Journal of Land and Public Utility Economics* 23: 428–32.

"Democratic Acceptance Speeches: Dukakis Pledges 'Era of Greatness'," 1989. *Congressional Quarterly Almanac 1988.* Washington, D.C.: Congressional Quarterly Press, pp. 83A–85A.

Demos, John. 1986. *Past, Present, and Personal: The Family and the Life Course in American History.* New York: Oxford University Press.

Egan, Timothy. 1995. "Many Seek Security in Private Communities." *New York Times* (September 3): 1, 22.

Ehrenhalt, Alan. 1995. *The Lost City: Discovering the Forgotten Virtues of Community in the Chicago of the 1950s.* New York: BasicBooks.

Elshtain, Jean Bethke. 1981. *Public Man, Private Woman.* 2nd ed. Princeton, N.J.: Princeton University Press.

Etzioni, Amitai. 1993. *The Spirit of Community.* New York: Touchstone.

Evans, Sara. 1979. *Personal Politics.* New York: Vintage Books.

Evans, Sara M., and Harry C. Boyte. 1986. *Free Spaces: The Sources of Democratic Change in America.* New York: Harper & Row.

Evard, Michele. 1996. "'So Please Stop; Thank You': Girls Online," in *Wired_Women: Gender and New Realities in Cyberspace,* ed. Lynn Cherny and Elizabeth Reba Wise. Seattle: Seal Press, pp. 188–204.

The Federalist Papers. 1961. New York: New American Library.

Feldman, Stanley. 1982. "Economic Self-Interest and Political Behavior." *American Journal of Political Science* 26: 446–66.

Forty, Adrian. 1986. *Objects of Desire: Design and Society from Wedgewood to IBM.* New York: Pantheon.

Fowler, Robert Booth. 1991. *The Dance with Community.* Lawrence: University of Kansas Press.

Francaviglia, Richard V. 1977. "Main Street USA: The Creation of a Popular Image." *Landscape* 21: 18–22.

Frank, Robert H., and Philip J. Cook. 1995. *The Winner-Take-All Society.* New York: Martin Kessler Books.

Frazer, Elizabeth, and Nicola Lacey. 1993. *The Politics of Community: A Feminist Critique of the Liberal-Communitarian Debate.* Toronto: University of Toronto Press.

Frazier, E. Franklin, and C. Eric Lincoln. 1974. *The Black Church Since Frazier.* New York: Schocken Books.

Freire, Paulo. 1970. *Pedagogy of the Oppressed.* New York: Continuum.

Frohnen, Bruce. 1996. *The New Communitarians and the Crisis of Modern Liberalism.* Lawrence: University of Kansas Press.

Garreau, Joel. 1991. *Edge City: Life on the New Frontier.* New York: Anchor Books.

Gaventa, John. 1980. *Power and Powerlessness: Quiescence and Rebellion in an Appalachian Valley.* Urbana: University of Illinois Press.

George, Stephen, and Arnold Weimerskirch. 1994. *Total Quality Management: Strategies and Techniques Proven at Today's Most Successful Companies.* New York: John Wiley & Sons, Inc.

Gert, Bernard. 1970. *The Moral Rules: A New Rational Foundation for Morality.* New York: Harper Torchbooks.

Gilligan, Carol. 1982. *In a Different Voice.* Cambridge: Harvard University Press.

Glendon, Mary Ann. 1991. *Rights Talk: The Impoverishment of Political Discourse.* New York: The Free Press.

Gozdz, Kazimierz. 1993. "Building Community as a Leadership Discipline," in *The New Paradigm in Business: Emerging Strategies for Leadership and Organizational Change,* ed. Michael Ray and Alan Rinzler. New York: G. P. Putnam's Sons, pp. 107–19.

Gray, John. 1992. *Men Are From Mars, Women Are From Venus.* New York: HarperCollins.

Greenfield, Meg. 1991. "The Fellowship of Patriotism." *Newsweek* (July 8) 118: 68.

Hagel, John, III, and Arthur G. Armstrong. 1997. *Net Gain: Expanding Markets Through Virtual Communities.* Boston: Harvard Business School Press.

Harrary, Keith. 1994. "The Truth About Jonestown," in *Religious Cults in America,* ed. Robert Emmet Long. New York: The H. W. Wilson Company, pp. 10–20.

Hayden, Dolores. 1984. *Redesigning the American Dream: The Future of Housing, Work, and Family Life.* New York: W. W. Norton.

Herszenhorn, David M. 1995. "Reflecting on the 4th, Many Draw a Blank." *New York Times* (July 4): Sect. A, 35.

Hillery, George A., Jr. 1955. "Definitions of Community: Areas of Agreement." *Rural Sociology* 20: 111–23.

Hiss, Tony. 1990. *The Experience of Place.* New York: Vintage Books.

Hochschild, Arlie Russell. 1997. "There's No Place Like Work." *New York Times Magazine* (April 20): 51–55.

Holsworth, Robert D., and J. Harry Wray. 1982. *American Politics and Everyday Life.* New York: John Wiley.

Jackson, Kenneth T. 1985. *Crabgrass Frontier: The Suburbanization of the United States.* New York: Oxford University Press.

Jameson, Frederic. 1984. "Postmodernism, or the Cultural Logic of Late Capitalism." *New Left Review* 146: 53–92.

Jeffres, Leo W., Jean Dobos, and Mary Sweeney. 1987. "Communication and Commitment to Community." *Communication Research* 14: 619–43.

Jordan, Winthrop D. 1968. *White Over Black: American Attitudes Toward the Negro, 1550–1812.* Chapel Hill: University of North Carolina Press.

Judd, Dennis R., and Todd Swanstrom. 1994. *City Politics: Private Power and Public Policy.* New York: HarperCollins.

Kariel, Henry S. 1977. *Beyond Liberalism: Where Relations Grow*. San Francisco: Chandler and Sharp Publishers.

Karlsen, Carol F. 1987. *The Devil in the Shape of a Woman*. New York: W. W. Norton.

Kerber, Linda. 1989. "Women and Individualism in American History." *The Massachusetts Review* 30: 589–609.

Kerber, Ross. 1993. "Watching Profits Rocket on the Fourth of July." *Washington Post* (July 6): Sect. E, 1.

Keyes, Ralph. 1973. "I Like Colonel Sanders." *Newsweek* (August 27) 82: 8–9.

Kirk, Jeffrey. 1972. "The Family as Utopian Retreat from the City." *Soundings* 55: 21–41.

Klemm, Mary, Stuart Sanderson, and George Luffman. 1991. "Mission Statements: Selling Corporate Values to Employees," *Long Range Planning* 24: 73–78.

Kotler, Milton. 1969. *Neighborhood Government: The Local Foundations of Political Life*. Indianapolis: The Bobbs-Merrill Company.

Kowinski, William Severini. 1985. *The Malling of America*. New York: William Morrow and Company, Inc.

Kunstler, James Howard. 1993. *The Geography of Nowhere*. New York: Touchstone.

Lasch, Christopher. 1975. *Haven in a Heartless World: The Family Besieged*. New York: Basic Books, Inc.

———. 1979. *The Culture of Narcissism*. New York: W. W. Norton.

Laslett, Barbara. 1973. "The Family as a Public and Private Institution: An Historical Perspective." *Journal of Marriage and the Family* 35: 480–92.

Leakey, Richard E., and Roger Lewin. 1977. *Origins*. New York: E. P. Dutton.

Lewis, George H. 1990. "Community through Exclusion and Illusion: The Creation of Social Worlds in an American Shopping Mall." *Journal of Popular Culture* 24: 121–36.

Lincoln, C. Eric, and Lawrence H. Mamiya. 1990. *The Black Church in the African-American Experience*. Durham: Duke University Press.

Long, Norton E. 1991. "The Paradox of a Community of Transients." *Urban Affairs Quarterly* 27: 3–12.

Machiavelli, Niccolo. 1950. *The Prince and The Discourses*. New York: The Modern Library.

MacIntyre, Alasdair. 1971. *A Short History of Ethics*. New York: Macmillan.

McGrath, Charles. 1996. "The Internet's Arrested Development." *New York Times Magazine* (December 8): 80–85.

McGregor, Douglas. 1985. *The Human Side of Enterprise: 25th Anniversary Printing*. New York: Warner Books.

McKenzie, Evan. 1994. *Privatopia*. New Haven: Yale University Press.

McKnight, John. 1995. *The Careless Society: Community and Its Counterfeits*. New York: BasicBooks.

McWilliams, Wilson Carey. 1974. *The Idea of Fraternity in America*. Berkeley: University of California Press.

Mansbridge, Jane J. 1980. *Beyond Adversary Democracy*. New York: Basic Books.

Marcuse, Herbert. 1964. *One-Dimensional Man*. Boston: Beacon Press.

Merelman, Richard M. 1984. *Making Something of Ourselves: On Culture and Politics in the United States*. Berkeley: University of California Press.

Mill, John Stuart. 1910. *Utilitarianism, Liberty, and Representative Government*. London: J. M. Dent & Sons, Ltd.

Moon, J. Donald. 1993. *Constructing Community: Moral Pluralism and Tragic Conflicts.* Princeton, N.J.: Princeton University Press.

Mullins, Patrick. 1987. "Community and Urban Movements." *The Sociological Review* 35: 347–69.

Nieburg, H. L. 1973. *Culture Storm: Politics and the Ritual Order.* New York: St. Martin's Press.

Oldenburg, Ray. 1989. *The Great Good Place.* New York: Paragon House.

Owens, Virginia Stern. 1980. *The Total Image: Or Selling Jesus in the Modern Age.* Grand Rapids: William B. Eerdmans Publishing Company.

Paris, Peter. 1985. *The Social Teaching of the Black Churches.* Philadelphia: Fortress.

Pateman, Carole. 1970. *Participation and Democratic Theory.* Cambridge: Cambridge University Press.

Peck, M. Scott. 1993. *A World Waiting to be Born: Civility Rediscovered.* New York: Bantam Books.

Peters, Thomas, and Nancy Austin. 1985. *A Passion for Excellence.* New York: Warner Books.

Peters, Thomas, and Robert H. Waterman, Jr. 1982. *In Search of Excellence: Lessons from America's Best-Run Companies.* New York: Warner Books.

Peterson, Merrill, ed. 1975. *The Portable Thomas Jefferson.* New York: Penguin Press.

Power, F. Clark. 1989. *Lawrence Kohlberg's Approach to Moral Education.* New York: Columbia University Press.

Putnam, Robert D. 1995. "Bowling Alone: America's Declining Social Capital." *Journal of Democracy* 6: 65–78.

Rabrenovic, Gordana. 1996. *Community Builders: A Tale of Neighborhood Mobilization in Two Cities.* Philadelphia: Temple University Press.

Reed, Edward S. 1996. *The Necessity of Experience.* New Haven: Yale University Press.

Reich, Robert. 1991. "Secession of the Successful." *New York Times Magazine* (January 20): 16–17; 42–45.

"Republican Acceptance Speeches: Bush Takes the Lead and Defines His Mission," 1989. *Congressional Quarterly Almanac 1988.* Washington, D.C.: Congressional Quarterly Press, pp. 41A–44A.

Rheingold, Howard. 1993. *The Virtual Community: Homesteading on the Electronic Frontier.* New York: HarperPerennial.

Rhoads, Steven E. 1985. *The Economist's View of the World.* Cambridge: Cambridge University Press.

Ritzdorf, Marsha. 1984. "Challenging the Exclusionary Impact of Family Definitions in American Municipal Zoning Ordinances." *Journal of Urban Affairs* 7: 15–25.

Robbins, Thomas, and Dick Anthony. 1982. "Cults, Culture, and Community," in *Cults and the Family,* ed. Florence Kaslow and Marvin B. Sussman. New York: The Haworth Press.

Rosenstone, Steven J., and John Mark Hansen. 1993. *Mobilization, Participation, and Democracy in America.* New York: MacMillan Publishing Company.

Rousseau, Jean Jacques. 1950. *The Social Contract and Discourses.* New York: E. P. Dutton & Company, Inc.

Ryan, William. 1976. *Blaming the Victim.* New York: Vintage Books.

Sandel, Michael J. 1988. "Democrats and Community." *The New Republic* (February 22) 198: 20–23.

Schaef, Anne Wilson, and Diane Fassel. 1988. *The Addictive Organization.* New York: Harper San Francisco.

Schambra, William A. 1988. "Turf Battles: The Parties Clash Over Community." *Public Opinion* 11: 17–19.

Schiller, Herbert I. 1996. *Information Inequality: The Deepening Social Crisis in America.* New York: Routledge.

Schoenberg, Sandra Perlman, and Patricia L. Rosenbaum. 1980. *Neighborhoods That Work: Sources for Viability in the Inner City.* New Brunswick, N.J.: Rutgers University Press.

Schorr, Lisbeth B. 1997. *Common Purpose: Strengthening Families and Neighborhoods to Rebuild America.* New York: Anchor Books.

Schumpeter, Joseph A. 1976. *Capitalism, Socialism and Democracy.* New York: Harper Torchbooks.

Schwartz, Evan. 1995. "Looking for Community on the Internet." *National Civic Review* 84: 37–41.

Seabrook, John. 1997. *Deeper: My Two-Year Odyssey in Cyberspace.* New York: Simon & Schuster.

Sennett, Richard. 1970. *The Uses of Disorder: Personal Identity and City Life.* Vintage Books: New York.

———. 1976. *The Fall of Public Man: On the Social Psychology of Capitalism.* New York: Vintage Books.

Shawchuck, Norman, Philip Kotler, Bruce Wrenn, and Gustave Rath. 1992. *Marketing for Congregations: Choosing to Serve People More Effectively.* Nashville: Abingdon Press.

Sherry, Suzanna. 1986. "Civic Virtue and the Feminine Voice in Constitutional Adjudication." *Virginia Law Review* 72: 543–616.

Skolnick, Arlene. 1981. "The American Family: The Paradox of Perfection." *The Wilson Quarterly* 4: 112–21.

Smolowe, Jill. 1995. "Intimate Strangers." *Time* (Spring) 145: 20–24.

Somkin, Fred. 1967. *Unquiet Eagle: Memory and Desire in the Idea of American Freedom, 1815–1860.* Ithaca, N.Y.: Cornell University Press.

Spender, Dale. 1995. *Nattering on the Net: Women, Power and Cyberspace.* North Melbourne, Victoria, Australia: Spinifex.

Spock, Benjamin, and Michael B. Rothenberg. 1992. *Dr. Spock's Baby and Child Care.* 6th ed. New York: Pocket Books.

Stack, Carol B. 1974. *All Our Kin: Strategies for Survival in a Black Community.* New York: Harper Torchbooks.

Stevens, Hugh. 1984. "The Lost Art of Porch-Sitting." *Blair and Ketcham's Country Journal* 11: 84–85.

Sullivan, Deidre. 1991. "Targeting Souls." *American Demographics* 13: 42–46; 56–59.

Talbott, Stephen L. 1995. *The Future Does Not Compute: Transcending the Machines in our Midst.* Sebastopol, Calif.: O'Reilly and Associates, Inc.

Teixeira, Ruy A. 1992. *The Disappearing American Voter.* Washington, D.C.: Brookings Institution.

Thomashow, Mitchell. 1995. *Ecological Identity.* Cambridge: The MIT Press.

Thurow, Lester. 1995. "Why Their World Might Crumble." *New York Times Magazine* (November 19): 78–79.

Tocqueville, Alexis de. 1964. *Democracy in America*. New York: Washington Square Press.

Turkle, Sherry. 1995. *Life on the Screen: Identity in the Age of the Internet*. New York: Simon & Schuster.

Ulrich, Laurel Thatcher. 1982. *Good Wives: Image and Reality in the Lives of Women in Northern New England, 1650–1750*. New York: Alfred A. Knopf.

van Cleef, Eugene. 1970. *Cities in Action*. New York: Pergamon Press.

Van Horn, Susan Householder. 1988. *Women, Work, and Fertility, 1900–1986*. New York: New York University Press.

Wachter, Mary, and Cynthia Tinsley. 1996. *Taking Back Our Neighborhoods: Building Communities That Work*. Minneapolis: Fairview Press.

Wahlstrom, Billie Joyce. 1979. "Images of the Family in the Mass Media: An American Iconography?" in *Changing Images of the Family*, ed. Virginia Tufte and Barbara Myerhoff. New Haven: Yale University Press, pp. 193–227.

Wallis, Jim. 1995. *The Soul of Politics*. San Diego: Harcourt Brace.

Walzer, Michael. 1983. *Spheres of Justice*. New York: Basic Books.

———. 1990. "The Communitarian Critique of Liberalism." *Political Theory* 18: 6–23.

Warner, W. Lloyd, and J. O. Low. 1968. "The Factory in the Community," in *The Search for Community in Modern America*, ed. E. Digby Baltzell. New York: Harper & Row, pp. 22–39.

Waterman, Robert H., Jr. 1994. *What America Does Right: Lessons from Today's Most Admired Corporate Role Models*. New York: Plume.

Werner, Emmy E., and Ruth S. Smith. 1982. *Vulnerable But Invincible: A Longitudinal Study of Resilient Children and Youth*. New York: McGraw-Hill.

Willis, C. L. 1977. "Definitions of Community II: An Examination of Definitions of Community Since 1950." *Southern Sociology* 9: 14–19.

Wilson, Bryan. 1976. *Contemporary Transformations of Religion*. New York: Oxford University Press.

Wilson, William Julius. 1987. *The Truly Disadvantaged: The Inner City, the Underclass, and Public Policy*. Chicago: University of Chicago Press.

Winter, Gibson. 1962. *The Suburban Captivity of the Churches*. New York: The MacMillan Company.

Witten, Marsha G. 1993. *All Is Forgiven: The Secular Message in American Protestanism*. Princeton, N.J.: Princeton University Press.

Wolin, Sheldon S. 1990. "Democracy in the Discourse of Postmodernism." *Social Research* 57: 5–30.

Wuthnow, Robert. 1994. *Producing the Sacred: An Essay on Public Religion*. Urbana: University of Illinois Press.

Wylie, Jeannie. 1989. *Poletown: Community Betrayed*. Urbana: University of Illinois Press.

Zimmerman, Joseph F. 1967. *The Massachusetts Town Meeting: A Tenacious Institution*. Albany, N.Y.: Graduate School of Public Affairs.

Index

About the Author

John F. Freie is an associate professor of political science at LeMoyne College in Syracuse, New York. He has spent his academic career researching and writing about democratic participation as it applies to the practice of teaching, the development of citizenship, and the creation of community. This is his first book.